Kant, Deleuze and Architectonics

Continuum Studies in Continental Philosophy
Series Editor: James Fieser, University of Tennessee at Martin, USA

Continuum Studies in Continental Philosophy is a major monograph series
from Continuum. The series features first-class scholarly research
monographs across the field of Continental philosophy. Each work makes
a major contribution to the field of philosophical research.

Kant, Deleuze and Architectonics

Edward Willatt

continuum

Continuum International Publishing Group

The Tower Building	80 Maiden Lane
11 York Road	Suite 704
London SE1 7NX	New York, NY 10038

www.continuumbooks.com

British Library Cataloguing-in-Publication Data
A catalogue record for this book is available from the British Library.

ISBN: HB: 978-1-4411-6691-3

Library of Congress Cataloging-in-Publication Data
A catalog record for this book is available from the Library of Congress.

Typeset by Newgen Imaging Systems Pvt Ltd, Chennai, India
Printed and bound in Great Britain by the MPG Books Group

*In memory of Ruth Willatt, Duncan Willatt
and John Campion*

Contents

Acknowledgements

This book was written during my association with the philosophy department at the University of Greenwich in London. In particular I would like to thank Mick Bowles for being a huge inspiration and Matt Lee, with whom I edited a collection entitled *Thinking Between Deleuze and Kant* (2009). Their invaluable support, guidance, feedback, encouragement and friendship over the course of this project were essential to its completion. My great thanks are also due to Howard Caygill and Linnell Secomb, for their advice and encouragement. The philosophy department at Greenwich gave me the opportunity to take part in conferences and workshops held in the splendid surroundings of the university's Maritime Greenwich campus on areas closely related to my research. It has been a privilege and an immense pleasure to play a small part in the life of this flourishing department in the company of scholars from whom I've learnt a very great deal.

Fellow scholars from a number of different universities contributed to my research through discussion and comments in response to papers and presentations that I've given. In particular I would like to thank Brian Smith, Robin Williams, Scott Revers, Kath Jones, Jim Urpeth, Matt Astill, Nick Midgley, Neil Chapman, Bruce McClure, Raymond van de Wiel and Matt Travers. I would also like to thank Sarah Campbell and Tom Crick at Continuum for giving me the opportunity to publish my work and for their guidance. My thanks are also due to Candy, Bruce, Alex and Mycroft for their support without which none of this would have been possible. I am forever in their debt.

Abbreviations

The bibliography contains details of the editions and translations used for each text.

Works by Immanuel Kant

A   – *Anthropology from a Pragmatic Point of View*
CPR – *Critique of Pure Reason* (references to this text will give the standard *Akademie* pagination of the text with the 1781 edition indicated by 'A' and the 1787 edition indicated by 'B'. For example: CPR: A19/B33).
KRV – *Kritik der Reinen Vernunft*
L   – *Logic*
LM – *Lectures on Metaphysics*
MF – *Metaphysical Foundations of Natural Science*
P   – *Prolegomena to Any Future Metaphysics*

Works by Gilles Deleuze

DI   – *Desert Islands and Other Texts (1953–1974)*
DR – *Difference and Repetition*
ECC – *Essays Critical and Clinical*
KCP – *Kant's Critical Philosophy*
NP   – *Nietzsche and Philosophy*
PS   – *Proust and Signs*
KS1 – Kant Seminar of 14 March 1978
KS2 – Kant Seminar of 4 April 1978

References to Deleuze's Kant Seminars will refer to the pages of the 'pdf' versions of the English translations of this text, which are available at : http://www.webdeleuze.com/php/sommaire.html

Works by Marcel Proust

CF — *The Captive, The Fugitive*
WBG — *Within a Budding Grove*

Other Frequently Cited Works

CK — Norman Kemp Smith, *A Commentary to Kant's* Critique of Pure Reason
IE — James Brusseau, *Isolated Experiences*
K — Paul Guyer, *Kant*
KCJ — Béatrice Longuenesse, *Kant and the Capacity to Judge*
KPM — Martin Heidegger, *Kant and the Problem of Metaphysics*
KTI — Henry E. Allison, *Kant's Transcendental Idealism*

Introduction

How We Read Kant's *Critique of Pure Reason* and Understand Its Relation to the Work of Gilles Deleuze

In this book I will give a unifying reading of Kant's *Critique of Pure Reason*. This means that rather than taking its parts in isolation, as independent arguments and concepts, I will consider the organization of the text as a whole. This will involve considering how this organization functions as an argument. How are the parts of the whole related in such a way that together they present, clarify and make convincing an account of experience? How do they carry forward an argument by being unified and forming a whole? I will need to consider why Kant found this way of arguing convincing and necessary to the account of experience that he seeks to provide in the *Critique of Pure Reason*. Parts of the *Critique* are often read in isolation and the value of a unified reading is doubted. A number of critical concerns arise. Is an account of experience that is given as a whole, that is presented all at once in a single text, rigid and constraining? If it internalizes its argument, relying upon nothing external, is it bound to be artificial and not at all dynamic? By relying only upon the relations of its parts it provides an exhaustive account of experience rather than being open to revision. Understanding this form of argument and assessing its value will be the major concern of this book.

In seeking to pursue such a reading I will build upon the work of Kant scholars such as Béatrice Longuenesse, Gerd Buchdahl and Henry E. Allison. These scholars attempt to make sense of parts of the *Critique of Pure Reason* by considering how all its parts relate. They argue that we do not understand any aspect of Kant's account correctly in isolation from the whole. The second task of this book will be to consider how this way of reading Kant contributes to our understanding of the philosophy of Gilles Deleuze. My focus will be on Kant's *Critique of Pure Reason* in order that I may consider how the unity of this text deepens our understanding of the thought of both Kant and Deleuze. The unified presentation of this text will, as it unfolds, provide us with a mode of argument and concepts that show Kant's account of experience in a new light. They will also allow me to develop Deleuze's thought in response to critical concerns over his account of experience.

In this introduction I will give a brief survey of the ways of reading Kant's *Critique of Pure Reason* that have emerged in Kant and Deleuze studies. This will show that there is a case for pursuing a unified reading of this text and assessing the contribution it makes. How could a reader of Kant's *Critique of Pure Reason* take account of the unity of the parts of this text? Gerd Buchdahl is a reader of Kant eager to discard the baggage that Kantian terms have collected because they have been considered in isolation. He writes that he wants to break through '. . . the usual idea of an "authoritarian timelessness" assumed to surround the transcendental approach' (Buchdahl 1992: 9). Rather than isolating and analysing the terms used in the *Critique of Pure Reason* from an external viewpoint, these terms are to be viewed, as Kant himself counsels, by '. . . someone who has gained command of the idea as a whole' (CPR: Bxliv). The reader's task is to gain an Idea[1] of the process of cognition as a whole, how it relates its terms and assigns them roles and meanings. This might seem to be an uncritical reading strategy but in this book we will argue that we can only be critical or evaluative when we have grasped and understood this Idea rather than forestalling it. This means that we locate and understand the terms used in the *Critique of Pure Reason* as various stages in Kant's account of the process of cognition as a whole. Buchdahl proposes that Kantian terms are to be understood by means of '. . . the dynamical imagery of "flow", enabling us to keep in focus simultaneously the various nodal points of the Kantian structure, . . .' (Buchdahl 1992: 38).

In order to understand this tendency in Kant scholarship it will be useful to put it in the context of opposing views. If we follow Buchdahl's reading then Kant's understanding of the process of cognition as a whole marks out the position of various terms within this whole. Let's pick out the term 'thing in itself' and consider how it is to be understood and assessed. Paul Guyer's strategy is to evaluate this term in isolation and as something external to Kant's account as a whole. Instead of considering its role in Kant's account of the cognition of experience he asks what it could be or what it could represent. He concludes that it refers to ordinary objects, such as tables and chairs, which exist both as we represent them and as they are 'in themselves' (Guyer 1987: 335). They exist prior to the process of cognition and are what it is unable to reach, what is lacking in its outcomes. We only have subjective representations of these ordinary objects, not knowledge of them as they are 'in themselves'. According to this reading these down-graded objects or 'appearances' characterize Kant's account as a whole whereas for readers like Gerd Buchdahl it is the whole that characterizes its parts. Guyer's reading is often referred to as the 'two-object' or 'two-world' view (K: 68; KTI: 3). It argues from the inability of cognition to reach ordinary objects or 'things in themselves'. From this it follows that Kant's system is characterized by an inability to secure the full cognition of reality. Certain outcomes of cognition are excluded because there are potential objects that cognition cannot reach. Henry E. Allison echoes Buchdahl when he argues that the notion of objects outside of the realm of cognition is vacuous in Kant's system (KTI: 62). There are for him two different 'aspects' of objects rather than an object we can reach and an object that we always lack. The same object is a 'thing in itself', insofar it is not involved in the cognition of experience, and an 'appearance', insofar as it forms part of the materials of cognition. Thus Allison's reading is distinguished from the 'two-object' or 'two-world' view as the 'two-aspect' view because it has behind it an Idea of the process of cognition as a whole. It allows the whole process of accounting for the cognition of experience to question the assumption that any objects of cognition pre-exist this whole and characterize it as lacking in some respect. This issue gives us a sense of the great importance for Kant scholarship of the way in which we read the *Critique of Pure Reason*.

Why seek to consider the relation of Kant and Deleuze in a new way, using the strategy for reading Kant's *Critique of Pure Reason* we will be developing? We will argue that Kant needs to be read in a new light in order that he may contribute in new ways to our understanding of Deleuze's thought. This is to question the ways in which the relations of these two thinkers have previously been developed. In Deleuze studies there is a strong tendency to break up Kant's *Critique of Pure Reason* when thinking about its influence on, and role in, Deleuze's thought. Thus, while in Kant studies there is a tradition of unified readings of this text alongside the tendency to isolate its parts, the *Critique of Pure Reason* is not read in a unified way when it is related to Deleuze's thought. This reflects the fact that Deleuze actively selected and made use of parts of Kant's text in order to develop his own thought. We as readers of Deleuze are led to understand Kant's text as necessarily dismembered. We take our lead from Deleuze who, as a reader of Kant, selects parts from the whole on many occasions. Should we therefore treat Kant's text only as a source of further useful parts, and not as a unity to be explored on its own terms, when we relate it to Deleuze's thought? We see Deleuze writing in *Difference and Repetition* of '. . . a precise moment within Kantianism, a furtive and explosive moment which is not even continued by Kant, much less by post-Kantianism' (DR: 58). This is a reference to Kant's understanding of the thinking subject but reflects Deleuze's overall concern to make use of parts of Kant's thought regardless of their wider role in his system. These are useful whether or not Kant continued to develop them and regardless of their role in his account of experience as a whole. If Deleuze's use of Kant is selective it seems that there is only so far we can go with Kant before throwing his text aside. This seems to be the only way of reading *between* Kant and Deleuze, of developing their relations, because it reflects the limits Deleuze himself imposed on his relation to Kant. He rejected aspects of Kant's *Critique of Pure Reason* and so reading this text in a unified way seems unproductive if we are analysing its relation to Deleuze's thought. Are the relations of these two philosophers ultimately limited by Deleuze's selective approach?

The tendency in Deleuze studies to respect the limits that Deleuze himself imposed on his relation to Kant is also supported by another feature of his thought. If Kant contributes something to Deleuze this is always in competition with the influence of other thinkers. We need to complete our understanding of Deleuze's thought not by reading more of Kant's text but by considering other influences on Deleuze such as Spinoza, Leibniz, Nietzsche and Bergson.[2] Thus we find that Deleuze draws upon Kant's philosophy of time and finds it to be revolutionary for philosophy. It opens the prospect of thinking time on its own terms rather than understanding it as a means of measuring space (ECC: 27–28). However, for Deleuze time is not given its full role in Kant's thought. Kant has opened up the prospect of making time superior to space but we need to add Henri Bergson's influence to understand Deleuze's full conception of time.[3] Thus the *Critique of Pure Reason* is the place where the prospect of time being thought on its own terms is uncovered but at this point we stop reading Kant and start reading Bergson. Deleuze is therefore seen to select parts from the Kantian whole and then connect what he has selected to different concepts from different thinkers. This brief survey of ways of reading Deleuze in relation to Kant gives us a sense of how neglected the unity of the *Critique of Pure Reason* is in Deleuze studies.

There is strong evidence in Deleuze's writings to suggest that he didn't find it worthwhile to think about Kant's *Critique of Pure Reason* as a unified whole. His criticisms of Kant suggest that, as Levi R. Bryant puts it, we need to locate Deleuze's '. . . doorway for jumping out of critical philosophy . . .' (Bryant 2008: 181). It is not then worthwhile to follow the unfolding of the *Critique of Pure Reason* as a unity. Deleuze's assessment of Kant's notion of critique suggests that a doorway or means of escape is being sought: 'He seems to have confused the positivity of critique with a humble recognition of the rights of the criticized. There has never been a more conciliatory or respectful total critique' (NP: 89). Deleuze's verdict is that Kant begins by believing in what he criticizes and then tries to justify his belief. This challenges the integrity of Kant's account. As we shall see, Kant holds that an account of experience must not assume what it is to account for. Deleuze alleges that he does not live up to his own standards of argument because he preserves things that are given in experience. He respects things that should be subject to a critical account. We will consider this mode of attack at different points in this book while seeking to argue that it should not dissuade us from exploring Kant's text further in order to develop his relation to Deleuze.

An alternative approach to Kant's *Critique of Pure Reason* has been developed in readings of Deleuze's 1968 book *Difference and Repetition*. This text is unified through its relation to Kant's *Critique of Pure Reason* rather than needing to escape its influence. This move is captured in Daniel W. Smith's claim that '[f]rom the viewpoint of the theory of Ideas, *Difference and Repetition* can be read as Deleuze's *Critique of Pure Reason*, . . .' (Smith 2006: 44–45).[4] This is strikingly affirmative in contrast to the conclusions we might draw from Deleuze's critique and selective use of Kant, and his reliance on other thinkers that draws us away from Kant. Advocates of this reading unify both texts by locating something that Kant and Deleuze both affirmed. Thus Smith finds the unity of both texts in the theory of Ideas that Kant and Deleuze were concerned to develop. We will explore this theory in Chapter 2 of this book but for now are concerned with how reading strategies for *Difference and Repetition* lead us to re-read Kant. In the following passage from an article by Ray Brassier we see how something that unites Kant and Deleuze can nevertheless result in their quite different accounts of experience. The parts of Kant's *Critique of Pure Reason* are re-arranged and developed in new ways by Deleuze's own concerns:

> Representation is subjected to a critique which annuls the mediating function of the conceptual understanding vis-à-vis reason and sensibility. In *Difference and Repetition* the tripartite structure of the first critique ostensibly undergoes an involution which folds the Transcendental Dialectic directly into the Transcendental Aesthetic. (Brassier 2008: 7)

Sensation is made intellectual because it incarnates the Ideas found in Kant's Transcendental Dialectic. The distance between the sensible and the intellectual, which for Kant needs to be bridged by concepts and their schematism, is annulled. By rejecting Kant's forms of conceptual possibility that mediate the relation of Ideas and sensation Deleuze offers us a different account of experience. A shared theory of Ideas unifies *Difference and Repetition* and the *Critique of Pure Reason* but with quite different results in each case. The point to be made here is that the text has been re-arranged; it has become a different whole, with the result that experience has a different character.

Constantin V. Boundas agrees with Brassier that the Transcendental Dialectic of the *Critique of Pure Reason* is folded into its Transcendental Aesthetic in Deleuze's account while arguing that Kant's text as a whole is nevertheless repeated or retained. While Deleuze re-organizes and revises Kant's text, he repeats Kant's unifying project: 'The fidelity is revealed in a striking display when we put Kant's *Critique of Pure Reason* and Deleuze's *Difference and Repetition* side by side' (Boundas 2005: 261). This is because the Kantian theory of Ideas is retained as the focus or inner problematic of *Difference and Repetition* but it results in a different way of organizing the text. As Boundas puts it, Deleuze is '. . . moving about Kantian blocks in a non-Kantian way . . .' (ibid.: 262). We have Kantian blocks but these now enter into new relations. The whole forms a new argument, it argues for a way of accounting for experience, but this is now an argument based upon the direct relation of Ideas and sensation. Elements of Kant's account are now related by Deleuze's concern with the role of sensation in incarnating and realizing Ideas rather than through the forms of conceptual possibility that are secured in the now discarded Transcendental Analytic of the *Critique of Pure Reason*. Does this count as fidelity to Kant's text? Boundas claims that by taking Kantian blocks and arranging them in a non-Kantian way, in order to form an argument over the course of *Difference and Repetition*, Deleuze is repeating and retaining Kant's account. However, we find that the moves made by Kant in the Transcendental Analytic are now neglected because of the new and selective arrangement of its parts. For Deleuze the Kantian theory of Ideas demands that we consider how Ideas are incarnated in sensation and this excludes certain aspects of Kant's own account of experience. This seems to be a valid move because Deleuze rejects the conclusions of the Transcendental Analytic of the *Critique of Pure Reason*. However, in this book we will argue that, while the forms of conceptual possibility that Kant put forward in his Table of Categories are rejected by Deleuze, the way in which he argues for such conditions of experience is highly relevant to Deleuze studies. This is to suggest that the *Critique of Pure Reason* has not made itself heard in these readings, even in those that claim to affirm Kant's text as a whole in the way they present Deleuze's *Difference and Repetition*. By seeing Kantian blocks as parts to be re-assembled we neglect the Kantian process of assembling and unifying an account of experience. What if the Kantian way of organizing the blocks is as important as the blocks themselves in understanding Kant's text and developing his relations with Deleuze? It is on the basis of this question that we shall proceed in this book.

A further question that we will pose is: What if we do not stop at points where Deleuze and Kant are at odds and do not move to other influences on Deleuze thought? We must accept that Deleuze rejects aspects of Kant's *Critique of Pure Reason* very strongly. However, we will not let this distract us from pursuing a more unifying reading of the *Critique of Pure Reason* that may be of use in understanding Deleuze. This is the argument we make for devoting the first five chapters of this book to developing such a reading of Kant's text. It will be given the space to unfold so that we may then consider its relation to Deleuze's thought on the basis of a well-developed reading. In Chapter 1 of this book we will consider how Kant's *Critique of Pure Reason* unfolds as a unity through its architectonic method. This will set the tone for the following chapters where we will consider parts of the text that seek to establish conceptual conditions of possibility for experience. Despite Deleuze's clear rejection of such an approach to experience we will seek to show, in Chapter 6 of this book, that the method and forms of argument it involves are of value for his thought. Very fruitful work has been done on how, for example, the part of the *Critique of Pure Reason* named the Anticipations of Perception as a single argument adds to our understanding of Kant and Deleuze.[5] However, we will seek to situate this principle, along with the other members of the Table of Principles, in the context of Kant's account as a whole in Chapter 5 of this book. We will ask how the whole forms an argument rather than isolating and considering individual arguments in the pages of the *Critique of Pure Reason*. The conclusion to this book will seek to show the significant contribution that a unified reading of this text can make to contemporary debates concerning the philosophies of Kant and Deleuze.

Before turning to Kant's architectonic method of presentation and argument, which we will explore in the first chapter of this book, we must offer some further justification for the textual focus we will be maintaining. Deleuze himself gives a unifying reading not of the *Critique of Pure Reason* alone but of Kant's critical system that comprises all three of his *Critiques*. He finds the basis of this unity in the third *Critique*, the *Critique of Judgement*. Insofar as this retroactively provides the basis for the organization of the earlier two *Critiques* it is a source of unity that Deleuze is willing to affirm.[6] If we seek to be true to Deleuze's intentions we should pursue this move in his thought rather than pursuing the unity of his first *Critique*. However, the argument for neglecting this aspect of Deleuze's relation to Kant is that the singular unity of the *Critique of Pure Reason* calls for much concentration. It demands our attention even though Deleuze did not see it as a worthwhile avenue in his reading of Kant. If the *Critique of Judgement* provides a way of unifying and accounting for the relations of the faculties in all three *Critiques* it must be recognized and explored.[7] However, this must not exclude the full exploration of a form of unity that is not taken seriously by many scholars or pursued by Deleuze in his reading of Kant. We will seek to show that the singular source of the unity of the *Critique of Pure Reason* is only uncovered by concentrating on the architectonic method employed in this text. Only on this basis can the full implications for both Kant and Deleuze studies be drawn from its account of experience.

Chapter 1

Kant's Architectonic Method of Presentation and Argument

In this chapter we will seek to define a form of argument from within Kant's architectonic method. This method is at work in the unfolding of his *Critique of Pure Reason* as a whole. It is realized in the unified form of this text. This means that we will not be relying upon an understanding of the arguments that Kant uses from outside of this method and its realization in the *Critique of Pure Reason*. We will instead be treating Kant's method of presenting and organizing the text as the source of the type of argument that characterizes the text as a whole. This method of presentation is therefore to be the source even of its own form of argument. If we understand Kant's method in this way we find that the architectonic must rely upon nothing external. The external here includes anything at all that is given in the course of experience which for Kant is what we must account for rather than assume.[1] This emphasizes the completeness and self-sufficiency of Kant's architectonic as a method of presentation and source of arguments that relies upon nothing external to its own unfolding. We will argue that this claim is worth taking seriously despite the great amount of baggage that the term 'architectonic' has accumulated. It is given meaning both by the philosophical systems that were current in Kant's time and by the way in which Kant scholars have understood his use of the term. Having considered the obstacles this presents to understanding the architectonic as proposing a valid form of argument, we will consider how this method can be said to be unifying and internalizing. The architectonic must relate its parts to form a whole in the course of providing a complete account of the basic forms of the cognition of possible experience.[2] Kant needs to show that an account that is unified and internalizing is more convincing than one that borrows from experience and leaves open the ways in which its arguments and concepts can be developed. We will explore this in order to understand how Kant's architectonic embodies a form of argument while at the same time being a method of presenting and unifying the text.

What is Kant's Architectonic?

The most straightforward way of understanding the term architectonic as it is used in the *Critique of Pure Reason* is as a method by which we present and organize a text in order to make it form a clear and convincing argument. Being clear and convincing will allow the text to move forward and take the reader with it. However, the architectonic is a method for producing an argument by attending to the internal organization and unity of its own parts. It is therefore an inward looking method. Its basis is internal and it is internalizing because it draws only upon its own parts and their relations. Can such a method provide an argument that is clear and convincing or does it provide one that is rigid and obscure? To understand the architectonic method better we may consider an example of an argument that was used by Kant in his *Prolegomena to any Future Metaphysics*. This particular argument entitles us to say that 'the sun warms the stone' (P 44, n12). Here Kant locates the role not just of the perception of experience but also that of a concept, the concept of cause and effect. If we were to argue merely on the basis of the observation of our perceptions we would say: 'when the sun shines on the stone, it grows warm' (ibid.). However, a concept allows us to say that the warmth of the stone is caused by the sun. In this argument the time order of this perception is a necessary ingredient because in the judgement made using the concept of cause and effect, the heat of the stone, as the effect, must come after the emission of rays by the sun. Therefore, to draw a conclusion about the cause of this heating of the stone, we need an abstract concept as well as a concrete time order. This argument might seem to depend entirely upon the order and organization of what is given in experience and not upon the internal organization of an argument. However, for Kant we must seek to account for scenarios that arise in the course of possible experience, such as the coincidence of the sun and the stone that is warmed. We must account for these scenarios in ways that do not presuppose what is given in experience. Such accounts must not then follow the order or organization of what is given in experience. Instead they are to be self-organizing and in a way to account for and make possible such scenarios of possible experience. How we define an argument is of course a huge philosophical issue but it is not so contentious to say that its organization is crucial to the argument working. The question raised is whether the order of an argument like the one we've just considered emerges in experience or is internal to an account of that experience. In other words, do we have to wait until we encounter a scenario like the one discussed above before we can establish the conditions of possibility for our cognition of experience?

When we compare the example we have just given to the task of Kant's *Critique of Pure Reason* we see that it clearly does not have the ambitions of Kant's architectonic method. It is one thing to unify many arguments, like the one which allows us to conclude that 'the sun heats the stone', but it is quite another to seek to unify and organize an account of all arguments that we could ever make about experience. However, for Kant we must unify the argument of the *Critique of Pure Reason* as a whole and then unify and organize all the work of cognition. This will involve assigning to their places disciplines like metaphysics, natural science and psychology once their founding principles have been secured. Kant's architectonic method is intended to make every act of cognition convincing and objectively valid insofar as it is part of and extends an organized and systematic whole. Single arguments like the one we've considered do not stand alone. Instead they must somehow have their basis in the way an account of cognition is unified and how they are then included in the organization of all cognition, of its various disciplines and bodies of knowledge. This is because the order of any argument is part of a much wider system that accounts for all our cognition of possible experience. This system must therefore include the necessary order of cause and effect where effect must follow cause if we are to have an experience in the first place.[3] Thus for Kant, whether we are making an argument using the concept of cause and effect, writing a book that is to account for the cognition of experience or organizing the work of all the disciplines involved in cognition, we are ultimately to be guided by his architectonic method. However, the ambitions of this method risk making its precise nature unclear to us. We need to keep in view the context of the real, concrete work of cognition that it must account for and organize. In seeking to re-found all the work of cognition does the architectonic risk losing sight of judgements like those concerning the heating of a stone?

The grand ambitions of the architectonic method mean that for Kant it provides the basis for a unified reading of the *Critique of Pure Reason* and looks beyond it. It must re-found the work of cognition that up to now has not been founded upon an account of how the cognition of experience is possible in the first place. It is on the basis of this new foundation that we can then organize all the work of cognition, all of its disciplines and bodies of knowledge. We first encounter Kant's use of the term architectonic in his introduction to the *Critique of Pure Reason* where it concerns how this particular text is organized, how its parts are ordered and how this ordering allows them to relate to one another and thus form a complete whole or a whole argument. Kant writes that '. . . a science that merely judges pure reason, its sources, and its bounds may be regarded as the *propaedeutic* to the system of pure reason' (CPR: A11/B25). We will refer to this as the narrower use of the term architectonic or as the architectonic of the *Critique of Pure Reason*. The broader use of the term architectonic refers to the systematic organization of all disciplines of cognition.[4] The major difference between the narrower and broader uses is that the broader use refers to what Kant envisages as a system of all the forms of a priori cognition that found different disciplines of cognition and the bodies of knowledge they develop. It has the task of formulating these principles in a system that secures a priori cognition in all its guises, providing what Kant calls '[a]n *organon* of pure reason [which] would be the sum of those principles by which all pure a priori cognitions can be acquired and actually brought about' (ibid.: A11/B24–5).

Gary Hatfield argues that we can better understand this project if we turn to another of Kant's works. He writes:

> The only worked out version we have of this body of doctrine is that found in the *Metaphysical Foundations of Natural Science*. Here Kant applies principles

from the Analytic of Principles [of the *Critique of Pure Reason*] to the (empirically derived) concept of motion and purports thereby to derive two of Newton's laws of motion in an *a priori* manner. (Hatfield 1992: 218)

Thus the architectonic in the broader sense provides principles for sciences such as those that need to rigorously analyse motion. This allows them to extend their cognition on a firm footing, on the basis of principles that are not derived from experience but provide an account of it.[5] It thus looks beyond the *Critique of Pure Reason* to the work of cognition and how we organize it into disciplines according to the founding and characteristic principles of each science. The narrower sense of architectonic is clearly the most concentrated because it concerns the organization of a particular text, the *Critique of Pure Reason*, that is to prepare the foundations for all cognition of experience. Our primary concern is with the role and nature of the architectonic in the narrower sense, in organizing the *Critique of Pure Reason*, in order that we may gain a new understanding of this text by reading it in a unified way. Kant is concerned with how elements of an account of possible experience unfold and relate to one another over the course of the *Critique of Pure Reason* so as to form an argument when this text is considered as a whole. We will consider at length how the internal organization of these elements constitutes an argument. However, before we do this we will discuss the reasons for doubting that the architectonic presents a valid argument.

The way in which Kant organizes the *Critique of Pure Reason* is often either rejected or neglected in Kant scholarship. This foreshadows our approach to the architectonic and demands that we show why it should be taken notice of and taken seriously as the source of a valid form of argument in accounting for experience. We find Norman Kemp Smith writing as follows: 'Architectonic, that "open sesame" for so many of the secrets of the *Critique*, is the all-sufficient spell to resolve the mystery' (CK 332–3). Thus, if we are puzzled about Kant's moves at different points in the *Critique of Pure Reason*, we can only contemplate the magical abilities of his architectonic method. It organizes the text with no basis in anything other than what Kemp Smith refers to, in a pejorative way, as magic. On this reading the architectonic method fails to meet any criteria that would show it to provide a valid form of argument, failing to make clear its moves or show them to be convincing. The organization of the *Critique of Pure Reason* does not clarify and lead us through the stages of an argument. It does not relate its parts in a way that carries the argument forward. Readers like Kemp Smith speculate that the architectonic was simply a hobby that Kant enjoyed or an aspect of his mentality (ibid.: 341; Körner 1955: 77). It was a tendency or quirk that needs no further investigation, except by Kant's biographer. He liked to come up with a structure that was not led by or related to the arguments he was making and how these developed over the course of the *Critique of Pure Reason*. It was not then a dynamic response to the progress of his arguments but a rigid expression of a certain mentality. Thus we might organize our possessions in a chest of drawers in a way that makes the things we use everyday hard to find simply because we enjoy employing this method of organization. Our organization of things in particular drawers has no relation to how we use these drawers over the course of our life. It is unrelated to the concrete concerns, problems and realities we have to deal with. Similarly, while Kant's *Critique of Pure Reason* does present arguments that develop with the end of accounting for experience in sight, these are not reflected in the way the text is organized. His rigid method very much puzzles readers like Kemp Smith because it doesn't reflect a valid form of argument that they recognize.

More recent works of Kant scholarship tend to ignore Kant's architectonic method rather than speculating about his personal biography.[6] This reflects perhaps more rigorous standards of scholarship because it avoids using speculations about Kant's personal biography to evaluate his philosophical method of organizing the text. If the puzzling nature of this method is put down to something non-philosophical it can be easily dismissed. It seems that such an approach is itself rigid and artificial in that it is not open even to considering the philosophical concerns and possibilities that the architectonic might realize. One alternative is a tendency to reduce the architectonic not to the narrow sphere of Kant's personal life but to the historical and philosophical context of his thought. Howard Caygill argues that '[w]ith his concern for the philosophical system Kant inherited the Wolffian project of encyclopaedic philosophy or *philosophia generalis*. This project was the form in which German philosophy defended its claim against the discrete sciences (and faculties) of law, theology and medicine as well as the emergent natural sciences' (Caygill 1995: 84–5). This could lead us to heavily contextualize Kant's concerns in the *Critique of Pure Reason*. It suggests that the architectonic method would be more compelling to someone living in Kant's time, in his intellectual and professional world where a pressing concern with the hierarchical organization of university faculties can be located.[7] Indeed, we've seen that the architectonic is concerned with organizing the different disciplines or faculties on the basis of a philosophical foundation. This concern with systematizing all knowledge by enumerating the basic and founding principles of cognition has lost much of its force in the present age of specialization where even the most interdisciplinary approach would not entertain such a vision. It is not simply that this seems a difficult undertaking but that it seems dubious if we are to learn from the specificity of different disciplines and their concrete subject matters. It could be argued that the practice of cognition should not be based on a complete system of foundational principles but should allow concrete practices to shape its abstract concepts and principles. This is a concern that Kant's architectonic has to meet and we will consider his response in the next section of this chapter. However, the most damaging conclusion that follows from historicizing the architectonic method, from reducing it to its historical context, is that it is now an argument that is not valid according to Kant's own criteria. It draws its strengths from its context rather than from the internal force of an argument based solely on the relations of its own parts. The type of argument that would characterize Kant's method has become known as a transcendental argument. This embodies the concerns of the architectonic as we have so far developed them. It is to account for experience without presupposing anything given in experience. We find that Kant's arguments are in danger of being historicized rather than being understood as transcendental or architectonic. This makes them responses to Kant's historical context, drawing their force from this rather than the internal relations of their parts.

A different approach to those we've considered so far is found in Diane Morgan's book *Kant Trouble*. The apparent weaknesses of Kant's method are here understood in a positive light. If we find it unconvincing to argue that the elements of an account of the cognition of experience should be systematically unified once and for all, it is because the foundation of any such unity is impossible. This problem with founding the architectonic is, according to Morgan, a problem that is actually at work in Kant's text. It was not fully uncovered by its author but is still productive in how the text was written and how we read it.[8] Thus we should not seek to ignore or compensate for this apparent weakness, for the impossibility of founding an abstract system in the concrete world of experience, but use it to produce a unifying reading. Such a reading would then be based on the lack of foundation for the systematic unity that Kant proposes. For Morgan this problem of foundation was not recognized by Kant because he saw his architectonic account as complete and yet its real incompleteness is reflected deeply in the text he wrote. We cannot re-found all of cognition by formulating the concepts and principles necessary for turning our beliefs about experience into objective knowledge. We cannot sum up all the ways of doing this in some kind of 'how to' book which would boast encyclopaedic completeness. There is always more to concrete reality than our abstract concepts tell us. However, for Morgan the architectonic is not to be rejected or ignored. Instead we are to take notice of how it is unsettled because its abstract grasp of what is possible in experience is inevitably exceeded by the concrete realities it faces. Kant writes about securing good foundations and constructing a sturdy edifice using his architectonic method (CPR: Axi; A65/ B90). However, he in fact builds upon a lack of foundation that will demand revisions and new concepts in response to the reality that basic forms of experience can never be summed up completely. He postulates a foundation that does not reflect the reality of the object of cognition but he is then really reflecting this instability, this lack of real foundation, in how he thinks and writes. This is a positive reading because it concerns how a text is unified and how this unity is productive. For readers like Diane Morgan: 'These reflections on blind spots are in themselves most illuminating: they open up theoretical possibilities misrecognized by Kant himself' (Morgan 2000: 3). If no complete account of the cognition of experience can be given, it does not mean that Kant's architectonic is irrelevant or out of date. Thanks to this very problem, it in fact has a life that exceeds the author's intentions and the reader's expectations.

Among Kant's alleged 'blind spots' Morgan lists the concept of affinity, the notion that concrete reality corresponds to, or will correspond to, the concepts we have of it. It is the affinity of concrete reality with the abstract concepts and principles that are to deal with this reality. Kant seeks to find the stability of his architectonic here because he will organize the *Critique of Pure Reason* and project the organization of all a priori cognition according to this affinity. The affinity of the abstract and the concrete is to be the basis of the sturdy and systematic construction of an account of the cognition of experience and the subsequent work of the re-founded disciplines of cognition. Morgan writes that in fact such '. . . moments prevent the Kantian project from being able to locate the secure foundations it needs to be architectonic' (ibid.: 7). The system is shaken and unsettled by them as we recognize that we have not envisaged all that concrete reality has to offer and seek to close the gap. We can never attain an account that is inclusive and internal, one that relies only upon the relations of its own parts without any troublesome remainder. Kant therefore begins a project in the *Critique of Pure Reason* that will always be trying to re-establish affinity, to make up for an inevitable lack of affinity with concrete reality. This reality always disrupts the abstract construction that seeks to sum up and organize the basic principles of our cognition. It unsettles this edifice but this only makes the *Critique of Pure Reason* more productive. Morgan's conclusion is that if you attempt to build a system with such grand ambitions as Kant's architectonic you will get constructions that are unbuildable and temporary (ibid.: 31, 55). This makes Kant's architectonic an exercise in 'experimental architecture', because when it seeks to be inclusive and internalizing, it necessarily experiments. Unknowingly, Kant constructs and re-constructs in experimental ways as concrete reality challenges the abstract pretensions of his architectonic. He is then always seeking new ways of building the unbuildable, the complete system that can never last but is all the more productive for this reason (ibid.: 54–5). Having considered Diane Morgan's reading it is important to evaluate her positive assessment of Kant's architectonic and her emphasis upon how the real impetus of this method was not revealed to Kant himself. This does not take into account Kant's own refusal to make the basis of his method explicit. He argues that we cannot have knowledge of the basis of our construction of an account of the cognition of possible experience. Thus we cannot know that an external reality is susceptible to being unified systematically under abstract forms of cognition, that it has any affinity with concepts and principles that are independent of experience. We proceed on the basis that basic forms of cognition grasp the objects of our experience but for Kant we must not look to anything external to the architectonic to guarantee this.

The affinity of the abstract and concrete within Kant's architectonic is something we shall consider at length in the next part of this chapter. We will question Diane Morgan's argument that we have to look to Kant's blind spots to locate the problems that animate his thought. As we shall see, his architectonic method organizes the text on the basis of a problem that he puts centre stage because '[m]uch is gained when we can bring a multitude of inquiries under the formula of a single problem' (CPR: B19). We will argue that this methodological precept is integral to the architectonic. The text is organized as an account of the cognition of experience on the basis of an internal problematic that relates all the elements of the account. The architectonic thus finds a source for the unifying organization it performs not in a blind spot, but in a problem that, as we shall see, Kant raises explicitly in the introduction to the *Critique of Pure Reason*. Thus while Diane Morgan's reading takes Kant's architectonic seriously, rather than dismissing it prematurely or ignoring it, her account of the role of internal problems in this method can be called into question. In the next section we will seek to understand the architectonic as a method explicitly based upon a single and unifying problem.

The Role of Synthetic A Priori Judgements in the Architectonic

If we consider Kant's concern with a single problem and how it unifies inquiry in the *Critique of Pure Reason* this will help us to understand his architectonic method more precisely. We've suggested that for Kant the architectonic is a clear and convincing argument because it is unifying. It is unifying because it is internalizing or inclusive rather than referring to or relying upon the forms of unity we come across in the course of experience. Now we see that, for Kant, to be internalizing or inclusive means responding to an inner problematic in relating parts to form a whole. This single problem is to be at the basis of Kant's architectonic, providing the reason for it to relate its elements so as to form an account of the cognition of possible experience. Kant formulates this single problem in the following question: '**How are synthetic judgments possible a priori?**' (CPR: B19). He here specifies the basis of his method of organizing the text. This single and problematic question provides criteria for judging whether the text has presented an adequate account of experience. This account must elaborate only what is concentrated in this question if it is to be inclusive and internalizing. This problematic question is then the key to providing a full account of experience, one that leaves nothing out and that is self-sufficient. It does not rely upon anything given in experience in its account because in this question we find sufficient basis for it to proceed. It follows that this particular form of judgement, synthetic a priori judgement, must be secured and elaborated in the course of the *Critique of Pure Reason* because for Kant this will secure the concepts and principles that make experience possible in the first place. These concepts and principles are to provide a complete account only because they embody the two elements concentrated in the synthetic a priori form of judgement. These two elements are the synthetic and the a priori. The account must then be unfolded on the basis of the relations of these two elements to the exclusion of anything external. In other words, the synthetic and the a priori must give rise to a complete and systematically organized account of experience through their relations at the different stages of this account.[9] We must seek to understand and assess this starting point for an account of the cognition of possible experience that demands a very great deal from a single unifying problem. In what sense does a starting point that concentrates the elements whose unfolding will secure such an account provide us with what Kant calls an Idea of the whole?

We've suggested that Kant provides a single problem as a highly concentrated formulation of the account he wants to give. The relations between two elements, the synthetic and the a priori, are to be unfolded in the organization of the *Critique of Pure Reason*. For this to be an internalizing and inclusive account the synthetic and the a priori have to be shown to represent the two poles of the cognition of experience. They must, in other words, together ensure that nothing is left out of the account and that we do not rely upon anything external to the process of accounting for experience. This is because, as the two poles of experience, they are combined in foundational judgements for all cognition of experience. In their unity they give us an Idea of the whole, a whole that is only realized through an account of the relation of the synthetic and the a priori in all cognition, and through the work of cognition that this makes possible. It gives us an Idea of the two elements that all cognition must embody. We've considered the example of the judgement that applies a concept of cause and effect. This makes the combination of the synthetic and the a priori in a judgement problematic in the sense that Kant recognizes and sets before us. Their relation in such foundational judgements is not given in experience but needs to be secured once and for all. These judgements present a combination of the synthetic and the a priori that now needs to be unfolded clearly and convincingly in order to secure an account of the cognition of possible experience. This is the problem Kant puts at the basis of his architectonic, presenting us not with a completed whole or sum of cognition but an Idea of the whole that is only realized in the ongoing and re-founded work of cognition.

In order to understand Kant's argument better we may consider further the argument whose conclusion is that 'the sun warms the stone'. We saw that cause and effect had to be ordered clearly and convincingly for the argument to work. What is the role of the synthetic and the a priori in this argument? One way of understanding their nature and their complementary roles is to define the a priori as the abstract and the synthetic as the concrete.[10] The relation of the concrete synthetic and the abstract a priori poses the problem in this argument. How can we expect that effect will follow cause no matter how different the concrete case is? For Kant an experience where effect didn't follow cause would not be an experience at all. It would not qualify as experience because it was not made possible by the combination of the abstract and the concrete. Abstract and concrete constitute the two poles of any experience and need to be related so that their relation secures this experience in the first place, making it possible.

We not only need to be able to think about or abstract from experience but also to refer to experience in all its concrete detail. Kant argues that cognition can only come about as a result of the union of the abstract work of the understanding and the concrete input of sensation (CPR: A51/B75–6). This helps us to understand how the relation between the synthetic and the a priori, in what Kant sees as the foundational judgements for all cognition, is the inner problematic of his architectonic account of experience. He will unify his investigation with this problem so that the disunity in experience of the parts of an argument does not obscure their ultimate unity in cognition. Thus, to return to our example, if there is no necessary connection between the sun and the stone in the concrete this is because the concrete is incomplete without the abstract concept of cause and effect. As we saw, we need a concrete time order and an abstract concept for the argument to work. The relation of the abstract and the concrete must be involved even before the stage at which we perceive the warming of the stone.

We've sought to understand Kant's concern with a single and unifying problem by considering how the synthetic and the a priori represent the two poles of cognition. The problem that is raised is that they lack unity insofar as they are merely given in experience but have it insofar as they are concentrated in the synthetic a priori form of judgement that makes experience possible. This is the key to understanding the scope of synthetic a priori judgements for Kant. Abstract knowledge would not be effective at dealing with concrete situations and particularities that are presented in space and time. Likewise, we would be limited to the concrete if we did not have an abstract grasp of what holds within and across very different situations.[11] In either case we would not provide a full and therefore convincing account of experience. We would either lack openness to concrete situations and particularities or lack the reach that the abstract has in encompassing different aspects of the concrete. Henry E. Allison sums this up when he writes that '[t]he essential point is that in order to recognize the possibility of judgements that are synthetic in Kant's sense, it is first necessary to recognize the complementary roles of concepts and sensible intuitions in human knowledge' (Allison 1992: 325). This is the complementarity or togetherness of abstract concepts and concrete sensible intuitions in forms of judgement that are necessary conditions for the cognition of experience. Thus judgements that are synthetic must reflect forms of synthesis that are a priori, that embody a priori forms when they unify or synthesize sensible intuition. At each stage of the account, in each stage of the *Critique of Pure Reason*, these two poles of the cognition of experience must be in play if this complementarity is to be realized. We will now turn to the a priori and see how Kant characterizes this pole of cognition in relation to the concrete or synthetic component of every foundational judgement. Thinking about the arguments he uses will allow us to consider how forms of argument are developed within the architectonic and may allow us to characterize it as a whole. Our concern will be with how the architectonic method moves forward by establishing and relating the elements of its account.

Locating the A Priori

At the start of the second edition introduction to the *Critique of Pure Reason* Kant commences his account by considering how cognition begins. He argues that cognition always begins upon the occasions presented by sensation (CPR: B1). This is when sensation rouses the understanding or sets it in motion by providing the material for cognition. The understanding responds to sensation by comparing '. . . these presentations, [it] connects or separates them, and thus processes the raw material of sense impressions into a cognition of objects that is called experience' (ibid.). Kant clarifies this picture, so that while experience here provides the starting point for cognition on a particular occasion, it does not give rise to cognition entirely from itself. He locates something independent of experience that is represented in the understanding's response to the promptings of sensation. Is he suggesting that there is something innate in the human mind, whether something that is already present at birth or an ability that develops through life? In fact he does not invoke an innate component or ability of the mind here because he is discussing the elements of an account of cognition. For Kant this account must be given in order to make it possible to cognize something as innate or as a component of the mind, as some kind of container or location, in the first place.[12] It is a necessary feature of his architectonic method that objects are to be assigned their places in a unity of cognition as either subjective or objective, or as innate or acquired, through the very account now being developed.[13] The architectonic is internalizing and inclusive in this sense. It is an account that does not start with or presuppose a place where innate things could be stored but seeks to account for any such thing. Thus the architectonic has at its basis the difference between the synthetic and the a priori because through this difference a full account of the other differences that characterize cognition is to emerge. The *Critique of Pure Reason* is not then to be organized or driven forward by the difference between innate and acquired or by a search for the origins of cognitive activity in the subject as opposed to the object. Its organizing principle is the relation and difference between the synthetic and the a priori. In order to evaluate this move we must see where it leads Kant.

Kant calls the non-empirical or pure component of his account of cognition, which we've sought to define carefully, the a priori. It must be what is expressed in the work of the understanding and not given in experience. In other words, it is expressed in the giving of experience, in how it is made possible, rather than in what is given and accumulated over the course of experience (ibid.: B2). While Kant calls this pure component *a priori* he calls the empirical or given component *a posteriori* (ibid.: B2–3). The a priori is here expressed in the comparison, connection and separation of what is presented a posteriori in sensation as the givens of experience. However, the work of the understanding upon what is given in sensation is not the only role of the a priori. These acts of the understanding actually reflect how sensation is already unified or synthesized in a priori ways when it is given to us. We noted the ubiquity of the a priori in the previous section of this chapter. This is an important point because when the understanding compares, connects and separates given sensations these have already been unified or synthesized in a priori ways. We might call this the 'silent work' of the understanding, prior to when sensation prompts us to noisily compare, connect and separate.[14] This shows that the a priori is involved with the unification or synthesis of sensation before we are aware of it, before we consciously respond to sensation's promptings. Thus the a priori does not merely come after the synthesis of sensation but instead the synthetic and the a priori are always already at work together. As a result the understanding's a priori forms of response to sensation reflect the ways in which sensation has already been unified. They reflect the 'silent work' of the understanding that precedes its 'noisy work' of comparison, connection and separation. This is something that we will continue to explore because it is crucial to the complementarity or togetherness of the synthetic and the a priori in an architectonic or unifying account of experience. Understanding compares, connects and separates in order to end up with concepts that extend our knowledge of experience. However, this has its basis in the a priori work of the understanding before sensations ever occur to us and prompt us to compare, connect and separate.

Kant qualifies the a priori forms of unity which are to be at work in all synthesis as strictly universal rules for producing concepts rather than being only comparatively strict (ibid.: B4). They are strict in the sense that they alone make experience possible rather than in the sense that they are stricter than any other possible way of securing this end. They are not then one way of making experience possible and thus comparatively strict, but the *only* way and thus strict because they are indispensable. They are also, Kant argues, absolutely necessary or necessary no matter what is met with on the occasions when sensation presents us with material for cognition (ibid.: B2–3). This reflects Kant's concern to make the a priori ubiquitous. It is silently at work before sensation prompts the understanding and therefore should always be reflected in its 'noisy' work. The a priori is then strictly universal and absolutely necessary because it is already at work in how sensations are unified or synthesized. It follows that when Kant uses the term 'possible experience' this reflects and projects the a priori forms of cognition or pure concepts of the understanding. These are secured by synthetic a priori judgements and are the conceptual forms of possibility that alone make experience possible (ibid.: A93/B125). For Kant we get a full account of experience only because it is possible experience, because it is always given form by certain abstract and a priori forms through its synthesis. His argument hinges on a key claim of the architectonic method that if anything exceeded the grasp of synthetic a priori judgements it would not actually be a loss to experience. If it exceeded the basic forms of possible experience it would undermine the conceptual unity of experience that makes it possible in the first place. Thus the concrete possibilities of sensation really presuppose the abstract forms of possibility of the understanding rather than exceeding them. This is a claim we will interrogate further because, for Kant, it is why we must not look outside of the relations of the synthetic and the a priori but remain within the unified account formed by the unfolding of their relations.

Before we move on to consider the nature of Kant's arguments for major claims, such as the one we've just considered, it will be useful to explore a point that Philip Kitcher makes in an essay on the a priori (Kitcher 2006). He argues that we can identify two senses of the a priori. This is something that reflects Kant's attempt to include all of cognitive activity within the horizon of his architectonic. The a priori must allow us to justify claims that form part of everyday knowledge. Thus while Kant wants to secure claims that are foundational for all cognition, such as the claim that an effect follows a cause, he also wants to secure claims that arise, wholly or in part, on the basis of experience. It doesn't undermine the possibility of experience that a particular event no longer causes another event, even if this has happened for as long as anyone can remember. However, this connection of particular cause and particular effect is still significant. It is significant in a weaker sense than the concept of cause and effect which makes possible all judgements concerning the relation of events that follow one another in time. Kitcher therefore distinguishes a weak sense from a strong sense of the a priori. He describes what Kant himself referred to as cognition through empirical concepts or empirical cognition as securing weak a priori knowledge (L: 97). This move reflects the fact that for Kant, foundational or basic forms of cognition, which are secured by synthetic a priori judgements, are only a small part of the sum total of cognition. Kitcher argues that in attaining the weak a priori, the subject is active and justificatory so that,

> . . . [a]s we undergo the stream of experience that constitutes our lives, we are able to engage in certain kinds of processes that justify us in holding particular beliefs, and we can do this whatever specific form the stream of experience takes. (Kitcher 2006: 31)

A life or total stream of experience undergone by a subject is a sufficient basis for beliefs that can be acted upon. These are justified in a weaker, but still significant, sense than knowledge that is based upon what is independent of experience and a priori in the strong sense. Thus the proposition that the sun will rise tomorrow is established as long as someone lives for a sufficient time to observe this event frequently enough to form an empirical concept of the sun in which its rising is included. While the concept of the sun and its attribute 'to rise at daybreak' is not one of the a priori concepts that makes the cognition of experience possible, it is necessary relative to everyday concerns and to disciplines such as anthropology and zoology that observe humans, other animals and other forms of life anticipating and responding to the rising of the sun at daybreak. This shows us how a priori concepts are the basis of all cognition of experience but are only a small part of its sum total. The majority of acts of cognition are empirical or a priori in the weak sense. This gives us a greater sense of the ambitions of the architectonic and their relation to the concrete concerns of cognition. In the next section we will interrogate more closely the arguments we have seen Kant making in his attempts to secure the a priori.

The Architectonic and Forms of Argument

In order to assess Kant's claims about the role of the a priori we will seek to define the form of argument that characterizes the architectonic account within which they arise. We note that he is not just making the claim that we need both abstract and concrete as elements of a full account for experience, as its two poles. We've considered how we can defend this claim by arguing that experience involves both concrete cases and abstract unities that range across these cases. However, Kant is also asserting that we cannot have the concrete without an a priori that has a certain character. This a priori places certain systematic limitations upon what is possible in experience that are strictly universal and absolutely necessary. He seeks to establish the basic or foundational forms of the a priori once and for all in his architectonic account rather than leaving open the nature, organization and number of these forms. The architectonic method now needs to provide the criteria of a form of argument if we are to defend it against the charge that it is rigid and artificial. These criteria need to be identified through the unfolding of the architectonic if we are to show that this method is inclusive and internalizing.

One form of argument that we encounter already in the introduction to the *Critique of Pure Reason* explores what we might call the ingredients of an account of cognition. Kant later refers to this as a process of transcendental deliberation. He argues that we can distinguish the influence of the faculty of sensibility upon the faculty of understanding only if we assign presentations to different faculties (CPR: A295/B351). Apart from locating the influence of different cognitive faculties, it is to distinguish their contributions according to whether these are a priori or a posteriori. Thus, if the understanding contributes a concept to our cognition of experience, is this an empirical and a posteriori concept or a pure and a priori concept? Quassim Cassam refers to this as an 'isolation argument' because it isolates the a priori ingredients of cognition in order to establish the elements of an account of cognition (Cassam 1999: 86). We can see this at work in the introduction to the *Critique of Pure Reason* when Kant suggests that we attempt to remove all that we have learnt from experience from our concept of any object (CPR: B6). We find that we cannot get rid of the object's status as a substance or as being attached to a substance. He concludes that the concept of substance is unavoidable, that it forces itself upon us when we carry out this thought experiment, and that its necessity shows that it has a priori status. In this way we isolate a priori ingredients by inspecting the products of cognition and seeing which have the character of the a priori. Thus when we consider again the stone that is warmed by the sun we are led to think about the forms of judgement that have unified this experience. We find that we are always presupposing the application of the concept of substance and the concept of cause and effect. Once we have applied the concept of substance we can then attribute predicate-concepts to a subject-concept. We attribute things to a subject because we secure it using this a priori concept. This allows us to continue to unify this experience by locating the role of cause and effect. We thus isolate the roles of a priori concepts as well as the concrete time order of events in organizing this situation. We orientate ourselves in a particular experience or concrete situation by deliberating on what makes it possible in the first place. Instead of being confused by changes of state, we make a judgement anchored in a subject-concept, converting our beliefs about causality into knowledge grounded in a priori forms as well as in concrete details like the time-order of events. We are locating the force or influence of the understanding in realizing certain a priori concepts in the spatio-temporal synthesis of sensation before sensation actually occurs to us. This force is also at work in the argument that convinces us that the heat of the stone is the effect of the sun's rays. Such an isolation argument takes us from the object of cognition to the forces or cognitive faculties that are at work in the synthesis of our sensations of this object.

Quassim Cassam argues that such isolation arguments present a weaker form of argument than others that we find in the *Critique of Pure Reason* (Cassam 1999: 85). He claims that the isolation argument is weaker because it is not validatory. Rather than justifying our use of a concept it inspects the work of cognition and reveals its ingredients or the forces at work in its synthesis. It might show that the understanding's concept of cause and effect was at work in this case but does not tell us that it must have been so. We are here directly inspecting the work of cognition on the basis of finished concepts of objects without this providing any justification of the a priori elements this reveals. They form a list of conditions that is neither shown to be complete or indispensible for the cognition of possible experience. The argument is not then inclusive or internalizing because it leaves open the possibility of other ways of securing the synthesis of possible experience. Cassam argues that the alternative form of argument to be located is one where . . .

> . . . [t]heir aim is not just to tell us how we do in fact think of and experience the world, but to show that we are justified in operating in the ways in which we actually operate when thinking about or experiencing the world. (ibid.: 86)

Isolation arguments are too limited in their scope, referring to the actual operations and outcomes that we have observed over the course of experience. They reveal the structure and contributions of our cognitive faculties in these actual cases rather than establishing conditions of possibility that are indispensible and form a system (ibid.: 85). The form of argument that would characterize the architectonic must include every possible act of cognition in its horizon if it is not to be liable to revision. This seems to be a valid way of reading Kant's notion of the architectonic method. It concerns an internal justification in the sense that we do not presuppose the givens of experience that are to be accounted for, including any outcome or achievement of cognition. The architectonic must include every condition of the possibility of experience rather than isolating some of these according to what is given to us in the course of experience. It must therefore not wait for the situation to arise which allows us to form an isolation argument. Instead the architectonic must present these conditions all at once in a system, re-founding cognition once and for all without this being vulnerable to the haphazard discovery and isolation of conditions. Therefore, while an isolation argument may have a role in showing how the a priori has been at work in cognition, it cannot characterize Kant's architectonic and its scope. Insofar as this is to account for the very possibility of experience, to justify its a priori forms in an inclusive and internalizing way, isolation arguments could only play a supporting role within its unfolding.

We are moving closer to a positive definition of transcendental arguments or arguments that for Kant characterize his architectonic method in the *Critique of Pure Reason*. If we consider isolation arguments further and why they in fact do not meet the criteria of a transcendental argument this will bring us closer to our goal. Gary Hatfield characterizes arguments that seek to isolate the a priori as starting from 'bodies of knowledge' or 'cognitive achievements' and then seeking to find out how these are possible (Hatfield 1990: 79). They ascend from what has been achieved in cognition to the cognitive processes that make this achievement possible. Kant defines what we are calling isolation arguments in this way in his *Prolegomena to Any Future Metaphysics* where he writes that: 'They must rest therefore upon something already known as trustworthy, from which we can set out with confidence and ascend to sources as yet unknown, the discovery of which will not only explain to us what we knew but exhibit a sphere of many cognitions which all spring from the same sources' (P: 19–20). Here Kant calls this method of investigation 'analytic' insofar as it is to analyse the achievements of cognition, working back from these to the ingredients of the process of cognition that achieved them. Its focus is upon achievements that are for Kant indisputable and its horizon is the possibility of these particular achievements.

In what sense could isolation arguments or analytic investigations play a role in the architectonic of the *Critique of Pure Reason*? A starting point for an isolation argument that is very much in evidence in Kant's text is Euclidean geometry. Georges Dicker writes that for Kant . . .

. . . [i]t is because of the nature or structure of space that a straight line not only is but also must be the shortest distance between two points. More generally, it is the nature or structure of space that accounts for the necessity or strict universality of all geometrical propositions. Furthermore, geometry is the science of space, in that geometrical principles describe the nature or structure of space. (Dicker 2004: 27)

Mathematics here isolates and exhibits the a priori and it does this because it constructs or synthesizes sensations under the rule of the a priori. It is thus involved in certain spatio-temporal syntheses that are otherwise always at work silently. It shows that these are constrained by a priori rules, rules that form the axioms of Euclidean geometry, and in this way tells us about the nature of space. According to Kant, mathematics constructs or synthesizes space in the only way possible, in the a priori way that sensations are always being constructed or synthesized in space and time. It is clear that he has a particular view of mathematics, one that makes it the starting point for an isolation argument. He has what has become known as an intuitionist or constructivist view of mathematics, seeing its role as constructing sensations in space and time and thus exhibiting its a priori truths or rules in sensible intuition rather than in abstraction.[15] It tells us about abstract a priori rules and the concrete or synthetic ways in which they are realized because it actually exhibits the togetherness or complementarity of the a priori and the synthetic. Mathematical cognition is not then made up of merely a posteriori ingredients that can be revised on the basis of experience but neither is it formalistic as it would be if its axioms or starting points were not derived from how sensation is constructed or synthesized.[16] It embodies the togetherness of the abstract and the concrete in the spatio-temporal synthesis of sensible intuition. This leads Kant to argue that sciences need a mathematical component to ensure that they can deal with their subject matter on the basis of a priori synthetic cognitions. The force of this argument for the necessary role of the a priori is drawn from the cognitive achievement of mathematics in exhibiting the a priori ways in which space and time actually construct or synthesize sensations. It isolates the a priori ingredient, the ingredient that constrains mathematics and provides its axioms. It thus reflects how all synthesis is constrained or ruled by the a priori. This is clearly a huge claim concerning the nature of mathematics and relies upon a Euclidean geometry that has now been supplemented by non-Euclidean hyperbolic and elliptic geometries (Kline 1981: 446–7). However, our overriding concern is to place such an argument as a supporting argument in Kant's architectonic of the *Critique of Pure Reason*, one that is not relied upon by the text as a whole. We will now consider how the isolation argument is distinguished from the form of argument we are seeking to define.

In seeking to compare the role of different arguments in characterizing the *Critique of Pure Reason* as a whole it is worth turning again to Kant's *Prolegomena* where he reflects upon this issue. He explicitly contrasts the isolation argument or analytic investigation that characterizes and unifies the *Prolegomena* with the type of argument and investigation that does the same for the *Critique of Pure Reason*. He refers to the *Critique of Pure Reason* as performing an inquiry into '. . . a system based on no data except reason itself, and which therefore seeks, without resting upon any fact, to unfold knowledge from its original germs' (P: 19). Here Kant makes it clear that his method is inclusive and internal, that it is to leave nothing out and to work by relating the elements internal to the account it is giving. This is not to suggest that the *Critique of Pure Reason* employs only one type of argument but it puts isolation arguments in context. They are supporting arguments. Their place in the text and in an account of cognition is to be assigned by the architectonic. Kant is here counselling us to seek the unity of his *Critique of Pure Reason* in an overall method even though we find different forms of argument in this text. He also makes it clear that the *Prolegomena* does not provide a competing form of argument to that of the *Critique of Pure Reason*. In its preface he explains why he published this 1783 text in between the first and second editions of the *Critique of Pure Reason*. The *Critique of Pure Reason* is '. . . dry, obscure, opposed to all ordinary notions, and moreover long-winded' (ibid.: 6).[17] The *Prolegomena* is therefore to be presented differently but not, Kant asserts, in a competing form. We cannot do the work of the *Critique of Pure Reason* in a variety of different ways or by using now this cognitive achievement and now that one. Thus Kant writes that the *Critique of Pure Reason*, '. . . which discusses the pure faculty of reason in its whole extent and bounds, will remain the foundation, to which the *Prolegomena*, as preliminary exercise, refer; for that critique must exist as a science, systematic and complete as to its smallest parts, before we can think of letting metaphysics appear on the scene, or even have the most distant hope of so doing' (P: 6–7). Kant here affirms the integrity of the *Critique of Pure Reason* as something indispensable for re-founding cognition and subsequently assigning places to bodies of knowledge like metaphysics and natural science. He argues that the *Prolegomena* makes it easier to grasp the *Critique of Pure Reason*'s account of experience because it is a more popular work. Some people find it easier to think on the basis of what is presented in sensible intuition rather than beginning with abstract concepts and their role in a system. Isolation arguments simply suit them better but do not replace the foundational work of the *Critique of Pure Reason* which they seek to make accessible (P: 8–9). Thus the integrity of the systematic account presented in this text is not questioned but its role in all cognition demands that this account be grasped in different ways to suit different minds.

Kant defines the type of argument that is to characterize his architectonic in the introduction to the *Critique of Pure Reason*. Here he significantly discards any reliance upon examples of cognitive achievements or from everyday understanding in the type of argument he is going to pursue. These are not needed if we are to established that 'pure a priori principles' are at work in cognition (CPR: B5). Instead these must be shown to be indispensable for the very possibility of experience and therefore a priori. This would ensure that such principles are genuinely first principles because they would not have their basis in the contingencies of experience. We see that the scope of such arguments is to be the very possibility of experience. They concern the conditions of possibility of all experience and challenge anyone who is a sceptic about the a priori nature of the foundations of cognition. As Robert Stern puts it . . .

> . . . they set out to show that something the sceptic takes for granted as a possibility (for example that we have direct access to our inner states but no direct access to the external world, or beliefs but no reliable belief-forming methods) must be abandoned, as the one is in fact impossible without the other, for reasons he has overlooked (for example, inner states alone cannot provide the basis for time-determination, or that beliefs by their nature must be generally true). (Stern 1999a: 4)

What the sceptic must come to accept for the argument to work is that experience as a whole is unified in certain ways. The example Stern gives in parenthesis shows how the conceptions the sceptic might have gained through their inner states or inner experience are inseparable from a wider system in which all conceptions of possible experience arise.[18] These include inner and outer experience. Thus if, as in the example we've been considering, the sun warms the stone this can never be an isolated experience, one confined to an inner state. It refers to a whole system that is the condition of possibility of this experience in the first place, that makes possible both inner and outer experience through a priori synthesis. Cause and effect form part of a wider system and the architectonic of the *Critique of Pure Reason* forms an argument that seeks to make this system the condition of possibility for 'experience as such'. Thus our access to the external world is not something we must establish after having had experiences like that of the sun warming the stone but is a condition of possibility of this very experience. The theory of time-determination referred to by Stern, which allows Kant to argue in this way, will be explored in Chapters 4 and 5 of this book. How does this differ from an isolation argument? The difference is first of all one of scope or horizon. Kant is concerned to argue without the aid of examples, even if these examples are as unique and powerful for him as Euclidean geometry. He wants to think about 'experience as such' and its conditions of possibility. This means avoiding reference to its outcomes, no matter how venerable, or to anything whatever that has been given in experience.

Let's summarize what we've learnt about the form of argument that is to characterize Kant's architectonic. Its criteria are as follows:

1. The argument must be validatory rather than revelatory.
2. The argument must be indispensable.
3. The argument must not assume what it is to account for and thus leave it out of its unifying account.
4. The argument must not rely upon cognitive achievements or bodies of knowledge to re-found cognition.

5. It follows from the previous criteria that the argument must be inclusive and internalizing, providing the conditions of the possibility of experience exhaustively and so without remainder. In this way it relies only upon its own elements and upon its way of relating them in order to carry forward its argument.

From what we've discovered so far we can see that isolation arguments are closer to these criteria than arguments from experience or from the a posteriori. Thus if an argument starts with cognitive achievements that exhibit or reveal a priori truths this is more productive for Kant's architectonic than one starting with the facts or givens of experience like arguments from resemblance or regularity. Arguments from experience can locate patterns of resemblance and regularity that secure what we saw Philip Kitcher referring to as the weak sense of the a priori. However, these arguments cannot account for resemblances or regularities, or justify the assertion of their absolute necessity and strict universality on the basis of certain a priori syntheses. In contrast, a cognitive achievement like Euclidean geometry does reveal the a priori syntheses that exhibit basic propositions or a priori truths that ground its activity and ground the activity of all proper sciences according to Kant. However, what is needed is the horizon or scope of all a priori synthesis, of possible experience as such, and a validatory argument that holds it together. This account must be unifying or internalizing to the extent that it is based upon the horizon of possible experience as such. We may call arguments that meet these criteria transcendental arguments on the grounds that they are concerned with conditions of the very possibility of experience. The architectonic, as a transcendental argument, draws only upon its own parts and their relations. It is because this whole is greater than its parts that it cannot focus upon a part of experience like isolation arguments do. It includes all of experience within its horizon, from everyday experience to venerable cognitive achievements that are founded upon mathematical truths. This reveals the overriding ambition of Kant's architectonic, its aim of securing the conditions of possibility for the cognition of experience once and for all. Over the following chapters of this book the nature and unfolding of this account in the *Critique of Pure Reason* will be explored and assessed.

Conclusion

In this chapter we have been able to offer some justification for the textual focus of this book. We've sought to show that for Kant the synthetic a priori form of judgement presents us with the basis of the architectonic because it prompts, unifies and organizes its activity. Thus, while we have to wait until sensation prompts us before we engage in 'noisy' cognitive activity, the 'silent work' of a priori synthesis is always already underway. This demands a fuller treatment than we would be able to give if our textual focus was wider because it must be explored in the moves made in the *Critique of Pure Reason* as a whole. We must continue to make the case for this textual focus as we explore Kant's architectonic in the chapters that follow. We will consider how Kant's transcendental arguments, as these are formed and unified through the unfolding of his architectonic, construct a system that is to be the condition of possibility for 'experience as such'.

Many significant questions concerning Kant's architectonic method have not been answered. These further test our understanding of his way of arguing over the course of the unfolding of his architectonic. The concrete nature of synthesis is something we've specified as spatio-temporal but this definition is something we will need to explain and develop further. Synthesis is always performed in and through space and time, through the a priori forms or relations they offer. As we've seen, rather than being given in experience they are involved in the giving of experience and so form part of an account of experience. Thus we move from the warmth of the stone in direct sunlight, from it being possible for it to be in the right place at the right time to be warmed by the sun, to considering the a priori concepts that apply to it. As we've seen, spatio-temporal synthesis must make the application of an a priori concept possible because it is always already related to the a priori. We need to consider further how for Kant the a priori is involved in synthesis and is not simply applied to experience after the event of its synthesis. We will pursue this in Chapters 4 and 5 of this book where we will seek to understand how the a priori is not just relevant or applicable to possible experience but is always already involved in its synthesis.

For Kant we need both the abstract and the concrete to make possible the rich activity of the cognition of experience, such as when heat is rigorously defined by chemistry or when the heat of the stone is recognized and can then be harnessed for different practical ends. These two elements are concentrated in the form of judgement that for Kant is basic to all cognition precisely insofar as at every stage and movement of his account of cognition, in every part of the *Critique of Pure Reason*, the relations of the synthetic and the a priori are at stake. Thus, as Kant puts it, '[t]houghts without content are empty; intuitions without concepts are blind' (CPR: A51/B75). Understanding this will be our concern in the rest of this book as we seek to grasp the unity of the *Critique of Pure Reason* and its relation to Deleuze's thought. In the next chapter we will consider, on the basis of what we've learnt so far, how a single and unifying problem actually organizes the *Critique of Pure Reason*. We will then take our first steps in seeking to relate this architectonic method and its precepts to the work of Gilles Deleuze.

Chapter 2

Ideas and Method in Kant and Deleuze

In the previous chapter of this book I argued that the basis of the architectonic, the starting point from which it unfolds, is the problem of the possibility of synthetic a priori judgement. I also considered how an argument that relied upon cause and effect – allowing us to conclude that 'the sun warms the stone' – makes use of a concept that forms part of a system for accounting for the cognition of possible experience as such. Such arguments are ordered, with effect necessarily following cause in each case, only as part of the whole system that forms the architectonic of the *Critique of Pure Reason*. In this chapter I will consider how this system is actually constructed on the basis of the problem of securing synthetic a priori cognition. I have investigated the form of argument that characterizes the architectonic but need to consider the relation of this form of argument to the presentation and organization of the *Critique of Pure Reason*. I will do this in the first section of this chapter and this will involve introducing a number of new terms and engaging further with the issues that confront Kant's architectonic.

The first new term is 'problematic Idea', a term which I will use to further define the single and unifying problem Kant is concerned with in his architectonic and its role in the construction of systems. By exploring this term in some depth I will seek to understand how Kant's presentation of the *Critique of Pure Reason* is inclusive and internalizing in the construction of a system for accounting for the cognition of possible experience. I will ask how it can secure such an account without relying upon anything external. I will then explore Kant's response to certain critical questions by considering how his notion of a problematic Idea can make clear and convincing his construction of an inward-looking system. We find that this system is to be complete. To evaluate this claim I will need to situate and define completeness carefully within the architectonic method. We will see that Kant is able to defend his complete Idea of a system against charges of being rigid or artificial, of over-determining what it seeks to account for, because it is also a problematic Idea. Finally I will ask how he grounds the activity of system building in a problematic Idea. How can we be sure that the system we are constructing provides a valid account of the cognition of possible experience if we cannot assume anything external to its own unfolding?

Having grappled with these critical questions I will turn, in the second section of this chapter, to Deleuze's account of problematic Ideas. I will recognize the major differences between their accounts but will focus upon their common ground. This will be found in the methodological role of problematic Ideas and I will seek to show that their relation can be broadened and deepened on this basis. Thus, while Deleuze's account of Ideas draws upon thinkers other than Kant, it takes from him the methodological and unifying function of Ideas. This common ground will be the basis of the comparison between Kant and Deleuze that we will develop over the remainder of this book.

Idea and System in Kant's *Critique of Pure Reason*

I noted at the start of the previous chapter that the basis upon which the systematic unfolding of Kant's architectonic proceeds is unknown and unknowable. It follows that we must seek to understand this basis through its role in the construction of systems. The final section of the second edition introduction to the *Critique of Pure Reason* provides insight into the way in which this text is to be presented architectonically. This section bears the following title: 'Idea and Division of a Special Science under the name of Critique of Pure Reason' (CPR: B24). The terms *idea* and *division* suggest that it will show how the presentation or organization of the *Critique of Pure Reason* can be said to be internal to an argument which is based upon an Idea. We've seen how a single and unifying problem is put at the basis of the activity of the architectonic method. Here this activity is specified as the division of the *Critique of Pure Reason*. There is an Idea behind the division of this text. Our understanding of these terms is crucial to our conception of Kant's account as a whole. Do we have a rigid and artificial division of the text based upon an Idea that determines the outcomes to all the problems cognition might face? In other words, does the Idea over-determine possible experience by leading us to formulate solutions to any possible problem? For Kant an argument is to unfold on the basis of the relation of the synthetic and the a priori in judgements that are foundational for all cognition of possible experience. The text as a whole is to represent a dynamic and convincing response to a problematic Idea when it formulates these synthetic a priori forms. To understand Kant's argument we have to distinguish the completeness of a system based upon a problematic Idea from a completeness that over-determines the outcomes of cognition. For Kant completeness must not tell us what to think or what to expect beyond the most basic conditions, those that make experience possible in the first place. He must therefore show that his account is *complete* in providing the conditions of the cognition of possible experience but not in specifying its outcomes. In what sense can completeness give rise to an open-ended cognition of possible experience?

We learnt in the previous chapter that for Kant the *Critique of Pure Reason* is a propaedeutic. He develops this further when he writes of what it is to prepare for:

> Transcendental philosophy is the idea of a science for which the critique of pure reason is to outline the entire plan *architectonically*, i.e., from principles, with full guarantee of the completeness and reliability of all the components that make up this edifice. (ibid.: A13/B27)

Here Kant distinguishes transcendental philosophy as being concerned with what we've called the architectonic in the broad sense, the organon of principles for all branches of cognition. The *Critique of Pure Reason* does not offer a complete system of all the a priori principles of cognition because it does not include '. . . a comprehensive analysis of the whole of human a priori cognition' (ibid.). Instead it sets out all of the 'root concepts' of which this pure cognition is comprised (ibid.). Such concepts are then to be the source of the growth of cognition, the only roots that can be at the basis of all cognition because they are conditions of its possibility. In this way Kant envisages the outcomes of the cognition of possible experience as inexhaustible (ibid.: A12–13/B26). Onora O'Neill understands this in the following way: 'The construction of reason is to be seen as process rather than product, as practices of connection and integration rather than as once and for all laying foundations' (O'Neill 1992: 292). The process referred to here is one that continues to respond to problems, including the founding problem of the architectonic, rather than seeking to solve them once and for all. Thus the relation of the synthetic and the a priori is always a problem because cognition deals with new sensations and needs to relate them to a priori concepts. However, we need to consider Kant's concern to set out the root concepts that make possible the open-ended process O'Neill refers to. For Kant we cannot be open to experience and extend cognition unless certain conditions of possibility make experience possible in the first place. We need to consider why, contrary to what O'Neill suggests, he understands the complete formulation of these conditions in the architectonic as the necessary foundation of all openness to experience. In other words, how is a complete Idea to ensure openness to experience in a meaningful sense?

How is the completeness of Kant's architectonic system to be secured without seeking to solve all problems and thus over-determine the cognition of possible experience? How can the inexhaustible and rich possibilities of the cognition of experience be realized? If we return to Kant's outline of the two senses of the architectonic, as propaedeutic and as organon, we will be able to see how he responds to this concern. In dividing these two senses Kant introduces a problem. If we ask why he does not seek to produce an organon right away, in the *Critique of Pure Reason* itself, he responds by pointing to the *precariousness* that concerns the propaedeutic. An organon would not be concerned with the precariousness of synthesis (CPR: A14/B28).

The precariousness of synthesis is its difference from the a priori, it is the challenge presented by concrete synthesis to the completeness of a priori concepts and principles. It is something that must be responded to by the architectonic as propaedeutic before we can think about constructing a complete organon of the a priori principles of all cognition. Thus, while the relation of synthetic and a priori gives us a 'complete idea' (ibid.) of the horizon of the activity of all cognition of possible experience, this completeness has to be qualified in a crucial sense. The completeness of the architectonic goes together with the precariousness of the relation of the synthetic and the a priori. Kant writes of the importance of having a unified plan (ibid.). We plan to respond to the precariousness of the relation of the synthetic and the a priori, and this plan takes the form of a system constructed by their relations. For Kant then it is not outside his architectonic that we find the challenge that ultimately characterizes it and ensures that it makes cognition an ongoing process of responding to the problem of relating the synthetic and the a priori. It is to include what challenges it rather than excluding this and then being undermined by what it has excluded. However, the notion that a system can include what challenges it does lead us to a serious criticism. If a challenge can be included within a system, does it really challenge that system? Does it not need to be external to have a genuinely challenging role? In assessing Kant's arguments so far we've seen that he makes his account inclusive or internalizing on the grounds that otherwise we fail to provide a transcendental argument. Without an inclusive and internal system, experience would never make itself known to us, but be undermined by something external. Therefore, any challenge must be included in the system and provide its internal dynamic or inner problematic. We will now consider whether Kant's inclusion of precariousness is convincing by seeing how this characterizes his systematic account.

We've seen that if we combine completeness and precariousness at the basis of Kant's architectonic, in the term 'problematic Idea', we can better understand how it unfolds without being rigid or inflexible. How does this division according to a problematic Idea actually take place in the text of the *Critique of Pure Reason*? If we remain in the final section of the second edition introduction to the text we find Kant making the following declaration:

> If, then, the division of the science being set forth here is to be performed in terms of the general viewpoint of a system as such, then this science must contain in the first place a *doctrine of elements*, and in the second a *doctrine of method*, of pure reason. (ibid.: A15/B29)

This is the viewpoint of a system that relates the elements of an account of the cognition of possible experience. It relates the contributions of the different faculties of cognition in the Doctrine of Elements so that an account of the cognition of possible experience is formed first of all. Sensible intuition contributes sensations, understanding contributes pure concepts, imagination contributes schemata, judgement contributes principles and reason contributes Ideas.[1] At each stage we have a precarious and problematic Idea of the relation between the synthetic and the a priori at work in relating these elements. Over the course of the *Critique of Pure Reason* this forms a system for accounting for the cognition of possible experience. This system is to be complete insofar as it includes and responds to the precariousness or inner problematic in question. We see that the Doctrine of Method must appear only after the Doctrine of Elements has responded to the problem of the possibility of synthetic a priori judgements. This is because it concerns itself with the cognition of possible experience that now has its foundation in the account of synthetic a priori cognition secured in the Doctrine of Elements. It must reflect the unity of the a priori and the synthetic at the basis of all cognition. Kant's projected division of the text continues when he writes that in the Doctrine of Elements sensation comes before the understanding as a source of the unity of the synthetic and the a priori. The a priori emerges in sensation first because objects of cognition are given to us before they are thought (ibid.: A16/B30). We encounter the a priori in the syntheses exhibited by mathematics before we can consider the role of a priori concepts of the understanding by reflecting on such things as the order of events in experience. Thus the Transcendental Aesthetic comes before the Transcendental Analytic in the Doctrine of Elements because of the order of our encounters with the a priori. Kant goes no further in his sketch of the division of the text but he has provided the dynamic. This is the response of this organization to a problematic Idea of the unity of the synthetic and the a priori at different stages of the account he is giving.

We can see that this unfolding has its reasons within Kant's architectonic, in the problematic Idea it raises. However, we must continue to confront important questions that arise about any account that is internalizing and inclusive, that is complete in the sense we've defined this term. The architectonic must provide us with reasons for its internal focus. For Kant the synthetic and the a priori are not unproblematically related but related in a way that needs to be accounted for through a well-presented argument. This means that, in the presentation of the *Critique of Pure Reason*, we first show where they are exhibited together, in the mathematical truths considered in the Transcendental Aesthetic. This part of the text is divided from the rest in order to be clarified and to convince us of the relation of the synthetic and the a priori through an isolation argument. As we saw in the previous chapter of this book, the work of mathematics allows Kant to isolate certain a priori ingredients of cognition. The work done by the Transcendental Aesthetic can then support a transcendental argument that begins in the Metaphysical Deduction of the Transcendental Analytic. Here the abstract use of the understanding in General Logic does not exhibit any connection with concrete experience. However, the need to relate it to the concrete is supported by the unity of the synthetic and the a priori as exhibited in the Transcendental Aesthetic and founded upon the problematic Idea represented by synthetic a priori judgement in the introduction to the text. The abstract a priori is isolated from the concrete synthetic in General Logic and this is a problem because Kant is investigating the possibility of synthetic a priori judgements in the *Critique of Pure Reason*. He needs to account for their closer relations as these have already been exhibited in the Transcendental Aesthetic but now must be secured using a different type of argument in an account of possible experience as such. It also follows that the schematism chapter of the Transcendental Analytic, which is concerned with involving the abstract directly in the concrete work of synthesis, must come later. Only in this way can it respond to this problematic without pre-empting the earlier stages of the argument that seek to justify the conclusion that the a priori is at least relevant to the synthetic. Kant seeks in this way to clarify the different stages of his account, to divide them in a way that convinces us that the a priori needs to be related to the synthetic in order to account for possible experience. However, while this allows us to make sense of Kant's division of the text, it still does not allow us to fully understand the basis upon which it proceeds. How is a problematic Idea the basis of the construction of a system for accounting for the cognition of possible experience?

We need to understand how the division of the stages of the *Critique of Pure Reason* is convincing precisely because it is systematic and based upon a problematic Idea. If this Idea unifies and organizes an account of cognition then for Kant it does this systematically. If it did not do this it would not be clear and convincing, it would not be a process in which we could have absolute confidence because it is a priori rather than a posteriori. Kant therefore begins his chapter on the architectonic in the Doctrine of Method by defining the term *architectonic* as 'the art of systems' (ibid.: A832/B860). As we've seen, the *Critique of Pure Reason* can be read and understood as Kant's attempt to construct a system for accounting for the cognition of possible experience that unfolds through the relations of the synthetic and the a priori at different stages of this account. The system constructed here is for Kant a condition of possibility for the cognition of possible experience as such. It is a propaedeutic that makes explicit the whole set of root concepts always already at work in its synthesis. Thus if cause and effect is part of this system, one of the root concepts it formulates, it must play a systematic part in making the cognition of experience possible. It does this only as one root concept among a system of root concepts. It is a condition of possibility but only as a part of a whole system. Thus, it is part of an architectonic unity rather than a technical unity that responds to problems as they arise in the course of experience (ibid.: A833/B861). Thus if we had a concept of cause and effect but no concept of substance then for Kant we would not have experience at all because we could not keep hold of an unchanging substance which would form part of a chain of cause and effect. We could not construct a technical unity of root concepts that responded to problems that arise in experience because without the whole system of root concepts experience as such would not be possible. Thus an architectonic unity or system focuses upon making experience possible and for Kant this means that it responds to its own inner problematic or problematic Idea. If it looked outside to what is given in experience it would presuppose what it was to account for and form a technical unity or aggregate of responses to problems that arise in the course of experience. This allows us to better understand the role of a system as a condition of possibility for experience and how for Kant problematic Ideas are distinguished from contingent problems that arise in the course of experience.

We see that Kant seeks not merely a more convenient or more effective way of responding dynamically to the problematic Idea but the only way of doing so if we are to provide an account of the cognition of possible experience. We remember that transcendental arguments are to be indispensable and the system Kant proposes in the *Critique of Pure Reason* is to form such an argument. This helps Kant to respond to a critical question that now arises. Can we really walk confidently on solid ground when we proceed on the basis Kant proposes? In the remainder of this section we will consider how his art of constructing systems seems to lack any grounding given that it is focused upon its own unfolding, upon its own internal problematic. Kant is concerned to show that we cannot know the basis of our systematic activity and this means that we do not stand upon the *solid ground* offered by something already known or given in experience. There is nothing known or knowable to support our construction of a system. However, for Kant we nevertheless proceed to treat nature as something that can be systematically unified. We *walk upon solid ground* and don't need to always worry that our system of a priori concepts and principles will be undermined or might not actually correspond to reality. His overall transcendental argument in the *Critique of Pure Reason* is that experience is only possible if it proceeds within the framework of a system. This system must be unfolded on the basis of the problematic Idea we have been concerned with. It must be the only possible system for accounting for the cognition of experience because otherwise we would always be unsure about whether it has any contact with reality. If it left anything out or left open the possibility of other methods for securing possible experience then it would not provide the solid ground that is needed for cognition to be re-founded. For Kant, our construction of systems would be plagued by uncertainty if it were not focused solely upon its own unfolding. We must consider whether, as a result of this focus, his construction of systems loses touch with the concrete reality it must secure and account for. Does his abstract system float free of reality, of the concrete pole of our cognition of possible experience?

We've raised the question of the *solid ground* walked upon by the architectonic in its construction of systems. If we are constructing an a priori system we must reflect the completeness, universality and necessity of the a priori in how we proceed. Therefore, Kant's art of constructing systems must be characterized by certainty and confidence rather than experimentation or doubt. However, this system must be internally grounded, through the relations of its parts, rather than referring to a ground external to itself. How does Kant respond to the problem of grounding his systematic account? He rejects certain possible grounds for his construction of a system as being external to his account. These are things we need to account for rather than presuppose. In a paper entitled 'Projecting the Order of Nature' Philip Kitcher explains Kant's approach by considering two alternative ways of ordering experience that are rejected. One is realist and the other is pragmatist. The realist alternative is a system that seeks to recapitulate the order of nature itself (Kitcher 1998: 219–20). It provides the principles that structure nature and this allows us to derive laws of nature, the laws of objective natural necessity. This, Kitcher argues, is an Aristotelian concern with the 'order of being' rather than with the 'order of thought' (ibid.: 220). This is precisely the 'solid ground' or basis in reality that Kant seems to be lacking when he focuses upon an internal problematic to the exclusion of anything external.

The other alternative, associated with pragmatism, concerns itself with an 'order of thought', with how we think about nature. It seeks the best or most pragmatic way of thinking about reality rather than seeking to grasp the order of a reality independent of our thought. This pragmatist alternative would lead us to understand the architectonic as providing '. . . a manual for anticipating experience. It is full of useful information about general regularities involving familiar characteristics of familiar things' (ibid.: 219). The pragmatic aim is to make anticipating future experience as easy and reliable as possible by considering how we deal with experience, how we systematize our thought. This establishes a seemingly inescapable dichotomy between an objective 'order of being' and a subjective 'order of thought'. While the pragmatic alternative sounds closer to Kant's approach, Kitcher argues that neither of them fits Kant's project of re-founding and re-organizing the cognition of experience on the basis of its conditions of possibility. Instead a middle way is followed in the *Critique of Pure Reason*. Kitcher argues that: 'Central to Kant's thinking about science is his conception of inquiry as guided by principles that enjoin us to introduce a certain kind of order into our beliefs' (ibid.: 221). This has to be distinguished from the pragmatic alternative. What distinguishes it is the idea that we are 'enjoined' to introduce order into our beliefs. This ordering is necessary as part of a system for all cognition of experience rather than being in any way provisional or open to revision. Thus cause and effect is a concept and principle within a system that holds for all cognition, it enjoins us to order our beliefs so that they form valid arguments as part of a greater whole. We are thus enjoined by a system whose necessity and completeness grounds the valid arguments we make about such things as the role of cause and effect in situations where a certain order of events is observed.

For Kant we cannot rely upon a reality external to an account of synthetic a priori cognition but we also cannot rely upon a subjective order of thought if we want to include the objective side of experience in our account. In the

Critique of Pure Reason's Appendix to the Ideal of Pure Reason, Kant specifies the unity of reason as a systematic unity (A680/B708). He argues that this does not allow reason to grasp all possible objects of cognition. Its role is not objective but subjective insofar as it provides a maxim for reason's use in all cognition of objects over the course of experience. However, he qualifies this subjective role when he adds that '. . . the systematic coherence that reason can give to the understanding's empirical use not only furthers the extension of this use, but at the same time verifies the correctness thereof' (ibid.). He concludes that this makes 'the principle of such a systematic unity' objective as well as subjective but only in an 'indeterminate' way. It is not then a principle for the constitution of objects but for the regulation of the inexhaustible work of reason in empirical cognition. This it does '. . . by opening up new paths unknown to the understanding, while yet never going in the least against the laws of this empirical use' (ibid.). Here Kant is re-defining the subjective and the objective. He seeks to avoid the dichotomy of a subjective 'order of thought' and an objective 'order of being'. As we saw in the previous chapter of this book, subjectivity and objectivity are assigned their places and roles, and defined as such, by the architectonic method. For Kant they must not precede the work of this method and show us how it is to be understood. It is not then a question of an alternative between what is 'in us' and what is 'in the world' because these locations have not been assigned by an account of the cognition of possible experience as such. Now Kant wants to secure an account of objective experience without over-determining it. The objectivity secured by this system is qualified because it does not constitute the objective outcomes of cognition, it does not tell us what objects we will come across, but makes possible the inclusion of these outcomes in experience. The system is therefore objective 'in an indeterminate way'. This follows from the need for the architectonic to be inclusive but without over-determining the outcomes of cognition, something that would make its concepts and principles 'constitutive'. The system is to make it possible to convert subjective beliefs into objective knowledge but not determine the objects thus secured beyond the conditions of their possibility. Thus Kitcher writes: 'This distinction [between belief and knowledge] is to emerge from our efforts to systematize our beliefs in accordance with the principle of unification. Certain claims come to be regarded as lawlike because they play a particular role in the systematization of belief' (1998: 236). We can therefore use cause and effect to solidify beliefs into knowledge because this concept is one that makes experience possible as part of a system of such concepts. If we want to ground the system we are constructing, and ensure that it is 'in touch with reality', we must build a system out of a priori elements, out of conditions of the possibility of experience as such. For Kant this accounts for and includes the subjective and the objective rather than being on the side of one or the other.

We've seen that Kant's architectonic seeks to formulate only the conditions of possibility for the cognition of experience but not the outcomes of this cognition.

It seeks a priori concepts which are the root concepts of cognition rather than empirical concepts that embody the outcomes and achievements of cognition. In this way Kant seeks to open experience to cognition on the basis of certain necessary conditions. Thus he considers how we are enjoined to systematize our experience in certain necessary ways when we pursue the rich and inexhaustible work of empirical cognition. In the next section of this chapter we will consider how these methodological concerns provide a link to Deleuze's account of experience despite their many differences.

Ideas and Concrete Cases in Deleuze's
Difference and Repetition

We have so far focused upon the unifying method that Kant employs in the *Critique of Pure Reason* and postponed any consideration of his relation to Deleuze in order to pursue this. In the introduction to this book, we argued that rather than looking at the particular concepts they employ, we should consider the overall method behind their accounts of experience. We may explore this by turning to their respective notions of 'critique'. This refers to a genuinely critical account of experience insofar as it avoids assuming what is to be accounted for. It subjects all potential elements of its account to a critique that prevents anything given in experience from being presupposed. As we've seen, the architectonic of Kant's *Critique of Pure Reason* is intended as just such an account. Critique must embody certain criteria that unify thought by ensuring that it is genuinely and consistently critical in its account of experience. However, Ian Mackenzie represents Deleuze's view of Kant's critique in the following terms: '*In Kant, reason transcends critique such that both the totality and immanence of critique itself are unrealizable*' (Mackenzie 2004: 20). In other words, if certain ends of critique, such as the ends of reason, are not subject to critique like everything else we do not have a total critique or one to which everything is immanent. These ends are transcendent because they rise above the critical interrogation to which all potential elements of an account of experience must be subject. We have used the terms 'internal' and 'inclusive' to characterize Kant's architectonic and these have a great deal in common with the terms 'total' and 'immanent'. A total account leaves nothing out, it leaves nothing uncriticized. It is immanent because it draws upon the internal relations of its parts rather than relying upon anything transcendent or external when it gives its account. Deleuze emphasizes the potentially destructive nature of critique because, if we are to have a genuinely internal or immanent focus, the external or transcendent must not get in the way. The ground must be cleared so that our account is a critical one.[2] Kant and Deleuze therefore have similar concerns but Deleuze proceeds to accuse Kant, as Mackenzie suggests, of failing to live up to his own standards.

We find that Deleuze shares Kant's concern with the transcendental and the critical standards it embodies but seeks to go further:

> The transcendent is not the transcendental. Were it not for consciousness, the transcendental field would be defined as a pure plane of immanence, because it eludes all transcendence of the subject and of the object. Absolute immanence is in itself: it is not in something, *to* something; it does not depend on an object or belong to a subject. (Deleuze 2001: 26)

For Deleuze we need to account for the subject and the object, to understand them as being produced at the same time or immanently. One does not come before the other and they both emerge through an account of experience rather than preceding this account. This is the sense in which for Deleuze critique is totalizing and inclusive. The subject and the object must not transcend our account and be imposed upon it from the outside. He argues that to realize Kant's critique, to make it total and immanent, we must be so rigorous that there is no uncriticized remainder. Insofar as Kant preserves anything of the subject and object of knowledge we are familiar with, in the concepts he makes a priori, he has failed to live up to the standards of critique. Deleuze accuses him of 'redoubling' the empirical when he preserves ends of reason which are in fact always given in experience (ibid.: 27). Reason seeks to understand the subject and the object in certain ways but for Deleuze these ends of reason always have an empirical origin. We must therefore move away from Kant's attempt to preserve the objects and subjects reason recognizes, we must abandon this understanding of experience in order to account for it fully.

This negative assessment of Kant is balanced somewhat by Deleuze's positive references to the notion of problematic Ideas he finds in the *Critique of Pure Reason*. These are both transcendent and immanent (Smith 2006: 48). Insofar as they refer to a regulative triumvirate of self, world and God they are transcendent. However, insofar as they refer to a certain methodology they are immanent and embody values that Deleuze shares. We will now seek to explain this distinction. Kant's Ideas regulate our cognition by leading us to proceed *as if* there is a self, a world and a God. These are the transcendent ends of reason, giving us an Idea of what the subject and object must be like. They are not in fact objects of our cognition, they are unknowable like all problematic Ideas, but we must proceed *as if* they do exist in order to coherently relate the objects we do cognize. They form part of Kant's method for systematically unifying experience so that, for example, we see the self as a simple and unified thing. We proceed as if a subject or 'thinker' thinks the thoughts we encounter in inner experience just as an object causes events we encounter in outer experience. However, only in the latter case do we actually cognize the object referred to. This returns us to Kant's concern with constructing systems but gives more personality to the problematic Ideas that guide systematic cognition. If we understand the self as the thinker of the thoughts we encounter in inner experience, this makes experience more coherent or systematic, but this does not mean that we actually cognize this thinking subject (CPR: A682–3/ B710–11). However, we've seen that Deleuze does not want critique to preserve a subject and an object because it should 'not depend on an object or belong to a subject'. We will seek to develop Deleuze's relation to the immanent and methodological role of Ideas in Kant's *Critique of Pure Reason* despite their disagreement over the ends these Ideas embody. In chapter 4 of Deleuze's 1968 work *Difference and Repetition* we find a theory of problematic Ideas whose lineage is broad and varied. Readings of this chapter explore and emphasize the very different influences that shaped it.[3] We argued in the introduction to this book that if we merely ask where Kant's influence ends and base our inquiry on this type of question we cannot gauge the scope of his relations to Deleuze. Our focus will not be upon how Deleuze selects from Kant's work and then moves away from Kant to the various other influences that shape the fourth chapter of *Difference and Repetition*. Instead we will consider how his interest in Kantian Ideas expresses a broader relation and a common ground when it comes to the methods that unify thought. Their shared methodological concerns are a unifying theme rather than limiting their relations to particular concepts or aspects of their respective accounts of experience.[4]

We've seen that for Kant a problematic Idea at the basis of the architectonic must embody both the abstract and the concrete. If we consider Deleuze's account of experience we find that he first of all emphasizes the concrete. In the introduction to this book we noted that some commentators understand his project in *Difference and Repetition* as a version of the *Critique of Pure Reason*. He re-writes Kant's text by folding the intelligible into the sensible or the Transcendental Dialectic into the Transcendental Aesthetic. This does echo Kant's concern with synthesis, with how the abstract is related to, and realized through, its relation to the concrete. However, Deleuze criticizes Kant for failing to account for the intelligible through its relation to concrete synthesis. Instead of securing the abstract and then relating it to the concrete he wants to start by paying closer attention to the concrete and see what this produces. This seems to put the methods of these two thinkers at odds, suggesting that for Deleuze Ideas are realized in concrete cases while for Kant, as we saw, an Idea is realized in a system for accounting for all cases of experience as such. Jean-Clet Martin develops Deleuze's concern with the concrete when he writes: 'To have difficulty, or rather to be in difficulty, is the position of philosophy mired up to its neck in the detail of the concrete' (Martin 1999: 241). Thus, rather than securing an ability to deal with concrete particularities in certain abstract and a priori ways, Deleuze is concerned with how we are put 'in difficulty' by the concrete. He is concerned with how we are overwhelmed and amazed by it, with how we are made idiotic by the failure of abstract abilities and forms of unity (DR: 130). Martin argues that Deleuze replaces a concern with how the abstract is secured and then applied to the concrete with a concern with how the concrete produces its own forms of unity (Martin 1999: 242).

Thus conceptual forms of possibility do not precede and make intelligible what we encounter in sensation. The concrete and its ability to make things unintelligible must be able to account for the abstract and intelligible forms of unity we recognize. Moments when we are put 'in difficulty' are therefore more instructive and significant for an account of experience than moments when we find sensation intelligible. In this way Deleuze seeks to account for experience in its abstract forms by relating them to something they don't resemble, to moments when the abstract fails to grasp the concrete.

This concern to learn from the concrete leads Deleuze to argue that: 'It is the excess in the Idea which explains the lack in the concept' (DR: 273). In other words, insofar as Ideas are incarnated and realized in concrete sensation they exceed concepts that we seek to apply to concrete cases. They show us a different form of the abstract, one richer than conceptual forms of possibility because it actually emerges through the concrete. At this point we must note that Deleuze is not suggesting that we acquire Ideas from what is given in experience. As we've noted, he agrees with Kant in this respect and is particularly concerned that this would lead us to focus wrongly on what is familiar and recognizable in experience. If we confined ourselves to what is given in experience we would focus upon patterns of resemblance rather than upon unintelligible and unrecognizable moments that produce new patterns or forms of unity. If we stick to what is familiar and recognisable then for Deleuze we do not learn about how experience is produced and we are not able to account for it. Instead we must be open to the unintelligible work of concrete synthesis but, unlike in Kant, this work of synthesis exceeds the grasp of concepts. This at once echoes and strongly differs from Kant's account. Deleuze wants to include what exceeds concepts while for Kant the coherence and continuity of a priori concepts in a system makes experience possible. However, Deleuze echoes Kant's concern that we do not rely upon what is given in experience in order to account for it. This shows how similar these two thinkers are when it comes to the methods by which they account for experience but also Deleuze's concern that Kant didn't go far enough in his critique.

The methodology that is associated with problematic Ideas in Deleuze's account of experience must be explored further if we are to develop the common ground he shares with Kant. If a problem were destined to be erased by its solution then, as Christian Kerslake notes, a problem would be a very general thing (Kerslake 2007: 98). Anything could be a problem because all it would have to do is elude cognition for some period of time. However, the problem Kant and Deleuze are concerned with is not simply lacking a solution. It is something that gives rise to different solutions which never erase the problem but do show us how productive it can be. We can illustrate this by considering the distinction between the problem of finding an object and the problem of learning more about an object. In the former case we erase the problem when we find the object while in the latter case we have an open-ended process of providing different solutions to the problem. Another way of putting this is to say that the former object is determined in advance, we know what it is and will recognize it when we find it, but the latter object is undetermined by its very nature. As the undetermined object of a problematic Idea it gives rise to different solutions. It is the unifying theme of these solutions, the theme that leads us to continue to explore concrete cases. Thus, for example, if our object is a particular zebra we would be able to erase the problem given sufficient time and resources. It is a determinate object that we can find and recognize, thus solving the first type of problem. However, if we are engaging with the second type of problem we would never exhaust the solutions to the problem of the zebra. To learn about this animal or about animal life in general is potentially a lifetime's work. It is potentially the unifying and inexhaustible theme of a life. Deleuze shows how the two kinds of problems are related when writing about Kant's theory of problematic Ideas: 'In effect, the undetermined object, or object as it exists in the Idea, allows us to represent other objects (those of experience) which it endows with a maximum of systematic unity' (DR: 169). In other words, the problems that are erased by their solutions occur within the context of problems that are never erased but which can organize and sustain a whole life of activity. Thus we may discover a determinate object, the zebra, but as part of a life unified by a problem that has no determinate object, such as the life of the zoologist. Deleuze's reading reflects the way in which, for Kant, Ideas must assist understanding's cognition of objects; they must be the basis for a systematic investigation into concrete cases. Thus, interacting with a zebra, observing it or reading books about its way of life are concrete cases but they form part of an abstract system for responding to an inexhaustible problem or problematic Idea. Deleuze's appreciation of this methodological role of Ideas in Kant's account shows us how we may relate them more closely. Let's see if their divergent accounts of experience can be drawn together if we focus upon the methods that unify them.

Deleuze refers to 'real experience' as the object of his account in contrast to Kant's concern to account for 'possible experience'.[5] Instead of conceptual forms of possibility mediating the relation of the sensible and the intelligible, the intelligible is to be directly incarnated and realized in the sensible. Hence the importance of unintelligible moments in the synthesis of sensations. These are moments when a problem forces us to look for solutions that extend Ideas by engaging more closely with the concrete. Thus, in the example we gave, we engage with the ways in which an animal occupies space and time rather than considering the possible ways in which such an object could occupy space and time given the concepts we possess. We do not begin by considering how experience can be made intelligible but learn from how it becomes unintelligible. This leads Daniel W. Smith to argue that '. . . whereas Kantian Ideas are unifying, totalising and conditioning (transcendent Ideas), for Deleuze they will become multiple, differential, and genetic (immanent Ideas)' (Smith 2006: 48). The mediation and conditioning provided by concepts in Kant's account distances him from Deleuze. Smith points to the 'multiple, differential, and genetic' nature of Ideas that are incarnated in the sensible. To follow an Idea in sensation is to follow the differentiation of an Idea in and across concrete cases. For Deleuze this is what constitutes and unifies real experience. A way of understanding this is to say that an Idea is a common theme of different concrete situations. It is the object we study across different cases but is an undetermined object, one that produces different things in sensation rather than producing resemblance or uniformity. It does not tell us what concrete situations will be like, or what is possible in sensation, but is realized in the differences that emerge. We have a differentiating theme or Idea but one that is differentiated and extended by sensation itself. We can explain this further by considering Deleuze's exploration of biological Ideas in *Difference and Repetition*. He is not talking about the identity of 'the biological' as some kind of classificatory category abstracted from experience. 'The biological' is a theme of different concrete situations, one that is realized in the emergence of different cases in sensation. Human beings and zebras are different cases of 'the biological' and it is through their common Idea that they are both unified and differentiated. In this way we find that Deleuze develops Kantian Ideas so that they can be realized in sensation and in the way we engage with experience without concepts playing a mediating role.

A further difference between the two accounts must also be registered. For Deleuze there are as many varieties of Ideas as can be realized in the synthesis of sensation. Thus, if sensation produces biological differences between animals, it incarnates biological Ideas. It is the variety that the concrete presents us with that dictates the variety of Ideas. Likewise, social differences are to be seen as the realization of social Ideas (DR: 186). They imply a further variety of Ideas. As we've noted, Kant presents three Ideas in the *Critique of Pure Reason*'s Transcendental Dialectic. We cannot know that there is a self, a world or a God but we pursue the work of cognition *as if* these things exist beyond the realm of experience. There is less variety of Ideas here and for Deleuze this follows from the transcendent role of Ideas in Kant's account. Ideas embody ends that are respected and transcend critique, with the result that the concrete cannot make us aware of many more Ideas. However, we've seen that the methodological role of Ideas is developed by Deleuze, leading us to use the example of the zoologist's inexhaustible engagement with animal life. He or she learns from the concrete ways biological Ideas are realized, the ways in which concrete cases tell us more about animal life than we can understand in advance. We never know or determine the object of an Idea but for Kant and Deleuze this is what makes it problematic and thus rich and inexhaustible. Therefore, despite the differences we keep encountering between their accounts we are able to keep sight of their common ground.

As we noted, Kant develops the immanent, methodological role of an Idea of the self in cases of introspection or inner experience. He writes that, while we proceed as if there is a thinking subject behind our thoughts, it remains the case that we never find the unity of the appearances offered to us in inner sense (CPR: A682/B710). It does not provide us with something that could become an object of cognition and that we might call a simple and unified self. For Kant this lack of an object of cognition is more than made up for by the role of a problematic Idea in cognition. We have '. . . the idea of a simple independent intelligence' (ibid.: A682–3/B710–11). Kant argues that this only gives reason 'principles of systematic unity' which are of use in explaining 'appearances of the soul' (ibid.: A682/B710). These instruct us to treat these appearances as belonging to a single subject. Kant argues that to proceed *as if* there is a thinking subject behind the appearances of inner sense is a valid method and is indispensable for the systematic work of cognition. However, our use of this Idea must be relative to '. . . reason's systematic use regarding our soul's appearances' (ibid.: A683/B711). As we saw, it is not an 'order of being' or a pragmatic ordering of our thought that grounds this activity. Therefore, we proceed *as if* there is a thinking subject behind inner experience but cannot determine it as an object of cognition. We then allow this assumption to regulate our practice for the sake of the system as a whole, for the sake of a system where a thinking subject is an indispensible and productive Idea. Thus if, instead of the sun warming the stone, a person throws a stone we do not have an object of cognition that can be located as the cause of this event. However, to make sense of this case and include it in our cognition of experience as a whole we need to proceed as if a thinking subject exists who can recognize a stone, decide to throw it and then do so. In other words, to systematically organize experience using cause and effect, one of the conditions of possibility of experience, we need a problematic Idea of the self. The unity of the system, a methodological unity, allows something unknown and undetermined to have a necessary role in the cognition of experience. For Deleuze this role of Ideas is immanent and valid within a critical account of experience even if Kant's Ideas are also transcendent ends of reason and too limited in their variety.

Conclusion

We may now remind ourselves of the common ground we have uncovered. What concerns do Kant and Deleuze share when it comes to the methodological role of Ideas? Ideas must ensure that the cognition of experience is productive and must allow us to account for it without presupposing what we are seeking to account for. Deleuze recognizes that he shares with Kant an understanding of the role of Ideas in producing different cases of experience. He writes in *Difference and Repetition* that for Kant '. . . the concepts of the understanding find the ground of their (maximum) full experimental use only in the degree to which they are related to problematic Ideas: . . .' (DR: 169). He adds that it is on the basis of Ideas that concepts are able to '. . . comprise more and more differences on the basis of a properly infinite field of continuity' (ibid.). By setting problems, Deleuze argues, Kant has set thought the task of realizing the scope of problematic Ideas in experience. Since they have no determinate object or final solution, these Ideas lead us to explore the richness of experience, to engage with differences that arise in sensation. There is a 'properly infinite field of continuity' because problematic Ideas are at the heart of a method for dealing with experience. They ensure that we continue to learn from the ability of sensation to differentiate experience because they are unsolvable. It is insofar as Ideas keep experience open in this way for Kant, allowing us to 'comprise more and more differences', that he shares a common ground with Deleuze.

In the following chapters of the book I will seek to show how the problematic Idea of synthetic a priori judgement is realized in the system constructed in the *Critique of Pure Reason*. In the next chapter we will see that the Table of Categories relates the abstract and the concrete in a Transcendental Logic. It responds to the problematic Idea of the relation of the synthetic and the a priori because its starting point is the abstract use of the understanding but this is shown to be relevant to the concrete synthesis of sensation. This combination of abstract origin and relevance to the concrete is problematic for Kant and must therefore organize the account he is giving in the *Critique of Pure Reason* so that it forms a system. In the fourth and fifth chapters of this book we will see how the schematism of the Table of Categories again seeks to relate the abstract and the concrete but at a different stage in this account. The a priori is now shown to be involved in synthesis from the start rather than relating to it from a distance. However, at all stages of the account it is a system that is being con-structed, a system that from the Metaphysical Deduction onwards is embodied in a Table of Categories. For Kant, as we've seen, putting systematic limitations or conditions upon what can form part of experience is absolutely necessary. He seeks to project a systematic unity of possible experience.

I will continue to be concerned with how, rather than simply arguing that we must relate the abstract and the concrete, Kant is also arguing that the abstract must comprise a particular system. I will explore the way in which Kant argues in favour of this system, one embodied in a Table of Categories, over the next three chapters of this book. This will allow me to return to Deleuze in the sixth chapter. I will there consider how he shares a concern not only with problematic Ideas but also with the form of argument that, over the next three chapters, we will see Kant using in the *Critique of Pure Reason*'s Metaphysical Deduction and Analytic of Principles.

Chapter 3

Kant's Metaphysical Deduction

In the *Critique of Pure Reason* Kant formulates a Table of Judgements and a Table of Categories (CPR: A70/B95; A80/B106). He claims that the Table of Judgements presents the basic logical abilities or functions of the faculty of understanding. From these basic abilities he derives a Table of the basic conceptual forms or categories under which all of possible experience must be unified. This process of unification through judgement and under categories is to make experience possible. His claim in this Metaphysical Deduction is that we can derive the basic conceptual ways in which experience can and must be cognized solely from what understanding can do entirely by itself (ibid.: A65–6/B90–1). He is therefore concerned with the pure use of the understanding and with its pure concepts or categories. It will not then be possible to revise or add to these tables because they are established solely by exploring the abilities of the understanding and establishing these once and for all. Kant later refers to this account in the following terms: 'In the *metaphysical deduction* we established the a priori origin of the categories as such through their complete concurrence with the universal logical functions of thought' (ibid.: B159). Despite the huge ambitions of this deduction in Chapter 1 of the Analytic of Concepts, where both tables are presented, is only 26 pages in length. This includes six pages which were added in the second edition of the *Critique of Pure Reason* but there is little explanation and discussion of individual judgements and categories (ibid.: A65–83/B90–116).[1] However, many readers have wondered why this deduction is so brief. They argue that it must be supplemented either by later sections of the *Critique of Pure Reason* or by more recent discoveries concerning the logical abilities of thought. The task in this paper will be to grasp the reasons why Kant found this brief but hugely ambitious deduction of the categories necessary and convincing. For Kant the ways in which experience is to be unified in cognition, in order to make experience possible, must be given a priori, systematically and all at once. He therefore presented these two tables with little discussion of the individual uses and merits of their parts. This very puzzling method will be the concern of this chapter and will add further to our understanding of the architectonic method of which it forms a major part.

In the previous two chapters of this book I concentrated on the Introduction and Doctrine of Method of the *Critique of Pure Reason*. The move is now made from the faculty of reason, whose problem-setting we've focused on, to the faculty of understanding and its singular response to the problem raised. The single problem of relating abstract and concrete is now re-cast by Kant's use of the phrase '. . . an *idea of the whole* of understanding's a priori cognition . . .' (ibid.: A64–5/B89). The concern is with what understanding can do, with forming an Idea of its basic abilities and embodying this in a Table of Judgements. This draws us towards the abstract pole of cognition, towards a concentration upon the abstract abilities and forms of unity that the understanding must contribute in order to make experience possible. Thus in the Metaphysical Deduction we are not focusing upon synthesis and its concrete concerns but upon the abstract that is nevertheless presupposed by the concrete in a full account of experience. The architectonic method and its criteria are at work in this exploration of the pure understanding. This brings with it an internal focus, a focus upon the understanding and its abilities to the exclusion of anything given in the course of experience. In this chapter we will argue that Kant sees it as vital to the success of his deduction that we limit inquiry to what understanding alone is able to do and that the deduction is a brief one because it is limited and focused in this way. However, the Metaphysical Deduction has proved an obscure and unconvincing form of argument for many readers. We only have to dip into one commentary, by Karl Aschenbrenner, to find it described as far-fetched and artificial (Aschenbrenner 1983: 117, 119).[2] Responses to the Metaphysical Deduction often have in common a rejection of Kant's Idea of the whole of understanding's a priori cognition. For many readers the parts do not refer to a whole that precedes them and justifies their deduction.

One response to the puzzling nature of the Metaphysical Deduction is to update Kant's tables of judgements and categories. We may draw upon the modern, post-Fregean logic that has replaced the logic that was generally accepted in Kant's time (Strawson 1966: 80). This approach assumes that Kant's Metaphysical Deduction relies upon the logic of his day, it historicizes the argument he makes. The history of logic has seen general or formal logic become more abstract. This means that it is even less concerned to provide abstract abilities and forms that are in any way relevant to the concrete and synthetic content of cognition. We can therefore be selective about Kant's Table of Categories on the basis of a superior grasp of the abstractness of thought as it is formulated in logic. Logic no longer presents rules for the understanding but is now '. . . the science of objective relations of implication between thoughts . . .' (Longuenesse 2006: 158). It is now logical inference or truth functionality that is the concern, leading to the exclusion of judgements and categories that are relevant in any way to the concrete content of cognition. We can then drop components of Kant's two tables that express his concern to relate the abstract and the concrete.[3] On this reading any Idea of the whole we might have, one that would precede and relate its parts, is dependent on the history of other disciplines. We saw in Chapter 1 of this book that the history of mathematics threatens the integrity of Kant's architectonic. Now the history of logic threatens to re-formulate the two tables that for Kant are to be complete and exhaustive. However, we found in Chapter 1 that we should be wary of reducing Kant's arguments to the history of any discipline. We saw that isolation arguments based on the achievements of mathematics support Kant's transcendental arguments but are not indispensable. Béatrice Longuenesse points out that Kant's logic, as this is expressed in the two tables, does not agree with any of the logic text books of his day (KCJ: 3).[4] We will explore further the supposed dependence of Kant's Idea of the whole of understanding's a priori cognition upon another discipline as the nature of his Metaphysical Deduction becomes clearer.

Another approach that we will assess is a concern to bring the categories 'closer' to experience and to ordinary knowledge claims. This follows from the apparent need to overcome the abstractness of Kant's two tables, their distance from the concrete and its concerns. Rather than making the Table of Categories more abstract, like the history of logic would seem to do, we must relate it more closely to the concrete. We do this by dropping the criteria of the architectonic method that conditions of possibility must be complete. It could be argued that this would allow the understanding to respond dynamically to the concrete. Sebastian Gardner argues that 'Kant need only show that the conceptualization of an objective order plays some transcendental role. On this reading, Kant does not need to rule out other, logically possible metaphysics of experience' (Gardner 1999: 121). It follows that we should treat the two tables as lists of a priori judgements and categories that could be added to in response to experience. We must seek to understand why for Kant it is more convincing to argue that these two tables form a whole to which no addition is possible. We will consider whether being related dynamically to the concrete requires that abstract conditions be open to revision. We've seen that Kant is concerned to relate the abstract and the concrete at every stage of the unfolding of his architectonic. On this basis we will argue that Kant does not begin from a wholly abstract standpoint in the Metaphysical Deduction but one that is related to the concrete concerns of cognition as these emerge through synthesis. He argues that the timelessness of conditions for the cognition of possible experience, their being impervious to change, is not opposed or closed to the concrete. We will consider how these critical approaches to the Metaphysical Deduction could be responded to. The relation of abstract and concrete that for Kant must characterize the different parts of the *Critique of Pure Reason* must be brought into play. This relation emerges within his architectonic rather than through the relation of his arguments to something external, to what is given in experience or in the history of other disciplines.

The Ambitions of the Metaphysical Deduction

In our account of Kant's architectonic method we've emphasized his concern to avoid any reference to what is given in experience. His argument is that we have to avoid making reference to the empirical in order to fully account for it. This is a concern we would therefore expect to see reflected in the formulation of the tables of judgements and categories. We expect to see another inward looking argument, one responding to the single and unifying problem that Kant re-names an Idea of the whole of the understanding's a priori cognition. How does Kant here relate what the pure understanding can do, and the conceptual forms this involves, to the concrete side of experience? Kant argues that cognition always produces an object, that this is the way in which judgements and categories are extended or realized. They secure more and more objects in cognition, objects made possible by the input of both the abstract and the concrete. However, the term 'object' is not intended to provide an empirical basis for the Table of Categories. In his *Reflexionen* Kant writes that: 'An object, therefore, is only something in general which we think to ourselves through predicates which constitute its concept' (Kant 1882: 17: 616–17).[5] This term 'something in general' captures the strange notion of the categories accounting for experience without referring to anything actually given in experience. They have the horizon of 'something in general', of something that is both abstract and concrete so that both poles of experience are realized in it. This object of cognition is their focus, leading Béatrice Longuenesse to write of '. . . the objectifying function manifested in the very form of judgment . . .' (KCJ: 83). We can begin to understand this by considering the way in which Kant goes on to include this 'something in general' in every synthetic a priori judgement as one of two concepts that are compared with one another. This 'something in general' is the logical subject of a judgement. Kant writes: 'When I say "a body is divisible" this means that something x, which I cognize through the predicates that together constitute a concept of body, I also think through the predicate of divisibility' (Kant 1882: 17: 616–17).[6] Thus 'something in general', renamed here as 'something x', is referred to in every judgement or has a role in how cognition works. Cognitions are secured by judgements that refer to a logical subject that is never anything in particular. What are we to make of this strange something that is 'something in general' or 'something x', and is always involved in cognition?

Synthetic a priori judgements refer to experience but not in any specific sense. If such judgements, which make experience possible, specify what will occur in experience they either presuppose what they are to account for or over-determine it. We've seen in the previous two chapters of this book that for Kant these are two dangers to be avoided. In order to explore this I will be developing Kant's terminology by introducing the term 'situation'. This will allow me to explore the depth and complexity of the notion of 'something in general' or 'something x'. This is a move we must justify by showing how the Table of Categories for Kant presents the basic forms of any situation. It refers to concrete situations or situations that emerge through synthesis but it does so in an abstract way, without specifying situations beyond the conditions of their possibility. Categories are the basic forms of all objects of cognition, they therefore secure the objective situations we find ourselves in. They are the basic forms of 'something in general' or 'something *x*'. In Chapter 1 of this book we used the example of a situation where we are able to make the judgement 'the sun warms the stone'. This situation is marked out by a pure concept of the understanding, the category of cause and effect. The 'something in general' that arises through cognition is always a situation made up of objects of cognition and their objective relations, such as cause and effect. In this way, the term 'situation' helps us to capture the complexity of objects secured by judgements and categories. They are objects of cognition but not simple and self-contained objects. The 'something' referred to is also indeterminate in scale. It is more complex than could be captured by talking about this or that object. Thus common philosophical examples such as 'the desk at which I am sitting' or 'the book I am reading' do not capture the full scope or scale of this 'something in general'. The situation could be this room, this land mass, this planet or this universe. It would include both individuals and crowds as objects of cognition. The point is that these things must be left indeterminate if we are to realize an Idea of the whole of understanding's a priori cognition. If we view the horizon of the categories in terms of objects of a particular scale then they are reduced to, for example, the common experience of a scholar who tends to use as an example his desk or the book he is reading.[7] Kant wants to account for such ordinary experiences rather than assuming them or suggesting that they are more significant than any other. He therefore has in mind the openness, dynamism and potential for extension of concepts when he refers to 'something in general' as the logical subject of every judgement.

We've seen that Kant wants to refer only to the abilities of the pure understanding in the Metaphysical Deduction. He also wants to leave open the ways in which the abstract and concrete can be realized in an object of cognition. How is openness to the concrete secured by focusing upon the abstract in this way? We saw Sebastian Gardner arguing that we cannot get closer to concrete experience if we cannot revise our abstract ways of understanding it. However, Kant argues that the categories he seeks to secure in the Metaphysical Deduction cannot be established using proofs based upon experience. We must find out how such pure or non-empirical concepts refer to objects without borrowing these objects from experience (CPR: A85/B117). These concepts are not based on experience but are nevertheless open to experience in the sense of providing the basic forms of the cognition of any situation. They refer to objects and their relations in the widest possible sense by providing the a priori forms of objectivity as such. Thus any talk of openness to experience must be qualified because for Kant this openness can only be realized by the reference of abstract judgements and categories to an object that will be concrete as well as abstract. We must then refer to the abstract on its own terms in the Metaphysical Deduction but only as a stage in the architectonic's attempt to relate the abstract and the concrete. Henry E. Allison develops the concrete meaning of Kant's reference to 'something in general' when he writes that: '. . . every judgement involves a synthesis or unification of representations in consciousness, whereby the representations are conceptualized so as to be referred to or related to an object' (KTI: 87). The synthetic a priori judgement is derived by concentrating on the pure understanding alone but also by locating its outcome as an object that is both abstract and concrete. In the object of cognition the abstract abilities and forms of the understanding are realized and without it they are empty. With this in mind we will turn again to the role of general logic in Kant's Metaphysical Deduction.

Since we raised the issue of the relation between the Metaphysical Deduction and the history of logic we've seen that Kant's synthetic a priori judgements refer to the concrete in a certain way. They refer to it without specifying it, as 'something in general' or 'something *x*'. For Kant, the basic abilities of the understanding are presented in general logic and give a complete account of what the understanding can do. We move from the purity and completeness of understanding's basic abilities, as presented in general logic, to the purity and completeness of an account of how they unify experience in the most basic ways. Kant writes: 'For these functions of the understanding are completely exhaustive and survey its power entirely' (CPR: A80/B105). In his *Lectures on Metaphysics* Kant is concerned to focus upon the understanding to the exclusion of anything external: 'It is not research into a thing, but rather into an understanding, whose basic propositions and concepts must be open to study, for it all lies within me' (LM: 138, in parenthesis in the original). This makes it worthwhile to follow the example of general logic which has studied the understanding without any input from experience. Being formal it is concerned purely with the forms that thought can take and therefore abstracts from all of the content of cognition (CPR: A131/B170). It is focused upon what the understanding can do without referring to experience or even to the pure cognition of the understanding that makes experience possible. By avoiding any such reference it never relies upon something that can undermine our conclusions and be a source of doubt. General logic guides us by referring only to the understanding and for Kant this is something that we need to do before we relate the abstract to the concrete.

Kant's remarks on the history of general logic, located in the second edition Preface of the *Critique of Pure Reason,* suggest that this history comprises only one significant event. This is not then a history in the sense of a development over time but presents the discovery of what understanding has always silently been doing. For Kant we can get a complete Idea in general logic of what the understanding is capable of because of the one significant event in its history. This is the event of Aristotle's formulation of logic. Kant credits logic with proceeding like a science, with walking upon the solid ground that assures a discipline of its own progress and security (ibid.: Bviii). He argues that since Aristotle no revision or addition has been needed. No alternations to logic's canon have been needed expect for work to clarify and make succinct what had already been secured. Kant considers general logic to be complete because it formulates abilities of the understanding that were always already at work in

the a priori syntheses of experience. It reflects the completeness of the understanding's role in making experience possible. General logic thus presents the
basic abilities of the understanding just as we saw that Euclidean geometry
presents a priori truths about space. Both refer to forms of the a priori that were
already at work but by presenting them in abstraction they establish themselves
as sciences with a priori foundations. Kant argues that the success of logic in
proceeding upon solid ground is the result of its own restrictions. These
demand that it abstract from all the objects and details of cognition, ensuring
that it deals only with itself and its own forms of thought (ibid.: Bix). Logic has
the virtue of presenting the basic abilities of the understanding in complete
abstraction and without reference to experience. In the *Critique of Pure Reason*
Kant wants to use this cognitive achievement in order to grasp the abstract pole
of cognition in the most effective way. However, he does not rely upon this
discipline for his account of a priori synthetic judgement. These forms would
be at work even if no discipline had formulated them and presented them so
effectively. It is for this reason that the problem of the possibility of synthetic a
priori judgement, of relating the abstract and the concrete, occurs to reason.
It follows that we do not have to dispute the validity of the post-Fregean understanding of logic in order to show that Kant's Metaphysical Deduction is
complete. If logic no longer guides and supports Kant's account it also does
not challenge it. Having gone in a more abstract direction, logic remains silent
on matters that concern Kant in the Metaphysical Deduction. His logic, set out
in the two tables, is a transcendental logic. It responds to the relation of the
abstract and the concrete that unifies his architectonic.

We have then a transcendental logic that is not to be confused with a general
logic. It is made distinct by referring the abstract abilities of the pure understanding to the form of an object of cognition. This transcendental logic is
concerned with realizing the concrete content of cognition in the abstract
forms that an object must take. How is this effective in a concrete situation?
Thomas Kaehao Swing argues that: 'What is not so well known among Kant
scholars is that he claims the merit of making the first systematic attempt to
construct the science of material logic' (Swing 1969: vii).[8] This way of characterizing Kant's transcendental logic emphasizes the difference between a general
or formal logic and a transcendental or material logic. The latter refers to
the concrete pole of cognition without specifying its nature; it refers to it
as the object of cognition or 'something in general' that must be secured by the
two tables. Judgement now refers to the material constraints of a situation, to
the forms an object of cognition must take. It is then a logic that is related to
the matter or concrete content of experience but only in ways that make
experience possible. Swing illustrates the difference between a formal and
a material logic by considering the role of the term 'every' in a proposition
(ibid.: 11). This makes a proposition into a universal judgement, which is the
first judgement of quantity in Kant's Table of Judgements. This concerns

the whole proposition and not its subject-concept. Swing gives the following example: 'Every horse is an animal' (ibid.). In contrast, 'five' and 'a' are terms that concern the subject-concept and not the proposition. For example: 'Five horses are now running' or 'A horse is missing'. Swing argues that these quantitative terms have material functions while the quantifiers of predicate calculus, a post-Fregean form of logic, do not. They are not concerned with the content of knowledge, with marking out a situation in material ways, but only with the relations of judgements: 'Their function is not to represent any objects but to bring together the descriptive terms into propositions, and simple propositions into complex ones. Theirs is a connective function' (ibid.: 10). In formal logic we are concerned with the universal character of the judgement or proposition and not with making a subject universal. However, for Kant, pure cognition, with its two tables, makes possible the empirical cognition that grasps the details and particularities of the concrete. This means that any argument seeking to establish a transcendental logic must form part of an account of cognition that includes both its abstract and its concrete poles. It makes a material difference that the proposition has more or less abstract reach, that it includes more or less quantity. This is not to suggest that judgements themselves become concrete or seek to make a specific difference. Instead they mark out and secure a situation where it is possible for concrete things to be specified and developed. They remain abstract conditions of possibility for the concrete specification of possible experience. Therefore, what matters is that material situations are secured in the most basic and abstract ways so that an open-ended empirical specification of the concrete can take place.

Understanding the Metaphysical Deduction as an Argument

In Chapter 1 of this book we discussed the forms of argument that Kant employs in the *Critique of Pure Reason*. We may develop this by considering the following passage from the Metaphysical Deduction: 'In this treatise I deliberately refrain from offering definitions of these categories, even though I may possess them' (CPR: A82–3/B108). Kant then refers us to the method and aims of the *Critique of Pure Reason*. These do not demand the definition of the categories and it would introduce unnecessary doubts if we were to attempt it. It would distract us from the integral concerns of the architectonic. Here Kant refers us to the role of the *Critique of Pure Reason* as propaedeutic that we discussed in Chapter 1 of this book. He wants to make possible the cognition of possible experience as such rather than present a detailed organon of pure reason. We now find that this demands that we are brief in our arguments. We are to avoid doubt by not breaking up the two tables into their component parts. How does this help us define Kant's form of argument in the Metaphysical Deduction? Jill Vance Buroker offers a reason why Kant wants to be brief:

> Kant believes that it is simply a brute fact about humans that we judge by these logical forms. [. . .] Just as we cannot explain why we intuit objects in three-dimensional Euclidean space and one-dimensional time, so we cannot explain why our judging has exactly these logical characteristics. (Buroker 2006: 100)

If the Metaphysical Deduction relies upon a 'brute fact' it can be compared to the argument based on Euclidean geometry that we considered in Chapter 1 of this book. These both form what we defined as an isolation argument. We isolate the a priori ingredients of cognitive achievements in cases where we have the opportunity to investigate them. However, we noted that this means that no set of conditions can be indispensable, as the architectonic method demands, because we might uncover others in the course of experience. We've emphasized Kant's concern with completeness and with giving an exhaustive account. The brevity of his Metaphysical Deduction cannot then be explained by his reliance on a 'brute fact' that is already given to us and so needs no detailed explanation. How else can we understand Kant's concern to be brief?

Kant draws a distinction that adds a great deal to our understanding of his method of argument in the Metaphysical Deduction:

> When teachers of law talk about rights and claims, they distinguish in a legal action the question regarding what is legal (*quid juris*) from the question concerning fact (*quid facti*), and they demand proof of both. The first proof, which is to establish the right, or for that matter the legal entitlement, they call the *deduction*. (CPR: A84/B116)[9]

Deduction is tasked with establishing a right or legal entitlement. How is it distinguished from the question *quid facti*? If we build up a picture of the abilities of the understanding based on observations of matters of fact this would not establish a right or entitlement to use them in all cases. Kant seems to be concerned that doubt creeps in when we spend more time over a deduction in order to refer to facts. By referring to past experience we refer to what can always be doubted. Kant therefore defines deduction using the legal term *quid juris*. If we are to learn from this the reason for the brevity of the Metaphysical Deduction we have to relate it to the way Kant argues. We might wonder whether in legal practice it is not the case that precedent plays the major role. Something that precedes the present case may provide an authoritative example. Precedent, according to particular systems of law, must be worked through at length, building upon the achievements of legal practice just as isolation arguments build on what has been achieved by cognition. Can we then isolate the question of legality from the question of fact in legal practice as Kant suggests? We can do this if we uncover the true import of Kant's reference to what is now an obsolete form of legal practice.

Dieter Henrich provides much needed clarification of Kant's reference to legal practice (Henrich 1989: 29–46). He points to Kant's engagement with theories of legal deduction during his lectures on natural law at the University of Königsberg.[10] He uncovers in this literature a legal notion widely held in the eighteenth-century Holy Roman Empire:

> Since a deduction is not a theory for its own sake, but rather an argumentation intended to justify convincingly a claim about the legitimacy of a possession or a usage, it should refrain from unnecessary digression, generalizations, debates about principles, and so forth, which are of interest only to the theoretician. A deduction should be brief, solid but not subtle, and perspicuous. (Henrich 1989: 33–4)[11]

This is a legal practice that does not rely upon the authority of precedent but is focused upon a claim to possession or usage. By being brief, by avoiding explanation and not drawing upon precedent, we are to attain solidity. This will make sense only in its historical context, the context in which precedent was not a sufficient basis for a legal claim. We will seek now to show the relevance of this to Kant's Metaphysical Deduction without seeking to historicize his argument or render it outdated. In this sense we will take issue with Henrich's claim that: 'With regard to the *Critique* and its deductions, we can thus understand in a new light the old saying that books, too, have their destiny' (ibid.: 33). This seems to be a valid conclusion because this method of legal deduction writing became redundant following Napoleon's dissolution of the Holy Roman Empire in 1806, two years after Kant's death (ibid.). It was a practice based on competing claims over things like inheritance and rights of succession between the many states that made up this loose confederation during Kant's lifetime. However, this is not the only reason to avoid reducing Kant's argument to its historical context. He claims for the Table of Categories the dignity of embodying an Idea of the whole of the understanding's a priori cognition and this would make it non-historical. Its source is a problem posed by reason, a problem concerning the a priori synthesis of possible experience. It thus precedes and makes possible all historical cognition.

We have a historical context and a form of legal practice that responds to it. This provides a way of making sense of the philosophical method Kant employs but we cannot reduce this method to its historical context without undermining its claims. Henrich sketches the philosophical significance of Kant's reference to the legal methods of his time:

> A legal dispute originates when a party's claim has been challenged by an opponent, so that a court must be opened. This happened in philosophy when the sceptic challenged the claim of reason to be in possession of a priori

knowledge of objects. [. . .] To the extent to which a deduction can be produced, the claim of reason becomes definitely justified and the challenge of the sceptic is rejected. This is the aim of the Transcendental Analytic. (ibid.: 38)

This concern is reflected in Kant's *Lectures on Metaphysics* when he writes that: 'Enough systems have been composed which, even when they are in agreement, cannot withstand the onslaught of a mischievous sceptic' (LM: 126). His concern here is with defending an entitlement against '. . . an opponent who is no system maker' (ibid.). We saw in Chapter 1 of this book how Kant sought to construct arguments that began with what a sceptic must accept. The argument then moves to show the reliance of something they accept upon something they doubt. Thus, by being system makers, we relate what is accepted and what is doubted as parts in a wider system. We make them parts of a whole. We show that a sceptic may be no system maker but relies upon a system in order to have cognition of experience in the first place. The legal deduction writers of Kant's time worked on the basis that a right needed to be deduced in a situation where to do anything else would give rise to fatal scepticism regarding a claim. There is an emphasis upon securing a verdict in the context of the competing claims and lack of certainty in the political life of the Holy Roman Empire. There was no national unity in the Empire that would precede the work of legal deduction in order to make things predictable or secure.[12] In other words, there is no precedent to rely upon because no previous example or case has any source of permanent authority. That the power of the Emperor of the Holy Roman Empire was merely nominal and the role ornamental contributed to this situation (Hassall 1929: 11). Deduction writers were concerned with securing something against the tide of competing claims and lack of established authority. They could not appeal to facts and had to be brief in order to avoid relying upon anything outside of the argument they were making. A right or entitlement had to be justified on the authority of this argument alone. This gave rise to a method of deduction that Kant was very well aware of and that reflects his concerns. If we are to be system makers who defeat the sceptic we must construct systems by carrying out deductions that cannot be undermined by any reliance upon the givens of experience.

We've seen that if we take general logic as a precedent upon which to construct a deduction we are vulnerable to the history of logic. We have given too lengthy a deduction because we have taken the time to use general logic as the basis for our argument. When the history of this discipline moves forward the argument is undermined. We've seen that Kant did not think that general logic could be reformulated because he held it to be complete. However, since he did not rely upon it as the basis of his deduction his account is not undermined by its subsequent history. In the Metaphysical Deduction he ultimately refers to the basic abilities of the pure understanding and not to the discipline that had formulated these with apparent completeness. If we return to his concern with an Idea of the whole we will gain a better understanding of why this internal focus is important:

> Hence this completeness is possible only by means of an *idea of the whole* of understanding's a priori cognition, and through the division, determined by that idea, of concepts amounting to that cognition; and hence this completeness is possible only through the *coherence* of these concepts *in a system.* (CPR: A64–5/B89)

It is philosophy, as architectonic, that considers how abstract and concrete are always already related in order to provide an account of the cognition of possible experience. If we are not sceptics then for Kant this is because we practice architectonics which, as we saw in the last chapter, is the art of constructing systems on the basis of a problematic Idea of the whole. The two tables formulated in the Metaphysical Deduction are a complete system insofar as they secure the relation of the synthetic and the a priori in the basic forms of cognition once and for all. Kant argues that this provides . . .

> . . . a unity that is self-subsistent, sufficient to itself, and that cannot be augmented by supplementing it with any extrinsic additions. Hence the sum of pure understanding's cognition' will constitute a system that can be encompassed and determined by an idea. (ibid.: A65/B89–90)

It is brief in order to avoid the extrinsic, in order to formulate the abilities of the pure understanding rather than looking outside of the response of this faculty to a problem raised by pure reason. As we saw in the previous chapter of this book, a system is to secure and make possible the cognition of experience. We now see that in order to prepare for all such cognition it must be briefly formulated and so maintain the internal focus of the architectonic method. As we shall now see, being brief and systematic translates into the lay out of the two tables. It is for Kant a sign that the understanding's own abilities are being realized without any external interference. In the next and final section of this chapter we will consider whether the two tables show Kant's argument to be convincing. We will ask whether brevity can secure solidity or whether it leaves the tables vulnerable to the tides of history and experience.

The Two Tables

The unity of the two tables will help us to understand why they are presented all at once rather than piece by piece. Béatrice Longuenesse argues that '. . . each of the two tables sheds light on the other. The strength and coherence of each is established and buttressed by the other' (KCJ: 77). If we evaluate them or their components singularly we neglect the sense in which a system is being constructed on the basis of an Idea of the whole of the understanding's a priori cognition. They are at the centre of a system for accounting for the cognition of possible experience and will be involved in the unfolding of the architectonic in the remainder of the *Critique of Pure Reason*. Their systematic organization will direct this unfolding, it will direct the stages of the account where the abstract and the concrete are more closely related. How are these tables systematic? They each have 12 members and are both divided into four corresponding divisions. Kant is clearly concerned with proceeding systematically but how can this be related to the pure and basic abilities of the understanding? Henry E. Allison suggests a way of understanding this in the following passage:

> Appealing to a biological analogy, one might say that just as the function of the eye, namely, to see, may be broken down into several sub-functions, such as color, shape, and distance vision, so the function of the understanding, namely to judge, may be broken down into four (and only four) types of sub-function: quantity, quality, relation, and modality. (KTI: 137)

This might suggest that, like Jill Van Buroker, Allison sees the two tables as expressing a 'brute fact' about the nature of cognition. However, this does not necessarily follow from the analogy given. The Idea of an eye is an Idea of the whole that precedes all vision and opens the horizon of vision as such through the co-ordination of certain basic abilities. We ask what understanding can do and, just as when we ask this of an eye, this turns out to be a question with a brief but solid answer. It leads us to formulate a system of abilities, something co-ordinated and unified in purpose, which is briefly elaborated but is also very full and open ended in its account of experience. We rely for this not upon a empirical study of cases of the organ's use but purely upon a highly concentrated notion of this organ's basic abilities. These are complete because if they were added to it would disrupt the coherent, systematic organization of the eye that makes its functioning possible as such. It might be objected that scientists have been learning about the eye bit-by-bit and continue to do so. However, the analogy ultimately refers us to the conditions of possibility located in the understanding without which the activity of any science could not take place. Kant is seeking to provide a transcendental account of all scientific or naturalistic cognition, as we saw when we explored the broader role of his architectonic method in Chapter 1 of this book. The analogy suggests that if we think about the basic abilities of an organ, something which forms a system, we will find this to be a brief and solid notion. The possibilities opened by this are inexhaustible because we can never see everything there is to see, or know everything there is to know, but the foundation of seeing or knowing is exhausted briefly in a system of basic abilities. This analogy helps us to understand why Kant offers so little elaboration of the judgements and categories he presents in the Metaphysical Deduction.

While Kant's concern to be systematic in the formulation of the two tables can be understood in the way we've just considered, the particular system he offers has been the source of much puzzlement. The third judgement or category under each division is derived from the combination of the first two. This comes in for the charge of artificiality from many commentators and this reflects attitudes towards the architectonic method as a whole. Thomas Kaehao Swing describes this as a 'pervasive triadic obsession' (Swing 1969: 21). We've seen that Kant moves swiftly against scepticism on the grounds that it does not include more of experience in its viewpoint but undermines the very possibility of experience by having no system. If it is to be possible, experience must be included in an abstract system as well as being extended by all the detail and particularity of the concrete. Without a system there is no experience and without an Idea of the whole there is no system. Kant is arguing from within an Idea of the whole of understanding's a priori cognition that relates the abstract and the concrete from the perspective of understanding's pure use. It relates them in synthetic a priori judgements that refer to an object of cognition. However, being systematic is one thing while making one particular system complete and indispensible is quite another. Having considered the argument for being brief and systematic we will now interrogate the system Kant provides in detail. We will consider whether it responds to the need to relate the abstract and the concrete in an object of cognition.

The first division of the tables of judgements and categories is quantity and the first judgement of quantity is the universal judgement. An example of this judgement is the proposition 'all human beings are mortal'. This is a judgement where the predicate (mortality) contains all of its subjects (human beings). A predicate-concept subsumes a subject-concept. The role of 'something in general' or 'something x' in this judgement ensures that it refers to the material terms of an objective situation. These are the objects of cognition we know from experience to be human beings. Thus we know in the abstract that in different concrete situations anything we recognize as a human being is mortal. This particular fact is not necessary to account for experience because human beings do not all have to be mortal to make experience possible. However, the logical function is necessary. This synthetic a priori judgement makes experience possible. It corresponds to a category of unity that expresses the ability of the understanding to unify objects of cognition in the abstract despite the fact that they are also concrete objects. This abstract ability and corresponding conceptual form make it possible to include something concrete, such as a human being, in experience as a whole. The category derived from the judgement must provide an empty and abstract way of marking out concrete situations in terms of their quantities. We must be clear that this does not specify what the concrete will be, such as that human beings and mortality are involved, but it does specify the logical function that makes it possible to include human beings and mortality in experience. We can now abstract from concrete cases where we encounter humanity or mortality even though these might appear under very different guises. The second judgement of quantity is the particular judgement. An example is 'some human beings are mortal'. This is a judgement in which the predicate-concept (mortality) contains some of its subject-concepts (human beings). To this synthetic a priori judgement there corresponds the category of plurality. Again the understanding's ability to abstract from concrete experience is at the basis of experience. Although we meet with many objects of cognition that we class under the concept of a human being, we must be able to distinguish those who share a particular predicate and those who do not. For Kant we take this ability for granted because otherwise experience would lack the coherent and systematic organization that makes it possible in the first place.

The third judgement of quantity is the singular judgement, an example of which is the proposition 'Socrates is mortal'. In this synthetic a priori judgement the predicate (mortality) contains one of its subjects (Socrates). This gives rise to the category of totality or allness. As we've remarked, Kant derives the third judgement and category in each division from the combination of the first two, leading some to find his system artificial. We must also note the difference between a general logic and a transcendental logic when it comes to the make up of the two tables. This third judgement of quantity faces the charge of being both artificial, because every division of the two tables must have a third member, and outdated, because logic has developed in a different direction. Kant argues that singular judgements should have their own place in the Table of Judgements despite the fact that in general logic they do not need this (CPR: A71/B96–7). If the inclusion of a third judgement and category is to be convincing it will have to be shown to be a response to the difference between general and transcendental logic. It would then be a response to the need to account for both the abstract and concrete in a transcendental logic rather than expressing a rigid and artificial method of systematically presenting two tables. As we've seen, a transcendental logic must refer to the concrete content of experience without specifying it and in this way make a material difference. Kant argues that the singular judgement must be compared to other cognitions in terms of quantity (ibid.: A71/B96). Thus we ask what material difference the first two judgements and categories of quantity make and then see what else is demanded. The category of totality reflects the fact that in the concrete we can refer to one subject, such as Socrates, while in general logic we never encounter this need. It is compared to other cognitions of quantity and distinguished because in this case we commit ourselves to a single subject. Any predicates will be referred to this subject so that we have the unity in one subject of a potential plurality of predicates. It thus combines the first two categories, unity and plurality, but does this in a unique and indispensible way. It ensures that we can recognize and abstract from concrete situations in order to make many singular claims about a subject. This third judgement and category therefore respond to the problem of referring in the abstract to complex, concrete situations that arise in the course of experience.

The judgements and categories of quality form the second division of both tables. Kant explains that transcendental logic here considers what *value* or *content* is to be secured (ibid.: A72/B97). Unlike in general logic judgements are understood according to the contribution they make to cognition as a whole (ibid.). The first judgement of quality is affirmative and an example is 'Socrates is wise'. The corresponding category is that of reality. James Luchte argues that this ensures that each object '. . . has its own kind of being or existence, its reality' (Luchte 2007: 53). The notion of a unique 'kind of being or existence' is very rich without being attached to what is given in experience or the concrete details of experience. The 'value or content' secured by a judgement of quality refers us to the reality encountered in an object of cognition that is wise or not wise, hot or cold, red or blue. This extends experience but for Kant this is always coherent and systematic because the two tables provide the abstract abilities and forms that make experience possible. A change in the value or content secured by judgement can make a significant material difference but it does this only because we can first of all affirm the reality of a quality in the abstract. The second judgement of quality is the negative judgement, an example of which is 'Socrates is not wise'. The corresponding category is negation. In the abstract we must be able to rule out concrete realities that might crowd out our clear understanding of a particular subject. For Kant something is an object of cognition only if its qualities can be distinguished from anything that would cancel them out or make them unclear. In the example we've given, the wisdom of Socrates must stand out from other possible qualities that we might predicate. If we cannot know whether Socrates is or is not wise, given sufficient experience, then the lack of this ability would undermine experience as such. The third member of the second division of both tables refers to how the qualitative content of a judgement is secured in the context of a wider domain of qualities. The infinite judgement and the category of limitation are these third members. They allow us to place a limit upon the infinite scope of what is possible in experience (CPR: A72/B97). Kant argues that while infinite judgements have an infinite logical range or scope, they only have a limiting role when it comes to the content of cognition (ibid.: A73/B98). An example of the judgement of infinity is 'Socrates is non-wise'. This sounds like negation, the second category of quality, but for Kant it is the combination of a negative predicate and 'the infinite sphere of all that is possible' (ibid.: A72/B97) that makes this a unique and necessary judgement and category. It is a combination of the infinite sphere of what is 'non-wise' and the negation that distinguishes a subject from this infinite sphere. This is to consider the background against which objects of cognition must be secured. As Béatrice Longuenesse puts it, '. . . what they *are* is thought only against the background of what they are *not*' (KCJ: 310). In this way the third judgement and concept of quality reflect the concrete pole of experience, the range of possible qualities that characterize the concrete and so need to be dealt with a priori in the abstract. Again it is the ability to abstract and to provide the abstract forms of every concrete situation that makes the pure understanding indispensible.

If we turn to the third division of both tables we find that Kant is concerned with judgements that articulate relations of thought (CPR: A73/B98). These are abstract relations that, in common with the other members of the two tables, refer to the concrete in abstract ways. They concern the relation of the predicate-concept to subject-concept in synthetic a priori judgements. Kant names the first judgement of relation the categorical judgement, an example of which is 'this is snow'. The category that corresponds to the categorical judgement is the category of inherence and subsistence or substance and accident. Kant is concerned with whether the predicate is inherent in the subject, whether it forms part of its definition or is merely accidental. If it is true that 'this is snow' then it is true that the predicate, being what we recognize as snow, inheres in the subject referred to. Kant is concerned with securing this in the abstract or in the pure use of the understanding and not solely on the basis of experience. An example given in his *Lectures on Metaphysics* shows the systematic relation of the first and second categories of relation. It shows how judgements and categories form a system and work together in securing the cognition of possible experience. The example is 'snow has fallen' and Kant writes:

> Herein lies that snow is, substance; fallen means an accident, upon the earth means an influence, that is action [*actio*] thus belongs to cause [*causa*]. Today refers to time, fallen to space. If we omit all sensations, as well as space and time, substance remains, which acts in a certain way, thus they must be connected so that the concept of experience arises. If we posit that we had no such pure concepts of the understanding [or categories], then we could not think or speak at all. (LM: 158)

For Kant synthetic a priori judgement has been at work here, systematically making possible the empirical course of events by securing an inhering substance and a sequence of cause and effect. Substance remains because it is an abstract form and is not secured on the basis of experience.[13] For Kant we could never extract from experience a notion of substance that makes this very experience possible. The second judgement of relation is the hypothetical judgement and the second category is causality and dependence or cause and effect. Kant gives the following example of a hypothetical judgement: 'If there is a perfect justice, then the persistently evil person is punished' (CPR: A73/B98). He argues that this hypothetical judgement only gives us a relation of implication between two propositions. That the persistently evil person is punished if there is perfect justice follows from the coherence of a system of perfect justice. This only shows what is implied in a logical sense and refers to the logic that makes a system of justice coherent. However, it does not tell us whether these two propositions are true in a sense that is both abstract and concrete. The example of the fallen snow showed how relevant to concrete experience this hypothetical judgement can be when combined with the category of cause and effect. It makes a material difference whether or not something causes it to snow. It matters for meteorology that this holds in the case of snow and for all experience that effect follows cause in any situation whatever. Now we must consider whether there are convincing reasons to move to a third member of this third division of both tables. For Kant we need to construct a system that makes experience possible and, because this system must relate the abstract and the concrete in order to do this, we need to show that their relation provides reasons for the construction of this system. As we've seen, for Kant the problematic relation of the synthetic and the a priori is at the basis of all construction of systems. This is what would allow him to claim that his tables are not rigid and artificial but engaged in fully accounting for experience.

From the third judgement of relation, disjunctive judgement, Kant derives the category of community. He qualifies this category as the interaction of agent and patient (ibid.: A80/B106). The apparent lack of fit between disjunction and community has been noted in the secondary literature. There seems to be no relation between a judgement that excludes things through disjunction and a category that includes things in a community. Paul Guyer is one such critic and he argues that . . .

> . . . what Kant has in mind by the disjunctive form of judgment, that is, 'Either *p* or not-*p*', e.g., 'Either the world is just or the world is unjust' (cf. A74/B99) seems to be the exact opposite of what he has in mind with the category of 'community' or 'reciprocity': in the case of a disjunctive judgment, the truth of one disjunct is supposed to entail the *falsehood* of all the others, while in the case of community, the condition of one's object is supposed to entail that of another and *vice versa*, that is, we might say, the *truth* about one object is supposed to entail and be entailed by the *truth* of the other. (K: 78)

Kant's alleged 'pervasive triadic obsession' could be used to explain why he insists on a third category of relation but this would neglect the philosophical reasons he offers for putting together these two apparently mismatching things. Kant relates disjunctive judgement and the category of community in the following way: 'This community consists in the fact that the cognitions reciprocally exclude one another, and yet as a *whole* determine thereby the true cognition; for, taken together, they constitute the whole content of a single given cognition' (CPR: A74/B99). This reflects the complementarity of both tables that we saw Béatrice Longuenesse proposing. Kant argues that disjunction needs a community of substances if it is to do its work and community needs to be defined by the work of disjunction so that we are not confused about its nature because of the different concrete things it includes. Longuenesse writes that '[a] disjunctive judgment presupposes that concepts are already formed' (KCJ: 105). It relies upon a community or whole that exhausts all the possibilities for disjunction and can be divided by it (CPR: A73–4/B99). It then provides community with a disjunctive definition, with the clarity this brings when it comes to defining a community of substances. Thus, while Guyer's claim is valid when it comes to the generally accepted definitions of disjunction and community in logic, it does not recognize the nature of the transcendental logic presented in two co-ordinated tables. This third member again combines the first two. It combines inhering substances and the relations of determination between such substances. However, it shows the Table of Categories to be concerned with how substances can be related in other ways than the second category, cause and effect, will allow. A community presents relations of determination between substances but these are not relations where an effect depends upon a cause. Substances are equal rather than dependent upon one another when they interact and determine one another reciprocally. We will return to this issue in Chapter 5 of this book where the close involvement of this judgement and category in the synthesis of possible experience will develop the relation of disjunction and community.

The judgements of modality, the fourth and final division of the Table of Judgements, could be said to be concerned with the way in which an object exists. If our judgement is 'maybe Socrates is a philosopher' it is a problematic judgement or claim about an object of cognition. It is possible that Socrates is a philosopher but experience has not established this. If, however, we say that 'it is the case that Socrates is a philosopher' we make an assertoric judgement that has a basis in experience. We have read books by Plato, Xenophon and others that claim to report Socrates' words and classify them as philosophy according to what we know of the subject. However, if we say that 'it is necessarily the case that Socrates is a philosopher' we make an apodeictic judgement. In the example we are using we would have an idea of what philosophy is and if we did not classify Socrates as a philosopher this would be undermined. We would no longer know what philosophy is if Socrates were not classed as a philosopher. Of course it is not necessary to the possibility of experience that Socrates is a philosopher but there are certain conditions which are necessary in this sense. These conditions include categories but also include things like the laws of motion that we found to be a concern of Kant's architectonic in Chapter 1 of this book. The three categories of modality are possibility, existence and necessity. They pick out in turn those things that are possible but not established as part of experience, those that exist because they form a recognizable part of experience and those things that are necessary to the very possibility of experience. In this way we find that something can exist in different ways according to its role in cognition as a whole. This final division of the two tables allows us to distinguish in the abstract the role of different objects in our cognition. The first three divisions of both tables are the basis for these judgements of modality. We can then proceed to investigate experience and establish the possibility, existence and necessity of objects. We recognize an a priori principle as necessary and thus distinct from one that is established by experience and open to disproof, or from one that is merely possible and demands further investigation. In this way the judgements and categories of modality extend the

Table of Categories as a whole into all our cognition of experience. They do not mark out situations like the previous three divisions of the two tables but organize our cognition of such situations in the course of experience. Their role should not be downplayed because for Kant empirical cognition must reflect the system that makes experience possible. His architectonic method demands that we do not simply acknowledge the foundational role of the Table of Categories and then forget about them. As an indispensable response to the problem at the basis of the architectonic this table must shape all of the understanding's empirical cognition.

Conclusion

We've found that the interpretations of the Metaphysical Deduction we considered at the start of this chapter have their limitations. The history of logic goes in quite a different direction to Kant's transcendental logic and does not directly challenge its completeness. The other approach, to make the categories reflect experience more closely, neglects Kant's understanding of how the abstract and the concrete are to be related in his architectonic. His argument in the Metaphysical Deduction is that openness to experience is made possible by synthetic a priori cognition in its systematic completeness. I have sought to show the link between completeness and openness in the two tables he presents. James Luchte sums up the role of categories in making openness possible:

> Any 'thing' that we may experience can suddenly be illuminated in light of this conceptual schema. A class room, society, or an artwork, for instance: the quantity of students, citizens or aspects, their qualities, their relations, and the way of being of the group, its state or composition as such. (Luchte 2007: 54)

The divisions of both tables make possible the open-ended and rich cognition of experience insofar as they are complete. For Kant the abstraction and emptiness of the two tables means that they specify the forms experience can take only insofar as this makes experience possible. As we've seen, he argues for completeness in order to defeat the sceptic who would always be able to undermine the system if we left it incomplete or founded it upon givens of experience that are liable to change.

We have now considered the architectonic at its most abstract. We saw the relevance of the abstract to the concrete but emphasized that for Kant the two must not be confused. How should we pursue this unfolding of the architectonic? Kant does not refer to the members of his two tables in the first and second edition Transcendental Deductions which follow the Metaphysical Deduction. In order to explore the case he makes for his deduction of the two tables I will turn instead to the Analytic of Principles and thus miss out the two Transcendental

Deductions. This is a major omission because in these two deductions we find something that Béatrice Longuenesse has described in the following way: '*There is no* unity of self-consciousness or "transcendental unity of apperception" apart from this effort, or *conatus* toward judgement, ceaselessly affirmed and ceaselessly threatened with dissolution in the "welter of appearances [*Gewühle der Erscheinungen*]"' (KCJ: 394).[14] Longuenesse locates the unity of Kant's Transcendental Analytic by drawing upon the Transcendental Deductions. These present an impersonal subject which is behind the use of the categories. As we've seen, the a priori is at work silently before we are aware of it and so this subject is not a personal one. The transcendental unity of apperception is the impersonal operator of the apparatus Kant presents in the two tables with the end of securing objects of cognition.[15] For Longuenesse apperception is the effort towards judgement that makes possible the cognition of objects of experience (ibid.: 395). In neglecting this part of the text I offer the justification that the Analytic of Principles that follows it is concerned with the Table of Categories and its make up. While the Transcendental Deductions are concerned with the operator of these two tables they do not engage with the particular system they provide.[16] If we are to see how the architectonic method gives rise to an argument like the Metaphysical Deduction and then secures its place in an account of the cognition of experience as a whole we will need to concentrate on the role of these two tables in the text. To this end we will jump to the Analytic of Principles and in the next two chapters consider how Kant's schematism relates concepts to the synthesis of possible experience. We will see how these concepts are first of all those presented in the Table of Categories and that we cannot understand this part of the text without referring to this table. This will allow us to deepen our understanding of Kant's architectonic method in one of its most contentious moves, in the formulation of two tables and their continuing role in an account of the cognition of possible experience. If we are to fully assess a deduction that is brief but very particular in the system it proposes we must consider how this system is developed in closer proximity to the concrete side of cognition.

Chapter 4

Kant's Schematism

Kant's chapter on the schematism in the *Critique of Pure Reason* demands much attention in its own right as an argument concerning the relations between pure concepts of the understanding and sensible intuition or sensation. However, it is not an isolated argument and its role in the text as a whole foreshadows any engagement with it. In the first chapter of this book I sought to put all the moves made in the *Critique of Pure Reason* in the context of a single and unifying problem, that of synthetic a priori judgement. The title of the schematism chapter is 'On the Schematism of the Pure Concepts of Understanding' (CPR: A137/B176). Kant has clearly not lost sight of the Table of Categories or pure concepts of the understanding and the problematic Idea or Idea of the whole that this embodies. It builds upon the response of the Metaphysical Deduction to the single and unifying problem of the architectonic. Kant continues to pursue the systematic presentation of his arguments that we've analysed in the previous chapters of this book. The schematism takes forward the systematic completeness presented in the abstract in the Metaphysical Deduction so that it becomes the systematic completeness of a concrete account of the synthesis of possible experience in space and time.

Should we follow Kant's apparent strategy and understand the schematism first of all as continuing to embody the concerns and the methods of argument of the architectonic method? For many commentators we should not and should instead understand the schematism as a much more convincing argument for the categories precisely because it differs from the Metaphysical Deduction. The problem of the heterogeneity of concepts and sensations arises in the context of the whole process of securing the a priori synthetic cognition of possible experience. However, it has a very different position within this whole according to the way we read the *Critique of Pure Reason*. Does it extend and realize the Idea of a whole presented in the Metaphysical Deduction or replace it with a more convincing characterization of the whole?

At stake is the role of categories or pure concepts of the understanding in the ongoing synthesis or production of experience in space and time. How can they be at work in the very synthesis of experience while being first of all abstract and disengaged, as we saw in the Metaphysical Deduction? Showing that they have this immanent and concrete role is the task of the schematism chapter. Kant here finds the source of the closer relation of concepts and sensations in the imagination, as an ability, and in time, as the ultimate form of the synthesis of experience. The question is whether this move should be taken as a replacement for the Metaphysical Deduction or whether Kant is right to apparently develop it as an extension of his architectonic presentation of the *Critique of Pure Reason*. We will consider why the former option is popular among commentators, building upon our investigation in the last chapter into why many commentators dislike the Metaphysical Deduction. We will see that many seek the justification of the categories in the Analytic of Principles with its chapters on the schematism and principles that make the categories immanent to the ongoing synthesis of experience in space and time. We suggested that this denies us the possibility of considering the Table of Categories on its own terms, as something justified in the Metaphysical Deduction and applied systematically in the Analytic of Principles. The ways of reading the *Critique of Pure Reason* that we have considered so far raise the problem of whether aspects of Kant's system can be removed or downplayed in order to get closer to what Kant *really* meant or should have said. Can we re-read Kant's work *from within* in order to make it more consistent with itself despite Kant's actual words?

As we saw in the first chapter of this book, some commentaries go so far as to blame Kant's 'mentality' for the way he seeks to establish the categories without reference to their role in the synthesis of experience. This external factor led him to isolate or abstract pure concepts in their systematic completeness and then seek to apply them to the synthesis of experience. S. Körner discusses the proofs provided in the Analytic of Principles for the application of the categories to experience:

> The proofs (not all equally obvious and at times somewhat artificial) are symptomatic of a certain formalism which is characteristic of Kant's mentality, inclining him first to the conviction that the Table of Categories is complete and then to the expectation that their schemata lead to an equally complete table of the synthetic *a priori* principles of objective experience. (Körner 1955: 77)

The argument that was put forward in the previous chapter of this book, and that will be further developed and defended in the chapter after this one, is that Kant's architectonic mode of argument and presentation needs to be given a fair hearing rather than labelled an 'external' factor. We argued in Chapter 1 that speculation concerning Kant's mentality should not stand in for this type of evaluation and can in any case only ever be speculative. However, there is still a case to be answered. Kant himself sets standards for arguments that arise within his architectonic method. They must relate the synthetic and the a priori in a clear and convincing way. As we shall see, there is an apparent mismatch between arguments that are based upon the concrete concerns of cognition and the order of Kant's presentation of the text. The abstract and the concrete seem to pull in different directions. Many commentators take seriously and evaluate his arguments for the necessary roles of particular categories found in the Analytic of Principles but see his tendency to form complete and systematic tables as irrelevant to these arguments. They affirm his interest in matching particular categories to concrete problems in the cognition of possible experience and reject his concern to unify and present all his arguments in an architectonic.

Our first task in this chapter will be to consider the case for revising or replacing the Metaphysical Deduction using the Analytic of Principles. We will consider Norman Kemp Smith's argument that the schemata or schematized categories were what Kant meant all along, even when he talked about pure and abstract categories in the Metaphysical Deduction. We will then contrast this reading to Martin Heidegger's attempt to articulate Kant's Idea of the whole or inner problematic by bringing the imagination to the fore. Having seen how it is foreshadowed by such readings of the *Critique of Pure Reason* as a whole, we will turn to the schematism chapter itself. The differences between concept, schema and image will help us to elucidate the 'secret art' and irreducible ability that the imagination is for Kant in its transcendental power of schematism. We will then introduce Deleuze's particular use of Kant's schematism and the limits of his positive appreciation of it.

Placing the Schematism in the Architectonic

We will be concerned in this section to consider why it is a common tendency among Kant scholars to seek to complete or replace the work done in the Metaphysical Deduction using the schematism chapter. Why go against Kant's explicit move to involve what he claims he has already established, a Table of Categories, in the synthesis of possible experience? The architectonic that organizes the text seems to be designed to take us from categories to their schematism, to be animated by the problem of relating concepts and sensations. In this way it maintains a particular Idea of the whole. The difference between concepts and sensations seems therefore to be a difference internal to Kant's account of experience or a problem that animates it from within. It shows how the relation between the synthetic and the a priori is at stake at this stage of the account, in the relation of the faculties of understanding and sensation. However, Norman Kemp Smith finds in the schematism chapter the 'delayed definitions' of the categories that were presented quite out of context in the Metaphysical Deduction (CK: 340). Their proper context, he argues, is their role in the synthesis of experience that the schematism chapter belatedly presents. He blames the influence of the architectonic, as a method of presenting a philosophical account, for misleading both the reader and the writer of the *Critique of Pure Reason*. In the schematism chapter '[i]t forces [Kant] to preface his argument by introductory remarks which run entirely counter to the very point he is chiefly concerned to illustrate and enforce, namely, the inseparability of conception and [sensible] intuition in all experience and knowledge' (ibid.). It follows that their abstraction or distance from experience in a Table of Categories is not the 'internal' and productive problem that it might appear. It is an 'external' and false problem to do with how the categories are presented and how the text is organized. It does not then indicate a problem that must be responded to in the process of accounting for the cognition of possible experience. As we saw in Chapter 1 of this book, Kemp Smith goes so far as to claim that: 'This architectonic was a hobby sufficiently serious to yield [Kant] keen pleasure in its elaboration, but was not so vital to his main purposes as to call for stronger measures when shortcomings occurred' (ibid.: 341).

This argument is something we shall be testing in this chapter, and in the chapter that follows it, as we consider the Analytic of Principles. For Kemp Smith the architectonic's influence misleads us because categories and their involvement in the synthesis of experience are artificially separated by the way of presenting the text that the architectonic represents. Categories are always already immanent to the syntheses of possible experience in Kant's transcendental logic but his systematic presentation of the text fails to reflect this when it separates the Metaphysical Deduction and the schematism chapter. This takes a lot away from the schematism chapter, which is often seen as introducing a unique and necessary ability involved in securing the synthesis of possible experience. What is missing in the Metaphysical Deduction, according to Kemp Smith, is any proof that the categories presented there are the particular forms required for the cognition of possible experience. He argues that: 'This omission can be made good only by a series of proofs, directed to showing, in reference to each separate category, its validity within experience and its indispensableness for the possibility of experience' (ibid.: 333). This should have been done earlier because, Kemp Smith argues, Kant always thought of the categories in this way. He simply delayed his proof of this in order to pursue his architectonic presentation of the text and so made it appear that a new power or ability was needed. Kemp Smith argues that Kant uses the term 'category' when more often than not he means 'schemata' or 'schematized category' (ibid.: 339). His complaint is that Kant should have started talking about schemata rather than categories earlier in the text, avoiding the confusing delay.

To begin to assess this reading of Kant's *Critique of Pure Reason* we need to consider Kemp Smith's understanding of what is internal to the text. He criticizes its architectonic presentation because he finds that consistent and valid philosophical arguments are obscured by it. We've seen him speculating that Kant was influenced by the enjoyment of systematizing, as something equivalent to the enjoyment provided by a hobby, in order to explain why he obscured his own genuine arguments. We will need to engage with the schematism chapter and the chapters on the principles in order to assess this fully because we saw Kemp Smith claiming that the architectonic method was not important enough to Kant's argument 'to call for stronger measures when shortcomings occurred'. The schematism chapter overcomes its own position in the architectonic and in spite of this method of presentation shows itself to be the delayed supplement to the Metaphysical Deduction. However, while remaining at the level of the *Critique of Pure Reason* as a whole we can begin to question Kemp Smith's argument. When we do this we note that Kant explicitly presents the categories as abstract and isolated from their involvement in the synthesis of possible experience. This seems to go beyond the mere enjoyment of presenting his work systematically insofar as he makes a key claim concerning the relation of the faculties. Kemp Smith acknowledges this and points to Kant's philosophical and historical context and to a strategy that responds to it. He argues that Kant, like his contemporaries, understood concepts '. . . as in all cases a mere concept, *i.e.* an abstracted or class concept' (ibid.: 338). This leads him take abstraction for granted as a starting point and this creates the false problem of showing how the categories are engaged in the synthesis of experience. We are then misled by the apparent need to move from abstraction to concretion, by Kant's strategy for responding to the debates of his times. This strategy, Kemp Smith claims, betrays the movement of Kant's own arguments in the course of writing the *Critique of Pure Reason* because categories actually function differently in the transcendental logic he has been developing. He has come up with a logic always already engaged in the cognition of experience. It is as if the dynamics of the text, the learning process of the author in and through the text he writes, have taken Kant on a journey. It takes him beyond his hobby of pursuing an architectonic presentation and beyond his historical and philosophical context to categories that are always already schematized. Kemp Smith's criticism is that Kant does not clear the ground fully as he should and start with a schematized category. His conclusion is that with proper clarity and consistency the text would be re-organized in the following way:

> The table of categories, in its distinction from the table of logical forms [or the table of judgements], would then have been named the table of schemata, and the definitions given in this chapter would have been appended to it, as the proper supplement to the metaphysical deduction, completing it by a careful definition of each separate schema. For what Kant usually means when he speaks of the categories *are* the schemata: and the chapter before us therefore contains their delayed definitions. (ibid.: 340)

We have then a reading that re-organizes the *Critique of Pure Reason* on the basis of the claim that understanding and sensation are inseparable if we follow the development of Kant's transcendental logic. A concern that arises with this reading is that it leaves no room for a productive dynamic between what is grasped by the understanding and what is not. We defined this dynamic in terms of the relation between the synthetic and the a priori. On the basis of this single problem Kant relates understanding's a priori concepts to the sensations that arise through synthesis. Kemp Smith emphasizes the role of the understanding in dealing with sensation but fails to acknowledge the challenge presented by the synthesis of sensation on the occasions when it prompts the use of cognitive powers or faculties and their a priori forms of cognition. It is a reading of this sort that we find in Martin Heidegger's *Kant and the Problem of Metaphysics*.[1] He seeks to locate the power that unifies the a priori synthesis of possible experience in the imagination. He sums up his strategy in this way: 'The following interpretation will not follow each of the twisted paths of the Transcendental Deduction, but will lay bare the original impetus for the problematic' (KPM: 49). From the start an Idea of the whole is at work and Heidegger refers to this as keeping '. . . the whole of pure, finite knowledge in view' (ibid.: 55). Kant is seen to provide the setting in which cognition can take place, the transcendental horizon where pure forms of the understanding and sensation are unified in the a priori synthesis of possible experience. This is the ultimate unity of categories or pure concepts of the understanding and the a priori forms of intuition, space and time. They are unified in a common project that can only be pursued in the context of their unity. Such a unity is therefore 'in view' before all cognitive activity can take place and for Heidegger this demands the unique power that is the transcendental imagination.

A word of explanation is needed regarding Heidegger's terminology. This reflects the nature of his own thought but is worth exploring here because it can also help us to understand Kant's concerns. We saw that he articulates the Kantian Idea of the whole as 'the whole of pure, finite knowledge'. There is a combination of finitude and cognition here, placing the a priori unity of cognition in the finite context of space and time as a priori forms of sensation. This combination is developed by Heidegger's use of the term 'transcendence' and the notion of transcendence within finitude. It is a transcendence immanent to the finitude of the human situation, to situatedness in space and time. It is then a situated transcendence or a transcendence within finitude. Heidegger echoes Kant's concern with the precariousness of the relation between the synthetic and the a priori when he writes of: '. . . the lasting premonition of the finitude of transcendence . . .' (ibid.). It is the difference between our finitude, our situatedness in space and time, and our ability to transcend it that drives forward the work of cognition. The subject, the transcendental unity of apperception, rises above sensation in order to cognize it but always cognizes things as sensible, as characterized by space and time. However, this also involves a power of the imagination that is immanent to the synthesis of possible experience in space and time, and yet secures transcendence because it realizes the categories in the process of cognition. At this point we must assess the relevance of Heidegger's reading to the inner problematic of Kant's *Critique of Pure Reason*. He uses the term finitude to reflect the concrete and synthetic pole of experience, the material without which our a priori forms of cognition would lack content. With the term transcendence he captures the need to go beyond the givens of experience in a priori ways but recognizes that for Kant we can only ever cognize objects of possible experience. We never cease to be finite beings or beings located in space and time, no matter how much of this experience we grasp in abstract ways. Deleuze affirms this reading of Kant when he writes in *Kant's Critical Philosophy* that '. . . when we "know", we employ these words; we say *more* than is given to us, we go *beyond* what is given in experience' (KCP: 11). In this sense the 'finitude of transcendence' that Heidegger talks about seems relevant to Kant's architectonic. Our exploration of the a priori in the first chapter of this book showed how its ability to rise above the concrete did not undermine its relation to the concrete at every stage. The abstract wants to go beyond concrete cases but can never achieve anything without the concrete.

Heidegger makes an interpretive claim that, as well as being a necessary and unique ability that is not merely a supplement to the power of the understanding, the imagination actually provides us with an Idea of the whole for Kant's *Critique of Pure Reason*. He also claims that this is a reading '. . . which grew from the inner problematic of the *Critique of Pure Reason* itself, . . .' (KPM: 95). For Heidegger this is the problem of securing transcendence within finitude, through the combination of concepts and sensations, that persists in the ongoing cognition of possible experience. Kant presents a unifying image that Heidegger uses to represent the unity he finds in the *Critique of Pure Reason*. The image in question appears in the introduction to the text: 'Human cognition has two stems, viz., *sensibility* and *understanding*, which perhaps spring from a common root, though one unknown to us' (CPR: A15/B29). What is at stake is the ability of the understanding to deal with sensation, to deal with its own finitude using forms of cognition that transcend particular cases and yet are immanent to them. This is a transcendence that is not distant from finitude, that is engaged in the synthesis of possible experience itself as well as surveying it from the standpoint of the transcendental unity of apperception and the Table of Categories. Heidegger then points to places where Kant names three sources of cognition in order to interpret the unifying image of an unknown common root and its two stems. Thus in section three of the first edition version of the Transcendental Deduction Kant writes: 'There are three subjective sources of cognition on which rests the possibility of an experience as such and of cognition of its objects: *sense, imagination and apperception*' (ibid.: A115). For Heidegger Kant's acknowledgement here of the role of the imagination alongside sensation and understanding is still inadequate to the 'inner problematic' of the *Critique of Pure Reason*. He argues that we can interpret the unknown common root of the two stems, sensation and understanding, as the imagination. The imagination, he argues, shows itself to be more than one faculty alongside two others in accounting for experience. If we follow Heidegger's reading we find that this common root is to be the genesis of cognition and must therefore not be confused with what we meet in sensation or the forms provided by the understanding. It must instead be the source of their unity, something they rely upon because of its unique and unknown ability. Therefore . . .

> . . . the transcendental power of imagination is not just an external bond which fastens together two ends. It is originally unifying, i.e., as a particular faculty it forms the unity of the others, which themselves have an essential structural relation to it. (KPM: 96)

It is what understanding and sensation depend upon in order to secure transcendence within finitude. How does this imagery show that the imagination is an original power, that it allows cognition to account for rather than presuppose the givens of experience?

As we saw in Chapter 2 of this book, Kant refers to 'root concepts' in order to show that concepts are productive but also that they don't over-determine experience. They are not based upon what has already been given in experience and they don't tell us what will happen in it. Heidegger continues to develop this imagery to full effect. In order to show that the imagination is unique and original in its power to unify, Heidegger denies that this ground of unity is comparable to a 'floor' or 'base'. If it were like such things, Heidegger argues, it would provide no account of experience but be similar to things already given in experience. A floor or base is something already determined as part of experience, something fixed and present to us in the way it grounds other things given in experience. This distracts us from how experience is given or produced in space and time, a grounding that for Heidegger is more originary because it accounts for what it grounds. We think in terms of something extracted from this process so that it is merely present or 'at hand' as Heidegger puts it (ibid.: 97).[2] Instead this original ground must be involved in the giving of experience itself, in the growth of experience in space and time. We need the source of growth, the root or genesis of cognition, rather than something that already forms a part of experience. As Kant's unknown common root the imagination is to be original in the sense that '. . . it lets the stems grow out from itself, lending them support and stability' (ibid.). Thus the imagination is to be concerned with supporting and securing the cognition of experience but is not limited to how things are already given and present to us in experience.

We have found that both Kemp Smith and Heidegger seek what is internal to Kant's text and in this way challenge the architectonic presentation of the *Critique of Pure Reason* by re-interpreting the Idea of a whole that is behind it. Kemp Smith challenged the Idea of a whole whose origin is the difference between concepts and sensations. However, we've found that the relations of the synthetic and the a priori lead Kant to relate the faculties in different ways at different stages of his account. We will now continue to make the case for preserving the heterogeneity of concepts and sensations. We turned to Heidegger's attempt to take further this 'internal difference', locating in the imagination the root of the unity of concepts and sensations. He interprets

Kant's unknown common root as the transcendental power of the imagination on the grounds that Kant has left open its nature, as 'unknown', and that imagination must mediate in an original and 'unknown' way between sensation and understanding. A major obstacle to this reading is Kant's move, in the second edition version of the Transcendental Deduction, to down play the role of the imagination. As Heidegger acknowledges, the schematism is now described as the understanding's action upon sensation (CPR: B152). This leads him to claim that 'Kant shrank back from this unknown root' (KPM: 112). We might ask why Heidegger did not shrink back from his own interpretation of the role of the imagination given Kant's explicit move in the second edition of the *Critique of Pure Reason*. Again we find that the schematism is a notion that has the power to re-organize the text in spite of Kant's own words. Heidegger argues that even though Kant downgrades the role of the imagination in his second edition version of the Transcendental Deduction '. . . the accomplishment of its transcendental grounding according to the first edition must still be maintained' (ibid.: 113). There is then a unity to the text and to the account of experience provided by its first edition that is to be defended even against the intentions of its author. An internal problematic or Idea of the whole is at stake. According to Heidegger the problem that unified Kant's account, that of relating concepts and sensations through the imagination, made him shrink back. This led him to move away from the imagination in the second edition. We've so far avoided defining Kant's notion of schematism and this was in order to explore its situation in the text as a whole and how it is foreshadowed by this. We will return to the question of whether it can or should undermine Kant's architectonic as both Kemp Smith and Heidegger claim from their different standpoints. In the next section we will consider the schematism chapter itself and this will allow us to gauge the case for using it as a guide for reading or re-reading the *Critique of Pure Reason* as a whole.

The Schematism

The Analytic of Principles of the *Critique of Pure Reason* begins by introducing the *third thing* that Heidegger makes so much of. Kant argues that it is clear that '. . . there must be something that is third . . .' (CPR: A138/B177). This third thing must make possible the application of categories or pure concepts of the understanding to appearances. Kant argues that it must therefore be homogeneous with both the categories and appearances. However, this is not identified with the imagination at first but is rather presented as being at work in judgement. It is introduced under the heading 'On the Transcendental Power of Judgement As Such' (ibid.: A132/B171). A unique and original ability is invoked in response to how judgement differs from understanding's concepts and sensation's intuitions. Neither understanding nor sensation can fully account for their common project, for the unified cognition of possible experience.

How then is judgement able to apply concepts to sensations? The first way in which Kant seeks to show how categories are actually involved in the cognition of concrete situations in experience is to refer to rules. Understanding is our 'power of rules' while judgement has a unique ability to '*subsume* under rules' (ibid.). These are rules for the synthesis of experience, ways of ensuring that conceptual forms of determination are applicable to experience rather than irrelevant to its spatio-temporal forms. The search for a definition of the ability to apply rules supplied by the understanding now animates the text, producing at first negative definitions that emphasize the uniqueness of this ability rather than reducing it to the abilities of the understanding and sensation. We saw Heidegger uncovering an unknown common root behind these moves, where Kant gets closer to the imagination as the source of the ultimate unity of cognition. The unique and unknown role of the schematism does indeed take centre stage, as we shall now see.

In the schematism chapter itself Kant provides a definition of the imagination's transcendental power of schematism that needs to be interrogated because of how little it seems to tell us about this unique and original ability. He describes it as a '. . . secret art residing in the depths of the human soul, an art whose stratagems we shall hardly ever divine from nature and lay before ourselves' (ibid.: A141/B180–1). First of all we must consider Kant's use of the German term *Seele*, which is here translated as *soul* (KVR: 178). This requires our attention because two German terms in the *Critique of Pure Reason*, *Seele* and *Gemüt*, are translated as *soul*. In the Transcendental Aesthetic Kant writes that '[a]lthough inner sense provides no intuition of the soul [*Seele*] itself as an object, yet there is a determinate form under which alone [as condition] we can intuit the soul's [*Gemüth*] inner state' (CPR: A22–3/B37).[3] The soul's inner state is time and we will consider the pervasive role of time later in this chapter. However, this passage is of immediate help in allowing us to define *Seele* as an actual or potential object of cognition. Howard Caygill analyses this distinction and defines *Gemüt* for Kant as '. . . a corporeal awareness of sensation and self-affection' (Caygill 1995: 210). Thus it is defined as an inner state in the above passage but can also refer to our outer state where we encounter sensations rather than our own thoughts (CPR: A22/B37). This leads us to define *Seele* as a substance rather than as the place where the faculties of cognition are centred. *Gemüt* is a term that brings together the different faculties of cognition, the capacity to sense, to understand, to imagine and to think.[4] We are both passive in receiving sensations and active in applying concepts, thanks to these faculties centred in the soul (Caygill 1995: 211). This might suggest that while we have to establish the number and nature of faculties or capacities concentrated in the soul as *Gemüt* we may treat the soul (as *Seele*) as something we can uncover like any other object or substance. However, this is to neglect the secrecy surrounding the schematism as an art of the soul (*Seele*). Why this secrecy if the soul, as *Seele*, is a substance or object?

In considering Kant's reference to a secret art of the soul (*Seele*) we also have to consider whether he is avoiding giving an argument. The reference to 'the depths of the human soul' seems to obstruct enquiry because in fact the soul in this sense is, for Kant, not open to cognition. He refers to the soul as something we cannot come to know despite the fact that as *Seele* the soul is something substantial rather than being the centre of different faculties as it is when the term *Gemüt* is used. In fact it is because the German term *Seele* refers to an object or substance that the secrecy surrounding it is appropriate. The soul as *Seele* is not something that should be transparent to us. We saw in Chapter 2 of this book that for Kant we only have a problematic Idea of the self as a 'simple independent intelligence'. He writes that '[t]he first object of such an idea am I myself, regarded merely as a thinking nature (soul [*Seele*])' (CPR: A682/B710; KRV: 544). However, as we saw, '. . . reason has before it nothing but principles of systematic unity that are useful to it in explaining the appearances of the soul [*Seele*]' (ibid.). It follows that this undetermined object of an Idea cannot reveal itself to us in the course of cognition but it can play a part in providing an account of cognition. We cannot know the soul (*Seele*) but we can have a problematic Idea of it. We saw in Chapter 2 that it is because the object of a problematic Idea is undetermined that it is able to play a productive role in the cognition of possible experience.

From this analysis of Kant's reference to a secret art of the soul we have learned how to put the schematism in context. The *Critique of Pure Reason* is concerned with the faculties involved in accounting for the cognition of experience and not with the soul as an object of cognition.[5] If it seeks to *know* the soul we find that it is concerned with what the soul (*Gemüt*) is capable of, its faculties, rather than with locating it as an object or substance (*Seele*). What follows from Kant's definition of the schematism is the re-direction of enquiry into this transcendental power of the imagination and decisively away from the soul as an object or substance. In order to give a positive definition of the imagination as a faculty, and not as an object to be discovered, Kant seeks to define it in terms of its role in accounting for experience.[6] Like other elements in this account it is to be understood in terms of what it does in securing the cognition of possible experience. For Kant this ensures that nothing is isolated from the process of cognition if it is to have significance for cognition. If it is isolated in this way it remains a mystery for cognition. However, as an ability rather than the attribute of a mysterious object or substance, the schematism is always involved in and understood in terms of a wider process. Kant also seeks to avoid confusing the unique ability of the imagination with the outcomes of cognition, with what we can discover in experience or 'lay before ourselves'. He dispels the mystery but does not do this by simply equating the schematism with what can be learnt on the basis of experience. As we've seen, Kant does not want to rely upon what is given in experience any more than on things that are outside or beyond experience. He seeks therefore to distinguish thoroughly this unique ability by giving negative definitions, to make it part of a transcendental account of the role and relations of the faculties insofar as it is not itself an object of cognition.

This process of clearing the ground by giving negative definitions brings us closer to the ability of judgement to subsume under rules. We've seen that this ability is not to be confused with the understanding even though it is charged with making its concepts applicable to the synthesis of experience in space and time. In contrast to the understanding, which can be taught and given rules, judgement is an ability that can only be practiced and never taught (ibid.: A133/B172). It is an ability that again seems to be mysterious but for Kant it is first of all unique and original. Without this 'natural gift' neither understanding nor sensation can fulfil their roles in the cognition of possible experience (ibid.). To maintain its uniqueness Kant argues that examples cannot instruct the power of judgement. They may 'sharpen' this power but if wholly relied upon they take us away from the universal scope of rules by being too close to a particular case (ibid.: A134/B173). These are rules that are involved in particular cases of experience but not limited to them. They must then embody the scope of the categories as well as being involved in particular concrete cases that are presented in examples. Thus no matter how singular and striking an example it is, it does not capture the scope of judgement in applying conceptual rules to experience. A singular example cannot tell us what else judgement is capable of or what it might come across. Judgement relies upon something quite different. Kant argues that this calls for something that mediates the conceptual and the sensible. It must be pure, and thus non-empirical, while being both conceptual and sensible (ibid.: A138/B177). Examples cannot make up for a lack of natural talent by reducing the unique ability displayed in judgement to what sensation presents us with examples. For Kant the insights provided by the understanding and sensation do not show us how they work together in the synthesis of possible experience.

Henry Allison seeks to explain this by pointing to the game of chess where we need to have an abstract grasp of the rules and goals of the game if we are to play it (KTI: 205). How is a chess player creative and successful given that anyone could acquire this rudimentary knowledge? This can only be in pursuit of victory, something that must exceed the images and examples anyone might have of possible moves if they know the rules and have studied previous games. The player must possess something that cannot be 'laid out' in any book of rules or manual. As Allison puts it: '. . . the fact that a move is legal does not make it a good move, that is, one that is called for by the particular circumstances' (ibid.: 206). Thus what a particular situation requires is still up to one's own judgement, something which one relies upon to become a 'good' chess player. Kant's conviction that judgement cannot be taught would seem to stem from situations like this that are at once abstract and concrete, demanding that an abstract strategy must be combined with openness to concrete circumstances. The present case is only similar to previous ones; it is too concrete to be exactly the same. To be concrete is to involve spatial and temporal relations so that '. . . even if the location of the pieces on the board were perchance identical, the opponent would be different' (ibid.). For Kant, Allison argues, '[i]t is rather a matter of immediately recognizing the universal (the winning strategy) in the particular, which, in Kant's terms, means possessing the schema' (ibid.: 208). If we are to make sense of there being grand masters in chess then something distinct from sensation and understanding is demanded. This sets the scene for a positive definition of the schematism as the transcendental power of the imagination. It seems to undermine Kemp Smith's reading which suggested that Kant did not really maintain the heterogeneity of concepts and sensations up to this point in the *Critique of Pure Reason.* We get the sense that this difference is an internal problem that animates the text with its succession of negative definitions whose purpose seems to be to stage the uniqueness of this 'third thing' in response to the heterogeneity of the first and second things.

For Kant we must not lose sight of judgement's ability to apply determinate rules. The move is to be made from abstract categories to the concrete synthesis of possible experience that involves these categories as rules. He talks about judgement at the start of the Analytic of Principles in order to emphasize his concern with the application of conceptual rules, with the move from the abstract to the realization of the abstract in the concrete. However, it seems that Kant's concern with imagination is behind these moves, as we saw Heidegger arguing, so that the concrete is not simply to be understood as being ruled by the abstract. The distinction that he makes between images and schemata shows that the concrete synthesis of experience is far from passive in its relation to abstract concepts. It is in fact a distinction between their different roles in this process. Kant defines images as products of the empirical imagination (CPR: A141–2/B181). He then locates schemata of sensible concepts, which would include concepts of spatial figures, as products of the pure or transcendental imagination (ibid.). This form of the imagination is what make images possible. It provides the link between images and concepts. Kant thus associates the empirical imagination with images, with something already part of experience and therefore not useful in accounting for experience. This follows from his concern with the limitations of examples for instructing judgement, with how they can exemplify images given in experience but fail to capture the scope of the synthesis of possible experience itself. They limit our ability to respond to sensation in judgement if we see them as exhausting the role of concepts in synthesis. This is because they are based upon what has already been given in experience and so are not open to the further extension of concepts in space and time. In contrast, transcendental or pure imagination is to account for the empirical images that populate situations across experience and for our ability to recognize them as belonging to objects of experience. While situations may be filled by a succession of images, no list of these could ever exhaust the possibilities of a situation or provide the means of securing recognition. We cannot imagine how a situation will look tomorrow on the basis of what it has looked like up to now or present a list of examples and images to show the scope of imagination in applying conceptual rules to sensation. Images characterize empirical situations and this means that they must be recognizable, being fixed and determined in recognizable ways. They must also be incomplete because further images will be needed, such as the images of possible moves in a game of chess that cannot be anticipated. The synthesis of recognizable experience under concepts is what needs to be accounted for. We are seeking, to use Heidegger's formulation, a source of growth and not something already grown or given in experience.

While we saw that Kant limited the role of examples in instructing judgement, he does use them to define the schematism positively. However, he does not suggest that the power of schematism can be summed up using images taken from experience. We will now consider two examples that he gives. The first is the example of a triangle. Kant argues that we could never find an image of a triangle that would be adequate to 'the concept of a triangle as such' (ibid.: A140–1/B180). It will be useful to consider the way Deleuze develops this in his 1978 seminars on Kant's philosophy using his own example, that of a ring. For Kant the schema of a ring would produce images but is not itself any particular ring or image of a ring. Deleuze gives his own interpretation of Kant's schematism using this example:

> The circumference is what allows us to make certain materials round. The ring must obviously be lived dynamically, as a dynamic process; [. . .] the ring implies an operation by which something in experience is rounded. It's a process of production of the circumference-type which allows the production in experience of things corresponding to the concept circle. (KS2: 5)

This suggests that concepts, as rules, are directly involved in the synthesis of possible experience in space and time. The schema of a ring is a universal way in which space and time is shaped, it connects a universal concept with diverse concrete instances where it is at work as a rule of synthesis. It does this by showing how a conceptual rule is productive, how it is '. . . what allows us to make certain materials round' (ibid.). No matter how diverse the circumstances the circle can be recognized because it can be produced by the imagination. Thus we have a recognizable rule of synthesis in the case of a ring that is worn by someone to symbolize commitment and in the case where a ring is traced in the night sky, and would be studied in different ways by an astronomer and an astrologer. The diverse ways in which it is realized in the synthesis of possible experience are held together by the abstract unity of the schema or rule of production that is at work in each case. This abstract rule must therefore be dynamic enough to be stretched by these different ways of occupying space and time so that recognition still works in each case. This interpretation of Kant's schematism does relate to the concerns of his account of experience as we've presented it. Deleuze shows how the abstract and the concrete presuppose one another, how there are both abstract and concrete reasons for having the schema of a ring. This is something I will explore in the next chapter of this book in the proofs of the principles that Kant provides. He is concerned to relate the abstract and the concrete in such a way that the a priori is directly involved in the synthesis of possible experience.

A second example that we find in the schematism chapter is the schematized concept of a dog. This suggests that a schema fills our perception with images, such as a wagging tail, four legs, a prominent and active nose, and so forth. We have here an empirical concept, its schema and the images that this produces. The distinction between pure concepts or categories and empirical concepts is something we must consider. Kant explores the role of the schematism of empirical concepts in cognition. He finds that we have the concept *dog* and that this concept refers to a rule which allows the imagination to trace the shape of such an animal in general. This means that we are not restricted to that which is given in experience, not even to all the possible concrete images of such a creature that we might have (CPR: A141/B180). The images produced by a schema show that the schema exceeds any list of images, any attempt to sum up the productive abilities of the imagination using images already given in experience. One cannot exhaust the things that can be met with but one can still recognize a dog, making this ability to subsume under conceptual rules something more productive than a manual for the recognition of a dog. The ability to recognize objects of experience through concepts is more original because it must deal with the complexity of the ways in which this animal occupies space and time. Thus Kant talks of tracing 'in a general way' (ibid.: A141/B180) the concept of a dog, invoking factors that go beyond a particular case and also beyond the concept of a dog that one possesses. The imagination must make the concept into a rule able to meet the challenges presented by experience, such as the dog whose tail is missing or who is deaf and so occupies space and time quite differently. The empirical concept must be extended without it being defeated by sensation when it presents such unusual images of a dog. Thus we extend the empirical concept and the rule has not failed, we still recognize a dog because we are able to register the possibility of a dog without a tail as it arises in experience. We will return to this example of the schematized concept of a dog once we have considered the other type of schematism that Kant proposes and the importance of this distinction. The other type of schematism involves pure, rather than empirical, concepts.

Kant continues the above passage by adding a further distinction to that between an empirical image and the schematism of an empirical concept. The schema of a pure concept cannot be presented or captured in an image (ibid.: A142/B181). While the schema of an empirical concept produces images the schema of a category or pure concept of the understanding does not. We thus have two different kinds of schematism. It is the distinction between the schemata of empirical and certain mathematical concepts, and the schemata of categories or pure concepts. The triangle and the ring are mathematical concepts, they belong to geometry and, as we saw, produce many images without being reducible to them. In contrast, the schemata of pure concepts or categories produce no images but are still at work in the synthesis of experience. As we saw in the previous chapter of this book, a transcendental logic must allow us to mark out material situations according to a Table of Categories or pure concepts. However, we now need to show that such concepts are actually involved in the marking out of such situations through their synthesis in space and time. Rather than being merely relevant to concrete experience they must be involved in how it comes about. However, this involvement of the Table of Categories in the synthesis of possible experience is something we cannot 'picture' (Dicker 2004: 216–17). Lauchlin Chipman sums up this distinction: 'One can call something a dog because of what it looks like – it presents a doggish appearance – but one cannot call something a cause because it presents a cause-ish appearance.' (Chipman 1982: 104). Thus we have no images produced by the schema of the category or pure concept of cause and effect as we do with the schema of the empirical concept of a dog. However, categories or pure concepts make possible the formation of all empirical concepts. They are the basis upon which empirical cognition proceeds. For example, a noise causes the ears of the dog to move and so opens for us a whole domain of the ways in which this animal occupies space and time. We might call the dog's way of occupying space and time 'territorial' because of the animal's concern with the noise that might come from an intruder. This allows us to recognize a dog and subsume images under the rule provided by the concept of a dog. It can do this because it allows us to engage with the synthesis of experience in space and time, involving ways of occupying space and time. However, empirical concepts emerge here because experience has the basic forms captured by the Table of Categories such as cause and effect. Thus the movement of the dog's ears can be understood as the effect of a noise nearby. This means that, while we could have experience without dogs and our empirical concept of them, we couldn't have experience without categories or pure concepts like cause and effect. We can only build upon the role of categories in the synthesis of possible experience in the course of empirical cognition. In this respect Kant's Metaphysical Deduction continues to play a central role by providing the ultimate rules of the synthesis of possible experience in space and time. It is directly involved in the ways in which this animal occupies space and time. How then does the schematism of categories or pure concepts work? If we cannot 'picture' it as we can the recognition of a dog under its empirical concept, does it remain a mystery to be contemplated rather than an element in a clear and convincing account of experience?

We are developing a positive definition of the schematism, of its role in the synthesis of possible experience. Kant provides a positive definition of a particular mode of schematism when he talks about counting. He asks us to consider the image of five dots one after the other (CPR: A140/B179). This is the image of the number five that has a role in experience, characterizing situations where space and time are organized by five points or moments. Then Kant asks us to think *number as such* in order to move from an image, the number five, to a schema. Thinking *number as such* gives rise to numbers that can be pictured, like five, and numbers that cannot, like a 1000. One cannot keep hold of a 1000 dots in one's mind and this leads us to seek a more productive ability. It is an ability to realize the scope of the concept because it is not tied to an image or our ability to form images. Again, Kant must explain rather than leave as a mystery the ability that he has invoked. He argues that we must locate the involvement of a concept in this ability to grasp numbers without the aid of images. We are concerned with a 'method for presenting' a multitude in an image according to a certain concept rather than with this image itself (ibid.). This method for presenting even that which we cannot picture in an image is to realize a concept in the a priori synthesis of possible experience.

An objection that might be made is that Kant is drawing upon psychological processes when he talks about counting. As a way of grasping situations that we come across in experience, in terms of the abstract concept of a number that organizes them, this appears to be a wholly psychological process. However, Kant seeks to give this process an autonomy that makes it part of the synthesis of possible experience that precedes and makes possible all psychological processes. This he does by understanding the schematism as the production of time, as a mode of time itself. Time is the ultimate form of the synthesis of experience, something that marks out the space and time of a situation. Counting is the generation or production of time that takes part in this marking out, that takes part in the synthesis of experience itself (ibid.: A143/B182). Thus, for example, a three-point-turn is counted out in space as a series of the points of the turn and the series of moments of the turn. It might seem that time is how we register the points of the turn in space, making it part of a psychological process. However, to understand such a concrete situation Kant does not focus upon what is given in experience, such as the vehicle which is undertaking this manoeuvre. He also does not focus upon the space in which it takes place or the psychological processes involved. Instead he seeks to focus upon time and how it precedes and makes possible these different aspects of the concrete situations we find ourselves in. We must seek to understand how he can rely upon time to account for the schematism of concepts and the things it produces in experience. How are schemata modes of time and concepts modes of determination in time?

We've found that in its power of schematism the imagination draws upon time's resources in order to mediate concepts and sensations. Counting generates

time and this marks out the space and time of a situation under the rule
provided by the concept. Kant sets out the direct role of time in the schematism
of concepts as the ultimate form of the synthesis of possible experience. While
the understanding provides a unity to be realized in synthesis, time is the form
of inner sense (ibid.: A138/B177). This means that time is always involved
in the reception of appearances. Kant then defines a 'transcendental time
determination' as being homogeneous with the pure concept or category
insofar as this time determination shares in its universal and a priori status
(ibid.: A138–9/B177–8). It is equally homogeneous with the appearances
received in inner sense, because time is involved in all experience, thanks to its
role as the form of inner sense. Kant then defines the transcendental time
determination as the schematism of pure concepts. It is what makes it possible
to apply a pure concept or category to appearances. Hence the imagination's
role is understood as the ability to relate things in time where time exceeds
the organization of the situation in which one finds oneself. If one is ultimately
situated in time, what Heidegger calls our finitude, it is only through time that
concepts are realized in the synthesis of experience. Thus the three-point turn
becomes a possibility drawn from time and the determinations provided by
concepts. This reorganizes the space and time of a situation that earlier were
characterized by the car facing in the wrong direction. In the move from an
image of the number five to 'number as such' we saw how time allows us to
mark out a situation and so apply a rule even when images fail us. With the
schematism of categories or pure concepts, where images are not produced,
time is our only way of grasping its role. Lauchlin Chipman understands this in
the following way: '. . . any general truth to do with time will manifest itself
in any appearances; e.g. through a necessary rule of synthesis' (Chipman
1982: 113). Thus when Kant talks about counting he is not referring to a
psychological process from which we can draw examples and images and so
sum up the nature and scope of the schematism. Instead he is talking about
a 'method of presentation' such as the three-point structuring of a situation.
This makes possible the attempt at a three-point turn and the recognition of
this manoeuvre only on the basis of schematized pure concepts like cause and
effect and empirical concepts like that of a three-point turn. The situation is
determined in time by the concepts according to which the vehicle's wheels
respond to the movements of the steering wheel and to the friction caused by
the road's surface, and three points are counted out. These hold no matter
how different the circumstances in space and time because this is a 'universal
procedure' for synthesizing experience (CPR: A140/B179–80). It is time's
resources, rather than those of space or psychology, that account for the
productive power of imagination in applying a concept even when an image
is lacking.

The emphasis upon time that we are exploring follows from Kant's concern
to make time the a priori form of inner sense that precedes space, which is the
a priori form of outer sense. Experience is ultimately temporal in form because

outer sense is encountered from the standpoint of inner sense (ibid.: B50–1). We've made some arguments for understanding this in non-psychological terms and as the ultimate form of the synthesis of possible experience. Kant emphasizes the autonomy of the elements of his account of experience so that his *Critique of Pure Reason* is animated, as we've seen, by the difference between the synthetic and the a priori rather than between the psychological and the non-psychological. He seeks to account for the cognition of things as psychological or non-psychological, for this difference, rather than presupposing it. We must now consider how in the schematism chapter, time is not situated as psychological time but is at work in the synthesis of experience. We saw Kant defining the schematism as a transcendental time determination. It is a rule of determination that embodies a concept in the very synthesis of experience whose form is ultimately temporal.

How does time in this sense differ from psychological time? Heidegger sums up the difference in the following way:

> . . . [T]ime must indeed be taken as pure sequence of nows in the horizon within which we 'reckon with time'. This sequence of nows, however, is in no way time in its originality. On the contrary, the transcendental power of imagination allows time as sequence of nows to spring forth, and as this letting-spring-forth it is therefore original time. (KPM: 123)

Heidegger argues that Kant is not reducing the role of time to registering the 'nows' or present moments in which we encounter empirical images. Just as the imagination is not to be reduced to the images it produces, so time is not to be reduced to the present moments it produces. Otherwise, the different images of a dog that we come across would be the source of our recognition of objects and sum up the productive power behind it. In this case time's role would be limited to presenting 'nows' and the images they offer us. It would have nothing more to offer to the imagination and to our cognition of experience. Instead time must bring about the determination under concepts that makes it possible to 'reckon with time' in the first place, as Heidegger puts it. The role of time in accounting for how we 'reckon with time' cannot be captured using images or considering how images occur to us, as if presenting a succession of images in psychological time was time's only role. Thus in our three-point turn example the role of a new type of vehicle does not undermine the concept even though it presents us with a different image to previous cases. This is because time does not realize this concept simply by registering a succession of images that correspond to the concept. We hold on to the concept of a three-point-turn rather than falling into an unrecognizable situation which exceeds the images we have of three-point-turns. We avoid a crisis of confidence in our ability to carry out the manoeuvre or to recognize it. Time must not just chart the images that occur to us in experience because then recognition in time would always be in danger of being undermined by our inability to form an appropriate image. Space, which is full of images, must be marked out by time so that it can be determined ultimately by the Table of Categories even when images fail us. New images can then be produced by the imagination when necessary because it forms new images on the basis of concepts and how these are realized in time. This shows how concepts are related to time by the schematism, to the time in which synthesis occurs and through which these concepts can become transcendental time determinations. For Kant this shows that concepts are never exhausted by the cases they are applied to but are able to give rise to new cases. They can do this because the imagination relates them to time. I will now turn to Deleuze's reading of Kant's schematism in order to further explore the scope of their relations. This will allow me to extend the comparison I made in Chapter 2 of this book where their common methodological concerns were considered.

Deleuze's Response to the Schematism

In *Kant's Critical Philosophy* Deleuze focuses upon the role of differences that are internal to Kant's account of experience as a whole. In Chapter 1 of this book I argued that the difference between the synthetic and the a priori provides the inner problematic of the *Critique of Pure Reason*. I reviewed Heidegger's case for focusing upon the difference between concepts and sensations in the first section of the present chapter. I will now argue that the concern, shared by Deleuze and Heidegger, to begin with the relations between the faculties in Kant's account has certain limitations. I will defend my reading, according to which it is the relation of the synthetic and the a priori that comes first. Deleuze writes that '. . . the problem of the relation of subject and object tends to be internalized; it becomes the problem of a relation between subjective faculties which differ in nature (receptive sensibility and active understanding)' (KCP: 14). It is therefore the difference between faculties, between their roles in accounting for experience, that animates Kant's thought in the *Critique of Pure Reason*. The schematism responds to the difference between concepts and sensation. However, Deleuze points out that while imagination alone schematizes, making it unique and original, we must recognize its subordinate role in Kant's Idea of the whole: '. . . it schematizes only when the understanding presides, has the legislative power. It schematizes only in the speculative interest' (ibid.: 18). This provides the basis for his critique of Kant in *Difference and Repetition*. While he recognizes the role of 'internal differences' in Kant's account of experience, differences between the faculties, he argues that we should critically consider how these differences emerge. In this way we can evaluate Kant's account of experience. He then seeks to go beyond Kant's project when writes of the spatio-temporal dynamisms that are at work in the synthesis of experience: 'Everything changes when the dynamisms are posited no longer as schemata of concepts but as dramas of Ideas' (DR: 218). The schematism is now to be realized in its own right because it *dramatizes* Ideas in space and time rather than referring back to the categories and their systematic presentation in a table. We sought to understand the nature and role of problematic Ideas for Deleuze in the second chapter of this book. The dramatization of Ideas in sensation moves beyond Kant's thought and its emphasis upon thinking categories or pure concepts in the abstract first of all. It makes them something external to what Deleuze regards as a valid account of experience.

For Deleuze then the synthesis of experience in space and time must be everything. It is not preceded by a Metaphysical Deduction or animated by differences that do not arise within the synthesis of experience through the dramatization of Ideas. This drama is '. . . a pure staging without author, without actors and without subjects' (ibid.: 219).[7] This excludes Kant's transcendental unity of apperception, the categories as basic forms of an object of cognition and even the self as a passive actor in the drama. This drama is the synthesis of experience in space and time but, unlike in Kant's thought, concepts are not specified prior to the drama and then applied to it. Thus the example of a three-point turn is a drama with a subject who wants to turn and others who want to avoid the path of a car. All are concerned to recognize the role of the concept in the situation. In contrast, Deleuze's dramatization of Ideas is without these conceptual forms of possibility. This appears to forestall the engagement between Kant and Deleuze that we are seeking to develop on the basis of the positive comparison we made in Chapter 2 of this book. In that chapter we saw how Kant and Deleuze disagree when it comes to the categories or pure concepts that mediate the intelligible and the sensible in Kant's account. Now we find that this disagreement gives rise to a further attempt to move beyond Kant. Deleuze seeks a dramatization of Ideas in sensation which is able to account for concepts rather than needing to presuppose them. The power of schematism is therefore not to be subordinated to categories or pure concepts, things not accounted for through this dramatization.

We might ask first of all why we should give up the determinations that Kant's abstract concepts provide. Indeed, we see no reason to deny that Deleuze wants to account for drivers doing three-point turns and others getting out of their way or assessing the manoeuvre as part of a driving test. Recognition must work and it must be dynamic if it is to meet the challenges posed by sensation. However, for Deleuze there is a need to disengage ourselves from recognition, to think without taking our bearings from it. We must do this in order to account for it. His criticism in *Difference and Repetition* is that Kant's schemata do not account for their own power to schematize. He seeks to avoid presupposing what is to be accounted for and therefore to account for the ongoing emergence of concepts through the dramatization of Ideas in sensation. According to Deleuze, Kant seeks to apply, to use Heidegger's terminology, a rootless concept which lacks any account of its own genesis in the synthesis of experience. The heterogeneity of concepts and sensations is therefore judged an 'external difference' since it is external to a full account of experience; it is something presupposed rather than accounted for (ibid.: 174). Deleuze proposes that instead we consider differences that are internal to the synthesis of experience itself, internal to the dramatization of Ideas in sensation. He writes that '. . . if the dynamism is external to concepts – and, as such, a schema – it is internal to Ideas – and, as such, a drama or dream' (ibid.: 218). Deleuze argues that the schematism chapter is where Kant calls upon a miracle that makes up for the lack of a full account of experience, one that includes an account of the emergence of concepts. It is a miraculous power to apply concepts to experience that do not arise in the synthesis of experience itself. He argues that '[a] concept alone is completely incapable of specifying or dividing itself; . . .' (ibid.). Therefore, for Kant imagination can only be productive in applying concepts that are formulated in abstraction in the Metaphysical Deduction. What is missed out is what accounts for concepts in the first place: '. . . the agents of differentiation [that] are the spatio-temporal dynamisms which act within or beneath [a concept], like a hidden art' (ibid.).

As we saw in Chapter 2 of this book, for Deleuze the intelligible is to be incarnated and realized in the sensible. In this critical account of Kant's schematism in *Difference and Repetition* Deleuze seems to want to escape the abstract limitations of Kant's account of experience. However, for Kant this reference to the genesis of pure concepts of the understanding has no meaning. It is only insofar as we make use of these concepts that cognition can have any meaning. His response to Deleuze would be based upon the necessary relation of the synthetic and the a priori in accounting for experience. If we sought to account for the a priori through the synthetic, as we've seen Deleuze proposing, possible experience as such would be undermined. Kant's concern to secure possible experience in the face of sceptical challenges, something we considered in Chapter 1 of this book, leads him to avoid all reference to something that precedes the a priori and makes it possible. Thus we find him conscious of the danger of seeking to locate that which is beyond experience. Instead of seeking to venture beyond the secure and solid ground of possible experience, we should be content with the richness provided by this fertile domain (CPR: A235–6/B295). Kant speaks of the possibility of us being content with the territory we have secured and in this chapter we have seen that, as well as being ruled by absolutely necessary conceptual forms, possible experience is a rich and fertile land. Thus in answer to Deleuze's critique Kant would point to the need to remain focused upon the relations of the synthetic and the a priori, and to do this by providing arguments that defeat scepticism. We must relate the synthetic and the a priori in necessary and indispensible ways, using arguments that establish the conditions of possible experience once and for all. Thus if we begin with the relations of the faculties we do not see what is at the basis of Kant's account. Faculties are related in order to secure the relation of the synthetic and the a priori at different stages of this account. This leaves us wondering whether we can relate Kant and Deleuze further. To do so we must show that Kant's concern to relate the synthetic and the a priori is relevant to Deleuze's account even if the ways he does this, for example by focusing upon the abstract use of the understanding, are rejected by Deleuze. In the next chapter of this book we will consider how for Kant the Analytic of Principles is shaped by the system embodied in the Table of Categories while also relating to the concrete synthesis of experience.

Conclusion

Our consideration of the role of time in Kant's account brings us back to a question which I raised in the introduction to this book. Levi R. Bryant argues that Deleuze uncovers in Kant's work '. . . a transcendental dimension more fundamental and deeper than those found in the understanding or the unity of apperception' (Bryant 2008: 181). Time is for Deleuze able to account for the emergence of subjects and objects through its role in the dramatization of Ideas. This undermines Kant's reliance upon a transcendental subject, or transcendental unity of apperception, and a Table of Categories. For Bryant this is Deleuze's '. . . doorway for jumping out of critical philosophy . . .' (ibid.). He seeks to go beyond Kant's concern with a finite subject, situated by the synthesis of possible experience in space and time, who relies upon the transcendental unity of apperception and Table of Categories to deal with experience. Bryant argues that the creative power of time manifested in the schematism ultimately takes us beyond the concerns of a finite subject. The schematism of the categories or pure concepts is not useful for Deleuze, only the schematism of concepts that emerge and develop through a relationship of reciprocal determination between the abstract and the concrete. As we've seen, the intelligible is incarnated and realized in the sensible in Deleuze's account. If time takes us beyond the role of a Table of Categories, opening up instead the reciprocal determination of the abstract and the concrete in time, this seems to take us beyond Kant's architectonic.

This verdict is not limited to those, like Levi R. Bryant, who seek to explore Deleuze's relation to Kant. Paul Guyer finds Kant's architectonic presentation of the *Critique of Pure Reason* an 'ill-digested addition'. However, what is fully digested and developed is: '. . . the basic theory of time-determination which really underlies Kant's theory of experience' (Guyer 1987: 189–90). This echoes Bryant's verdict since we find that time is said to make the Table of Categories obsolete in the synthesis of possible experience. However, by re-introducing, in the next chapter of this book, Kant's systematic tendency I will suggest the need to go much further with Kant. Rather than cutting short his systematic journey, or seeing time as a way of revising or exiting his system, I will argue that this provides an account of experience that is worth giving fuller consideration.

In this way I will part company with Deleuze in his rejection of the Table of Categories in order that I may fully develop Kant's architectonic presentation of his account of experience. Having done this I will consider, in Chapter 6, the positive role that this account of experience may have in Deleuze's own thought. As I have done throughout this book, I will seek to read Kant in a unifying way in order that we may be able to better understand his account of experience and relate it to Deleuze's thought in new ways.

Chapter 5

Kant's Analytic of Principles

It might seem that we have moved away from Kant's architectonic and its single and unifying problem in our discussion of the schematism. We found its role to be decisive in understanding the Metaphysical Deduction in the third chapter of this book. In the previous chapter we presented and evaluated the schematism as something that makes concepts immanent to the synthesis of possible experience. We saw that time is affirmed by Kant as the ultimate unity of this synthesis. Thus, while Kant begins with the abstract and moves to the concrete, he does not reduce the synthesis of possible experience to the simple application of categories to experience. We noted that for many readers of Kant, including Deleuze, we should make the most of Kant's elaboration of the determination of experience in time in the Analytic of Principles. We should not view it as extending the systematic tendency that characterizes the architectonic but as providing independent arguments for necessary and productive ways of cognizing experience.[1] However, when we recall our exploration of Kant's architectonic method of presentation and argument in the first chapter of this book we see that the relation of the abstract and the concrete is at the heart of the architectonic. Abstract concepts are involved in the concrete synthesis of possible experience in the schematism chapter. However, Kant goes further when he defines the nature and role of the abstract in a highly systematic way. He does this when he provides the schematism of the Table of Categories as a whole (CPR: A142–5/B181–5). This is followed by a Table of Principles (ibid.: A161/B200) whose four divisions correspond to the four divisions of the Table of Categories. Thus for Kant it is not enough that we involve the abstract in the concrete. This will not secure an account of possible experience. To do this we must extend the system that was set out in the Metaphysical Deduction in a Table of Categories. In this chapter we will continue to consider whether this is an artificial way of organizing the text or something integral to Kant's account of experience.

The Role of the Table of Categories

Returning then to the mode of argument we sought to highlight in the Metaphysical Deduction, we find that its systematic focus upon a Table of Categories is carried forward by Kant. He claims to move from the abstract to the concrete using this table as his guide. To do this he invokes the arguments and reasoning that, in the third chapter of this book, we found so curious and yet to be something that we should take seriously. Thus he does not simply take forward the outcome of the Metaphysical Deduction, the Table of Categories, but also its way of arguing. This is evident in the schematism chapter when Kant relates the schematism to the Table of Categories. He proposes that we do not spend time on a 'dry and tedious dissection' of the schematism of the categories or pure concepts (CPR: A142/B181). Instead he will connect these schemata to the Table of Categories and order them accordingly. A common complaint among Kant scholars is that this shows a lack of argument. However, as we saw in the Chapter 2 of this book, this brief mode of presentation can be understood as a form of argument that pursues solidity through brevity. Kant now speaks of avoiding dryness and tedium. This can be understood as referring to the same concern that we do not introduce external factors into the argument. Instead of elaborating the elements of an account of experience at length, or to the point of tedium, we must present the swift and lively unfolding of Kant's systematic Idea of the whole. The concern seems to be that a dry exposition would not invoke the impetus of Kant's architectonic, one that is drawn only from its own parts and not from anything that might arise, given more time, over the course of experience. A great deal is demanded of the Table of Categories. As a systematic whole it must carry us forward into a full and convincing account of the synthesis of possible experience in space and time. For Kant, as we saw in Chapter 3, it embodies the ideals of the architectonic. As an account of the basic forms of experience it leaves nothing out and it draws upon nothing external. For Kant this is because it is the outcome of an argument that is brief and inclusive in order that it should prove to be solid. How does this abstract and systematic completeness relate to the concrete work of synthesis? Matthew C. Altman writes that if we follow Kant's systematic presentation we will reach a table of '. . . the concepts as they are relevant to our kind of sensible experience (in space and time)' (Altman 2008: 146). We then move from relevance to involvement, via the schematism, with the Table of Principles. In this move from abstract to concrete the Table of Categories and time together provide the ultimate forms of unity, the transcendental time determinations, which allow the synthesis of possible experience to proceed. The former is the system and the latter its concrete realization. How do we include time along with the Table of Categories in Kant's account of possible experience?

In the previous chapter we considered the role of time and found it to be crucial to the schematism, providing the resources for the rich development of empirical cognition. However, we suggested in Chapter 3 that the Table of Categories is also crucial to the synthesis of possible experience for Kant precisely because it embodies and presents the basic rules of synthesis. Kant first relates schemata to time, as the a priori form of inner sense, and then relates the resulting transcendental time determinations to the Table of Categories.

He emphasizes the unity provided by time and argues that this is an indirect result of the unity of apperception (CPR: A145–6/B185). The role of apperception corresponds to that of inner sense insofar as both provide unity of a different sort, the former conceptual and the latter temporal. He concludes that the schemata of pure concepts or categories are the only means of relating such concepts to objects of experience (ibid.: A146/B185). Here we see that the ultimate unity provided by time does not exclude that provided by the categories but is held together by it insofar as it refers to objects of experience. Categories provide rules for determining different modes of time so that we have transcendental time determinations, as the example of counting showed in the previous chapter. How are we to understand the singular roles of the categories as Kant uncovers these in the modes of time determination at work in the synthesis of possible experience? In what follows we will consider the modes of schematism or transcendental time determinations, and how they lead us to the systematic presentation of the principles at work in the ongoing synthesis and cognition of possible experience. Our concern will be with the architectonic or systematic presentation of the principles while recognizing how singular and individually compelling each principle and its proof is. The challenge will be to keep Kant's architectonic in view, to treat the principles not as individual arguments but as principles for the realization of this Idea of the whole in the synthesis of possible experience. We will first of all ask how the architectonic unfolds rather than assessing each principle and its proof as independent arguments. However, we shall also evaluate this architectonic mode of presentation and argument by considering some objections to the way schemata and principles are divided according to the order of the Table of Categories. These come from commentators who think that the principles should be understood as independent or 'stand alone' arguments. Since we will be following the progress of Kant's architectonic mode of argument and presentation we will be able to make a fuller assessment than would be possible if, as is often the case, it is dismissed before it can make itself heard.

From the Schematism of the Categories to the Table of Principles

Modes of schematism or transcendental time determination are presented according to the order and division of the Table of Categories towards the end of the schematism chapter. This appears to be the basis for the elaboration of the principles that follows. The schemata provide the concrete basis for the categories to be systematically involved in the synthesis of possible experience as principles. Kant seeks to find in time ways of realizing the categories but always according to the systematic presentation of the Table of Categories as rules of synthesis. The section that follows the schematism chapter is thus entitled 'Systematic Presentation of All the Synthetic Principles of Pure

Understanding' (CPR: A158/B197). Being systematic here involves formulating a Table of Principles as the realization of a schematized Table of Categories in the ongoing synthesis and cognition of possible experience. In pursuing his apparently rigid architectonic method here Kant in fact seeks to realize the Table of Categories as a dynamic and open system of determination. As we shall see, he divides the four components of his Table of Principles into mathematical and dynamical or discursive principles, a distinction he originally made in the Metaphysical Deduction (ibid.: B110). He explains this in terms of the intuitive certainty of mathematical principles in contrast to the discursive certainty of dynamical principles (ibid.: A162/B201). As we shall see, both types of principles are dynamic or open to the production of experience but the second type is involved in how we respond discursively to this ongoing process. Jill Vance Buroker informs us that 'Kant recalls the Latin *discursus*, which means "running through"' (Buroker 2006: 81). The understanding '. . . operates by "running through" diverse representations and classifying them in terms of a concept' (ibid.). We will seek to understand how this can be a dynamic process when we consider the two dynamical or discursive components of the Table of Principles (the Analogies of Experience and the Postulates of Empirical Thought As Such). We will seek to show how this system of determination unfolds in the Analytic of Principles, in this way gaining a better understanding of Kant's rejection of any 'dry and tedious dissection'. This will allow us to understand the nature of these systematic divisions and to assess their contribution to a convincing account of experience.

The axioms of intuition

The first member of the Table of Principles is the Axioms of Intuition. It corresponds to the first division of the Table of Categories, the categories of quantity. The schema of the three categories of quantity is number (CPR: A142/B182) and we considered in the previous chapter how counting is the temporal process that marks out the space and time of a concrete situation. For Kant what is at stake in this transcendental time determination is the determination under a rule of a *time series* (ibid.: A145/B184–5). The time series is then a mode of time that must be determined under the rules provided by the three categories of quantity when they are schematized. First let's consider what this schema presents us with in experience. We have '. . . a presentation encompassing conjointly successive additions of one item to another (homogeneous item)' (ibid.: A142/B182). We saw in the previous chapter that this is the generation or production of time, something that participates in the synthesis of experience. Counting or successive addition is a concrete process but one that realizes an abstract concept in the unity and homogeneity produced by its synthesis of heterogeneous things. Kant argues that this unity is achieved because of our own role in making use of time in the course of experience (ibid.: A143/B182). It is the staging of schemata or transcendental time deter-minations in different situations that makes a time series into the source of a determinate unity in space. An example to add to that of the three-point turn, which we explored in the previous chapter, would be a measurable distance whose parts are presented successively in time. As a dynamic rule of synthesis this schema allows very different situations to become recognizable according to the abstract concept of a number that is to characterize them. If we return to Kant's divisions of the Table of Principles, carried forward from the Table of Categories, we note that as a mathematical principle the Axioms of Intuition must provide an 'intuitive' grasp of experience on the basis of the schematism involved. Sebastian Gardner interprets the distinction between mathematical and dynamical or discursive principles as pointing to a stage in the process of accounting for the objectivity of experience. Mathematical principles are not sufficient to give us objects of experience but provide a series of determinate parts or aspects of the object. These determinate intuitions include the extensive magnitudes generated by counting or successive addition (Gardner 1999: 166). Thus distances are built up in experience. These do not give us a complete object but a determinate intuition that is part of the ongoing determination of an object over time. They unify an object *here and now*, providing a series of its different determinations that are built up over time, but do not provide it with the ultimate unity of an object of cognition. The examples of a three-point turn or a distance covered, both allow us to recognize something about an object, they tell us what this body can do insofar as this can be counted or measured but no more. We will consider this further because it helps us to integrate the principles in Kant's full, architec-tonic account of experience. The Axioms of Intuition provide a partial account of the determination of objects of cognition and therefore look to other principles. This suggests that we have here something other than an argument that is confined to the role of successive addition in the synthesis of possible experience. We have instead a stage in the unfolding of Kant's architectonic.

How do we move from a schematized category to a principle in this case? Paul Guyer argues that Kant does not follow his architectonic strategy when he provides the principle and its proof, the strategy of moving from schema to principle on the basis of the Table of Categories and its relation to time. He argues that in the first two components of the Table of Principles, the Axioms of Intuition and the Anticipations of Perception, Kant does not draw upon '. . . the temporal re-interpretation of the categories of quantity and quality' (K: 101) that he presented in the schematism chapter. These are the transcendental time determinations that realize a conceptual rule in a mode of time, such as the time series that is ruled by the schematized categories of quantity. Guyer also argues that Kant does not show that the categories must be applied on the basis of the temporal structure of experience. Time does not provide an argument in favour of the necessity of the categories any more than the categories show how time is to be ordered. Thus if we find it convincing that mathematical operations like successive addition must take place to secure objects of cognition this is an argument about what mathematics can do and not about what time and the categories together are capable of. Guyer argues that . . .

> . . . what Kant actually does in these sections is to argue that the spatial as well as the temporal structure of our experience justifies the application of certain parts of *mathematics* to its objects, namely, the mathematics of 'extensive' and 'intensive' quantities. (ibid.)

We will now consider this reading that puts mathematics at the basis of Kant's arguments in the proofs of the two mathematical principles rather than involving the Table of Categories and its relation to time.

The principle of the Axioms of Intuition is that sensible intuitions are extensive magnitudes (CPR: A162/B202). Taking forward his schematism of the categories of quantity Kant defines an extensive magnitude as a magnitude where the presentation of the whole is made possible by the presentation of the parts. This is then a determinate unity because it is successively built up over a time series. Kant argues that one must draw a line in one's mind in order to be able to present it (ibid.: A163/B203). This involves the successive addition of parts of the line. He concludes that one is thereby thinking the progression in time involved in any production of a determinate magnitude. Here Kant moves from an example of how cognition actually works to time as the ultimate form of this synthesis of possible experience. He makes it clear that while his concern is with space or extension, the medium in which the cognition of extensive magnitudes is produced is time. There is the succession and progression in time that builds up parts so that a whole, an extensive magnitude, can be formed. Thus a distance in space has to be assembled through successive apprehension in time and is always open to being extended through time. This ensures that no extensive magnitude is discrete or self-contained. The unity of an extensive magnitude is the aggregate of parts presented in space but the role of time in the presentation of these parts keeps this extension open. It is then a principle of the synthesis of possible experience that extensive magnitudes are built up through time in order to make space determinate and keep open its determination in time.

It is clear that Kant is drawing upon mathematics and how it is necessary to our cognition of possible experience. We saw Paul Guyer argue that this makes the Axioms of Intuition an independent argument that is artificially presented through Kant's architectonic as following from his Table of Categories and the correlated modes of schematism. The arguments made concerning the Axioms of Intuition actually draw upon mathematics and stand or fall according to the evidence it draws from this source. Mathematics provides the rules that apply to the objects that we come across in experience and Kant therefore refers to what we do when we count rather than to the role of time and the categories in the synthesis of possible experience. However, if we follow Kant's architectonic mode of argument and presentation, mathematics is seen to participate in a wider process in the Axioms of Intuition rather than standing on its own. It is situated as something happening in and through time and the role of the categories in time. In Chapter 1 of this book we saw how it is a supporting argument when set in the context of Kant's architectonic method. It is nevertheless privileged because it shows what time and the categories can do in a unique way and so supports Kant's architectonic like no other cognitive achievement. To count is to produce time and in this way stage a transcendental time determination, to apply a rule that deals with time series. However, it is in time that this series has been able to arise as a succession of parts in space. It is also in time that the categories provide the ultimate rules for making this succession into the determination of an extensive magnitude or partial object. It follows that the synthesis of possible experience does not wait until someone learns or decides to count before this temporal operation takes place. Time and the categories are at work prior to the existence of a mathematician or to the evolution of life to the stage where counting is possible. It must make possible those situations where we can count by introducing number as the schema of the categories of quantity in the synthesis of possible experience. If we follow the architectonic, time and the categories come before mathematics as a practice but mathematics is privileged because it participates in synthesis like no other discipline.

It follows that while number is not a member of the Table of Categories, it is the schema of a division of this table, of the categories of quantity. If we follow this architectonic presentation of the text we find that mathematics informs us about how the synthesis of possible experience proceeds according to the system provided by the Table of Categories. However, we have not yet shown how the three categories of quantity are at work in the Axioms of Intuition. In his *Kant Dictionary* Howard Caygill sets out the role of each category of quantity in three rules for the determination of a time series (Caygill 1995: 90). They are the rules that turn a time series into a process of successive addition with an extensive magnitude as its outcome. The category of unity is realized in the instant or moment of time which forms part of the extensive magnitude that is being built up over time. The category of plurality is realized in the course of time that builds up the parts of an extensive magnitude. A plurality of unified moments is gone through in order to realize the first two categories of quantity in a concrete way. Finally, the category of totality is realized at the end of this time of the successive addition of parts, in the extensive magnitude they now form and its determinate unity. We see that the categories can be understood as structuring or determining a time series, providing a dynamic system of determination that produces extensive magnitudes in very different situations. A temporal interpretation of the three categories of quantity takes all three together and makes this part of a systematic unfolding of the schematized Table of Categories.[2] This is not to downplay the role of mathematics for Kant but to situate it in time and the work of the categories. It is very informative for Kant because it deals with appearances or partial objects, objects needing to be determined under rules. For Kant we cannot look beyond rules that deal with appearances in order to get to what is objective about space. In this sense, we must think about space like a mathematician does.[3] We need to envisage a mathematics of appearances that is always at work in the synthesis of possible experience. Thus appearances must be built up according to rules for securing unity, plurality and totality in the production of a magnitude just as in geometry the rule that two straight lines cannot enclose a space must always hold (CPR: A163/B204). These are partial objects, not complete ones that cannot be further determined in time under a priori rules. Mathematics then shows how objects are built up out of appearances that are only 'partial', as Sebastian Gardner suggested when he argued that mathematical principles do not give us complete objects. As extensive magnitudes they are open to change as well as being determined in time under rules. In this sense mathematics actually points to the involvement of objects in the synthesis of possible experience that necessarily involves the categories as rules rather than, as Guyer suggests, standing alone as a way of cognizing objects already given in experience. For Kant mathematics does not involve objects that come to an end but it does involve determination in time and under rules. This leads us to the open-ended determination of extensive magnitudes. In this way we can understand and situate mathematics within the unfolding of Kant's architectonic.

The anticipations of perception

We will now consider the second mathematical principle in order to see how it complements the first. We move from the building up of magnitudes in extension to differences in intensive magnitude. The systematic route that Kant takes is via the categories of quality and their schematism. However, he also draws upon the concrete role of intensive magnitudes which we've seen Guyer emphasizing so that the abstract and the concrete both play an indispensable role. Kant seeks to put the categories of quality in touch with the concrete synthesis of possible experience in space and time in the schematism chapter. Reality is a concept that indicates the being of something in time while negation indicates the non-being of something in time (CPR: A143/B182). It follows that the distinction between reality and negation corresponds to the difference between full and empty time (ibid.). Here the categories of reality and negation are involved in synthesis but they are schematized and so are translated into the ways in which they occupy space and time. They occupy space and time as fullness and as emptiness respectively. This is because the mode of time to be dealt with by the schematized categories of quality is *time content* (ibid.: A145/B185). Kant makes it clear in the Anticipations of Perception that the role of the schematized category of reality is not to be cancelled out by the role of the schematized category of negation in the ways in which these rules deal with time content.

The production of reality in experience, of spaces and times full of sensation, is not to come to an end with negation and nor is it to start from nothing.[4] It is instead what is always already underway because experience is always ultimately in time and so being continuously filled with degrees of reality. However, negation is necessarily involved in this determination of time content while not being something we ever perceive. We only perceive degrees of reality or spaces and times full of sensation. Kant describes the schema of the category of reality as the way in which quantity fills time, which is a continuous and homogeneous production of reality or of the being of an object in time (ibid.: A143/B183). He understands this process as the descent from a certain degree of reality to the vanishing of this sensation or the ascent by degrees from this vanishing to a particular magnitude. The categories of reality and negation deal with time content by keeping it full of degrees of reality but also open to changes in degree of reality. We have then continuity in the production of degrees of reality and a vanishing or negation that prevents any stoppage in this production because any particular degree will always be *negated* in favour of another. Negation thus ensures that our perception of degrees of reality flows rather than coming to an end, that we perceive further partial objects determined under rules and in time. How does this complement the Axioms of Intuition and so play a part in the unfolding of Kant's architectonic?

Kant argues that it is possible to abstract from extensive magnitudes in sensation and yet find in a single moment 'a synthesis of uniform ascent' from a zero degree of reality to what is given in experience (ibid.: A176/B217–18). Here Kant suggests that in one moment a synthesis can, as it were, *come from nowhere* in the sense that it is not accounted for by the building up of the parts of an object over time. An object may still have exactly the same number of parts in extension, the same extensive magnitude, but something has changed. Kant is concerned that recognition can keep up with a change in the way space and time is marked out for us by intensive magnitudes. This means that it needs a principle dynamic enough for this process to be anticipated. We do not anticipate the particular degree of reality but we do anticipate the role of the schematized categories of reality and negation in keeping perception full and flowing with degrees of reality or intensive magnitudes (ibid.: A170/B211–12). These categories keep reality full of different degrees, ensuring that the production of intensive magnitudes is open ended. An example would be an object that is perceived as 'too hot' to hold whereas a moment before it was an object that could be held. The object's role in possible experience thus exceeds any particular degree of reality. Kant describes the necessary role of negation here in terms of the production of magnitudes in sensation which begins with a zero degree of reality and ascends to a particular magnitude (ibid.: A166/B208). The role of the schematized category of negation is here further specified as the zero degree intensity that opens situations to the different ways in which things can occupy space and time. It does not specify the number of degrees by which the temperature of the object rises or how the person holding it reacts, something that will depend upon the psychology and physiology of the individual concerned. However, behind each change of degree we anticipate the role of the zero degree, ensuring that intensive magnitudes flow and so keep open what can happen in a situation in relation to the degrees of reality that characterize it. Thus, in order for recognition to be adequate to the synthesis of possible experience, it must anticipate a continuous production of degrees of reality. Only in this way can it account for the unpredictable ways in which we occupy space and time. Recognition is in this way armed with a principle that allows it to envisage a sudden and perhaps frightening or alarming change in intensity which is nevertheless a determinate change in magnitude.

This brings us to the role of the third category of quality, the category of limitation. We saw in the Axioms of Intuition that the three categories of quantity together form a dynamic system of determination for possible experience. This is echoed in the Anticipations of Perception where we find that limitation in space and time is the combination of the first two categories of quality. Here Kant extends the system presented in the Table of Categories. As we saw in Chapter 3, the third category in each division is derived from the combination of the first two. We found that if this is to be convincing, rather than rigid and artificial, it must play a necessary part in providing a full account of possible experience. In the case of the third schematized category of quality (limitation) and the principle derived from it (the Anticipations of Perception), Kant seeks to ensure that determinate unity is the outcome of a dynamic process of continuously producing the content of time. Limitation is to enclose a degree of reality within limits, within the limits of a situation where it might make things 'too hot' and where it has a definite, measurable degree. A degree of reality needs limitation to make it relevant to a concrete situation where it matters whether the content of time makes us retreat from an object that is now 'too hot'. This must realize the production of degrees of reality in a situation but not neglect the role of negation in keeping this process open. Thus the result of limitation in space and time is that we have a measurable degree of reality or intensive magnitude, such as a temperature. We can compare its role to the third category of quantity, totality or 'allness', in the Axioms of Intuition which ensures that the temporal process presents a unified extensive magnitude, something determinate in experience. For Kant the abstract and systematic guidance of the Table of Categories is necessarily complemented by concrete reasons for involving these three schematized categories in the synthesis of possible experience. Together the categories of quality form a dynamic system of determination that keeps experience full of sensation, of degrees of reality, but that also breaks this continuous flow. This determines the situation we find ourselves in as 'too hot' or 'too cold' or 'just right' and as so many degrees higher or lower than before. Limitation must not then limit us to a particular degree but make sure that we can account both for the surprise of finding something too hot and the accuracy of our measurement of this change in intensive magnitude.

It is important to note Deleuze's assessment of this part of the *Critique of Pure Reason*. We saw that he is concerned with differences internal to an account of experience provided by sensation. The Anticipations of Perception contributes to his understanding of their role. In *Difference and Repetition* he envisages . . .

. . . a step-by-step, internal, dynamic construction of space which must precede the 'representation' of the whole as a form of exteriority. The element of this internal genesis seems to us to consist of intensive quantity rather than schema, and to be related to Ideas rather than to concepts of the understanding. (DR: 26)

The construction of space as a concrete process introduces intensive differences into a situation. As we saw, this leads the inhabitants of this space to occupy it differently. However, for Deleuze this must not rely upon categories or pure concepts that he understands as external to this concrete process. Changes in temperature represent an open-ended process that results in different ways of occupying space and time ranging, for example, from a rapid but temporary retreat to a permanent change in way of life in response to the onset of an ice age. For Deleuze this does not have to do with three schematized categories of quality and how they form what he understands as an 'external' system. Instead it is the dramatization of Ideas directly in sensation. This selective affirmation of the *Critique of Pure Reason* echoes Paul Guyer's reading insofar as it takes the argument of the Anticipations of Perception in isolation, leading Deleuze to make use of it in his own account of experience in *Difference and Repetition*.[5] Our focus will remain on the unfolding of Kant's architectonic rather than upon a selective approach that would evaluate the components of the Table of Principles in isolation. Understood in this way, the Anticipations present part of the unfolding of the abstract Table of Categories in the concrete synthesis of possible experience. They show how the abstract and the concrete presuppose one another as part of a wider account. Therefore, while concrete reasons for the necessary role of principles in the production of experience are crucial, they are not isolated in Kant's account from abstract reasons. Kant's answer to Deleuze's criticism would be that we don't apply categories from outside, that there is a system of determination always already at work in the synthesis of possible experience. We will continue to consider how for Kant the abstract is realized in the concrete, and vice versa, as we consider the two remaining components of the Table of Principles.

The analogies of experience

The third component of the Table of Principles, the Analogies of Experience, introduces us to dynamical or discursive principles. In the schematism chapter Kant refers to the schematized categories of relation as providing the rules for

dealing with *time order* (CPR: A145/B184–5). At stake is our discursive understanding of experience in space and time rather than how magnitudes are built
up or how they occur to us in space and time. In the Analogies of Experience
a certain discursive activity is demanded in response to a time order presented
to us by the production of experience. They bring us to how experience is to be
thought through time rather than how it is given in determinate magnitudes
through time. However, the basis for this is still the synthesis of possible
experience in time through the system of determination presented in the
Table of Categories. These principles demand certain discursive activity when they
make us look for the relation that holds a situation together, a relation that
determines a time order in the very production of experience. This leads Béatrice
Longuenesse to locate a certain genesis of cognition in the presentation of a
time order in space. This must be understood in terms of the determination of
this time order under a rule if cognition is to move forward:

> We shall acquire a determinate cognition of it only by means of the indefinite,
> never-completed process of corrections and specifications of our discursive
> judgements in actual experience. Nonetheless, this process finds its initial
> impulse and its first step in the mere consciousness of the *simultaneous
> existence of things in space*. (KCJ: 390)

We will consider how in each Analogy a time order, something that makes
things simultaneous in space, prompts us to seek the role of a schematized
category in the synthesis of this experience.

Before considering each of the three Analogies of Experience we must
remember that for Kant time alone cannot show us the necessary relations that
hold in the synthesis of possible experience. The initial impulse to look for a
necessary relation arises because we cannot rely upon time to show us how
things are related in their synthesis. We saw in the previous chapter that for
Kant, while the schematism draws upon time, it is a power that cannot be
located or laid out before us. If it could, then we would find the power of time
presented or laid out in space. We would then fail to account through time for
what Longuenesse referred to as the 'simultaneous existence of things in space'.
The relations that arise in space in the course of experience, which are 'laid
out' before us, are what need to be accounted for. Therefore, space must not
show us its time order but prompt us to look for it. Kant therefore preserves the
non-spatial character of time. Time itself cannot be perceived. As a result its
role in the synthesis of possible experience is to be understood in terms of the
connection of perceptions, which involves concepts that connect them in a
priori ways (CPR: A177/B219). Thus determination in time does not remain
a mystery despite our inability to perceive it in space, despite the fact that
time is not 'laid out' before us. We should not be left merely contemplating
the mysterious abilities of time but instead be prompted to seek the role of
the categories in schemata or transcendental time determinations. It is this

role of categories that allows necessary relations to be discovered and time to be demystified through its role in synthesizing experience under the rule of these pure concepts. Thus while we cannot perceive time as a whole, this is because what time *is* can be presented only in terms of what it *does* and what it does here is the realization of the categories. This gives us our only *view* of time but it is one that must orientate discursive thought, as we shall see. We must respond to the simultaneity of things in space as a time order whose determination under a category we must discover. Rather than perceiving or contemplating time we are challenged to seek the category of relation that is being realized in the ongoing synthesis of possible experience.

In his 'General Comment on the System of Principles' Kant suggests the dependence of the three categories of relation upon the concrete synthesis of possible experience for their realization. He argues that concepts alone cannot teach us about the way in which things can exist only as subjects and not simply as attributes of others things, something which gives them the status of a substance. They also cannot tell us how it is that the existence of one thing causes the existence of another. Finally, concepts alone cannot allow us to understand how it is that among several things the existence of one of these things affects the others, a reciprocal relation that shows there to be a community of substances (ibid.: A235/B288). It follows that time, as the ultimate form of the synthesis of possible experience, enables the categories to occupy and determine space and time. Heidegger sums up the role of time when he writes of the first Analogy, where the abstract logical subject becomes a substance in a concrete situation, that: 'Time thus shows its own permanence' (KPM: 75). Thus, while we cannot perceive time as a whole we can perceive its role in the first Analogy in realizing the permanence of a substance as a rule for the determination of a time order. Heidegger argues that the permanence of time itself is the basis for the application of the category of substance and accident. The permanence of a substance, which distinguishes it from accidents that befall it, is ultimately provided by the permanence of time as the realization of this category. For Kant this follows because, given that we cannot perceive it as a whole, time is not subject to change. Time itself does not change but that which changes is in time. From this it follows that changeless and enduring time corresponds that which stays the same in experience. Kant defines this changeless and enduring thing as substance. Only by referring things to substances can we understand them in terms of time, as simultaneous or as successive (CPR: A144/B183). Thus, while time cannot be perceived, its role in the production of experience can be presented when it realizes the category of substance and accident in a concrete way. Equally, while the schematism of the category of substance and accident cannot be presented using images, it is here presented in the concrete, spatio-temporal form of a substance which we distinguish from its accidents. Change is now objective or belongs to an object as the substance to which various accidents are attributed. Thus, while extensive and intensive magnitudes are partial objects, we need complete objects or substances to which they can be attributed. We keep hold of the object through change because, while it is perhaps larger in extension than before or suddenly 'too hot', recognition is dynamic enough to be able to keep hold of it over time. Recognition seeks something permanent that allows us to say that something has changed rather than losing sight of the subject of change over time because we cannot tell it apart from the accidents that befall it. Thus for Kant we must draw both upon time's permanence and upon the Table of Categories that has guided us to a third member of this Table of Principles. This adds to the first two members of the table a discursive principle that leads us to seek permanence when we encounter a time order.

Kant's examples in the second Analogy draw upon the successive nature of our experience of the permanent substances established in the first Analogy. If we encounter a house, or a ship floating down stream, in experience we do so successively and therefore in time (ibid.: A190/B235–6; A192/B237). However, the two examples are different insofar as the succession is reversible in the case of our experience of a house and irreversible in the case of a ship floating down stream. This difference takes us to a further requirement of recognition but takes with it the need for the permanence of a substance if we are to recognize changes as belonging to one and the same object across a time order. We are again directed to how we are led by time in the cognition of objects, how it contributes to the means by which we recognize what is objective about a situation because it realizes a category in a concrete way. The schematized category of cause and effect rules in the time order if it is an irreversible time order, like the ship floating downstream. Thus it doesn't matter for cognition if we experience the roof or a window of the house first because this time order is reversible. All we need here is the permanence of the subject-concept of the judgement, 'the house', in order to attribute the different attributes or predicate-concepts to something objective or substantial in possible experience. However, things are quite different in the example of the ship sailing downstream. If we don't see the ship upstream before it appears further downstream recognition doesn't work. We do not recognize a change which is objective thanks to its irreversible order as well as its permanent substance. For Kant this is not simply a matter of how we make sense of objects or of the order of psychological time. It is first of all a matter of the synthesis of possible experience in time according to a priori rules. A time order leads us to seek the conceptual rules at work in this synthesis. In this unfolding of the Table of Principles, a second Analogy combines with the first Analogy and this now leads us to a third Analogy. It thus forms part of a dynamic system of determination whose outline or plan is the Table of Categories and its tripartite structure.

Rather than considering the objections that could be made to the arguments for the first two Analogies, or to the need to have a third one, we will move forward with Kant's architectonic. The argument for doing this is that the first two Analogies alone are not the full account Kant gives us in the Analogies of

Experience. To stop now and make assessments would be to consider something unfinished. As we've seen, Kant's architectonic is offered to us as a whole that is greater than its parts. For this reason we will seek to complete the model provided by the Analogies of Experience by adding the third Analogy before turning a more critical gaze upon this system of determination. We have sought to show that Kant's architectonic is concerned with its own unfolding and not with anything external to this. We have consistently argued that we must not pre-empt this unfolding if we are to assess it fully. W. H. Walsh argues that we do need to keep an Idea of the whole in view if we are to understand the involvement of the schematized category of community in the Analogies of Experience. He writes that: '. . . the story about substance both gains support from and lends support to the story about causality, and the same is true *mutatis mutandis* of the story about reciprocity in its relation to each and both of the others' (Walsh 1975: 147). Yet Walsh also bemoans the lack of development by Kant of '. . . the internal or systematic connections of the individual categorial concepts that he had put forward' (ibid.). This makes the point that for Kant's architectonic to work as an account of experience it would have to convince us that only this dynamic system of determination, taken as a whole, can account for experience fully. Echoing the concerns I considered in Chapter 3 of this book, Kant is seen to have been in a rush to present his account of experience and so does not develop internal and systematic arguments as he should. This criticism is important for us because it concerns the unfolding of Kant's architectonic.

The schema of the category of community, the third category of relation, is presented as the simultaneity of the determinations of two different substances according to a universal rule (CPR: A144/B183–4). The first Analogy provides the substance that persists and the second Analogy provides chains of cause and effect that relate persisting substances to past causes and future effects. However, if we only consider how substances are related in chains of cause and effect we have a system for determining a time order that excludes any community of substances. Kant is concerned with how time relates things here and now, in a unified space and time that makes up a concrete situation. Thus rather than a model that envisages only substances isolated in chains of cause and effect he includes communities of substances. How can this be said to develop 'the internal or systematic connections' of the categories that W. H. Walsh is rightly concerned about? Kant seeks to show that his Metaphysical Deduction presents categories that are presupposed by the concrete synthesis of possible experience just as these abstract categories presuppose this process of production in order that they are realized and do not remain empty. The abstract and the concrete presuppose one another, each allowing the other to be realized in the only way possible. The three Analogies are to show the necessity and completeness of the Table of Categories as conditions of possibility. They are therefore presented systematically according to this table. However, they must also show that this table is necessarily realized by being open to, and involved in, the synthesis of possible experience. The third Analogy is then to follow internally and systematically from the first two principles. To do this within Kant's architectonic it must follow both from the abstract order of the Table of Categories and the concrete concerns of the synthesis of possible experience.

The reciprocal determination of substances interacting in a concrete situation must then complete the dynamic system of determination presented in the Analogies. Kant uses an example from experience and again is concerned both with the discursive activity of the understanding in response to what we perceive and with the synthesis of possible experience itself. He defines the simultaneity of things in experience in terms of a reciprocity that does not occur in the second Analogy where things are in a relation of temporal succession. His example is of the simultaneous appearance of the earth and the moon, allowing one to perceive either the earth first and the moon second or vice versa (ibid.: A211/B257). He understands this reversible order as a sign of reciprocity and of the existence of two things in the same time (ibid.). The emphasis is again on time as the ultimate form of the synthesis of possible experience. We have a single stretch of time which will provide the basis for the application of the schematized category of community. This is because it makes it possible to determine substances as simultaneous under the rule of this category. For Kant the result is that the law of interaction holds and this reference to law is meant to show that the lack of a necessary order in the perception of the moon and the earth is not a sign of a lack of determination in time. Simultaneity is in fact a determinate time order that is highly significant because it makes us look for the relation at work in the synthesis of possible experience. It asks what rule of determination holds in this time order as distinct from an irreversible succession where cause and effect is the rule. In simultaneity in time the reciprocal determination of substances is revealed to us, to use Kant's example, because there is no priority in time to the perception of either the moon or the earth. Each substance is influenced by each of the others rather than one asserting itself as the cause of the existence or character of the others. We have a unified and law-governed scene without the onward march of chains of cause and effect undermining this particular form of determination and unity. This makes the schematized category of community the simultaneous interaction and reciprocal determination of substances. There is then no cause that imposes itself upon our attention first, that draws us away from interaction in the here and now. A community of substances is the outcome of the category which does not elevate one thing to be the cause of others but presents them as equal in their reciprocal determination. However, we see that it must also be a structure that is dynamic because it is grounded in how these substances interact. It must be grounded in how substances relate in space and time since it does not tell us what the outcomes will be of a community of substances.

When we explore the role of the concrete in Kant's formulation of the third Analogy we do indeed find that it is not an addition dictated solely by the order of the Table of Categories and without basis in the synthesis of possible experience. In other words, the abstract does not simply dictate to the concrete. However, this has been disputed by some commentators. Arthur Melnick uses the example of two billiard balls to show that we can understand substances sufficiently in terms of causal chains and without using the Table of Categories as our systematic guide (Melnick 1973: 103; cited in KTI: 268f). In this sense, the concrete synthesis of possible experience rebels against the unfolding of Kant's architectonic where a third category necessarily complements the first two. This echoes Guyer's argument that Kant's proofs in the Analytic of Principles are based solely upon the concrete role of each principle. Melnick points to a situation where two billiard balls are hit by a third billiard ball and then move off in different directions. Now if we were to use the category of community to understand this scene we would talk about a game of billiards as a community of substances and so situate the balls in relation to one another, their surroundings and the players. However, Melnick argues that chains of cause and effect allow us to account for the position of the two balls (which he refers to as b and c) on the billiard table: 'We thus have two series of successive states: 1) b at place p1, b at p2 . . . , b at pn; 2) c at p1', c at p2', . . . , c at pn' ' (ibid.). What he seeks to do here is to understand a game of billiards by talking separately about the two billiard balls that are hit simultaneously. He talks about them in terms of two isolated causal chains. This has to include variables like the elasticity of the billiard balls and the direction of the acting force and its magnitude.[6] Thus the wider situation is included but only in relation to the causal history of each of the two balls that are hit. The community of substances represented by the game is then the outcome of these separate causal histories rather than being involved in accounting for the situation as such. Henry E. Allison objects to Melnick's argument on grounds that are very important for our investigation. He does not deny the validity of his analyses of each ball taken individually and indeed being able to isolate a billiard ball is crucial to recognition. This is especially important if we want to recognize a winning strategy that separates one ball from all the others so that it allows us to win the game. However, Allison points to the difficulty of predicting the relations between the two balls at particular times if we think about each one in isolation. He argues that '. . . this cannot be done apart from a determination of the temporal relation of b and c at their respective locations, which, [. . .], presupposes their reciprocal influence' (KTI: 269). We cannot separate each ball into a causal chain without losing touch with their positions. The game necessarily involves the unity of a community, without which we lose a determinate grasp of where each ball is at a particular time. The two billiard balls are therefore only determinable through their relation to one another in time. This makes Melnick's analysis of the billiard balls a perfectly valid outcome of a more original process, that of the synthesis of possible experience in which the category of community is involved along with the category of cause and effect. This makes possible the charting of the separate causal histories of substances which is also necessary to playing a game of billiards. Allison argues that Kant seeks to distinguish subordination and co-ordination by having a second and third Analogy, reflecting the difference between the categories of cause and effect, and community (ibid.: 271). This shows that there are concrete reasons for the inclusion of the third Analogy; for drawing upon the abstract order of the Table of Categories. We will now develop the sense in which the third Analogy develops the relations of the abstract and the concrete, meeting the concerns of both as Kant's architectonic demands.

We have suggested that there must be concrete, as well as abstract, grounds for viewing the three Analogies as the systematic unfolding of the third division of the Table of Categories. For Kant the Analogies have to be shown to take forward the Table of Categories, to show how it is at work in the synthesis of possible experience rather than being artificially imposed upon it. For readers like Paul Guyer and Arthur Melnick the Analogies stand or fall as arguments in their own right. Guyer argues that Kant '. . . can be seen as finally proving the objective validity of the category of substance from his proof of the conservation of substance, rather than vice versa' (K: 108). He finds here an argument based on the necessary structure of experience, suggesting that in the Analytic of Principles, the Table of Categories becomes a list of possible categories and something open to revision. However, for Kant the architectonic mode of argument and presentation is convincing insofar as it is able to show that the abstract and the concrete presuppose one another. Thus Guyer's recognition of the concrete importance of rules of determination is not lost but made into a sign of the presupposition of the abstract by the concrete. Béatrice Longuenesse seeks to argue in favour of this reading and she develops the insights we have been uncovering about how categories are involved in providing an open and dynamic system of determination in the Analytic of Principles. She wants to think about how . . .

> . . . in his argument, Kant calls upon all three forms of relation in judgment, and thus all three categories of relation together with their schemata, to account for our generating our own representation of a unified space and time in which empirical objects may be cognized through their relations of universal interaction. (KCJ: 378)

Thus we cannot consider the three Analogies individually but only as together relating abstract categories of relation to a concrete domain. Substances relate only in '. . . the context of their universal interaction' (ibid.: 384). Her point is that whether substances interact successively or simultaneously, through cause and effect or reciprocal determination, they belong to this concrete context. Kant has not then started from three necessary features of experience that each

stand alone but with the third division of the Table of Categories and its realization in a dynamic model for securing determinate relations in the context of
universal interaction. Interaction in space and time is universal in the synthesis
of possible experience. Out of interaction must come not confusion but
determination that is secured by the permanence of a substance, chains of
cause and effect, and reciprocal determination. Kant's arguments in the
Analytic of Principles therefore rely upon the mutual presupposition of the
abstract Table of Categories and the concrete context of universal interaction.
These must convincingly presuppose and determine one another and in the
process provide a full account of possible experience.

We considered, in Chapter 3 of this book, the debate over the derivation of
the category of community in the Table of Categories from the disjunctive
judgement in the Table of Judgements. We may add to the points we made
in that chapter now that the role of the concrete has been developed in the
Analytic of Principles. What does this tell us about the relation between disjunctive judgement and the category of community? If the interaction or reciprocal
determination of substances in the Third Analogy makes objects recognizable,
then their recognizable 'marks' allow them to become objects of disjunctive
judgement (ibid.: 386). A situation is thus 'marked out' in the concrete context
of 'universal interaction', something reflected and formulated in the abstract
by the category of community. The schematized category of community now
makes possible the work of disjunctive judgement in experience because it
provides concepts to be combined in disjunctive judgements. While chains
of cause and effect put different states of objects one after the other, in
community opposites meet one another and are thus material for a disjunctive
judgement. This provides concrete material for disjunction or material that
arises from the context of universal interaction. However, the abstract does
not simply reflect the concrete and its universal interactions. The disjunctive
judgement provides the category of community with its 'totalizing character'
(ibid.). A full account of community in space and time relies upon disjunction
to totalize or individuate a community given the danger that if a community
includes everything it will lack any individuality and significance in experience.
This reflects the fact that being dynamic is not simply about being open to what
happens in space and time or in the context of universal interaction. It is about
being able to define a community in terms of what it is or what it is not, through
exclusive disjunction. A completely open community could be said to be no
community at all insofar as, lacking in distinction, it means nothing to its
members and adds nothing to experience. Disjunction then totalizes a community; it secures something very concrete by being very abstract. A community
'lives' it's distinctive and totalized character, it exists through being exclusive
and different, through exploring its own disjunction as a community of
substances. However, it provides the material for this disjunction and so allows
cognition to respond dynamically to the universal interactions among substances. A community can thus develop in concrete ways but is always made

distinct in the abstract by disjunctive judgement. In this way the mutual pre-supposition of the abstract and the concrete, in the unfolding of Kant's architectonic, characterizes the third component of Kant's Table of Principles as it did the first two.

The postulates of empirical thought as such

Now we come to the fourth and final component of the Table of Principles. It can be said to carry forward Kant's Idea of the whole because it very clearly draws upon the previous three components of the Table of Principles. However, it is unique in its concern with the empirical use of the understanding. We've noted that for Kant the pure use of the understanding is only a very small part of the total work of cognition. The a priori does not take over all cognitive activity and stifle its creativity by setting out the outcomes of cognition beyond their most basic forms, the forms that make cognition possible in the first place. In the schematism chapter Kant concludes his presentation of the schematized Table of Categories with the categories of modality. He defines the schema of the categories of modality as 'time itself', time as that to which objects belong and in which they are determined (CPR: A145/B184). It follows that the mode of time that is to be dealt with by the schematized categories of modality is *time sum total* (ibid.: A145/B185). This makes time, as sum total, the horizon of the empirical use of the understanding. Now we've seen that time is ruled by schematized categories. Time as sum total is the sum total of the ways in which time realizes the categories in concrete or synthetic ways. Thus it is time and the Table of Categories together that become the transcendental horizon of possible experience. The Postulates now demand that we ask if an object belongs to time, making this the horizon of all our thought about objects of possible experience. Turning to another systematic division of the Table of Principles that is carried forward from the Table of Categories, we see that the Postulates are dynamic or discursive principles. They call for thought in response to what is met with in experience but, unlike the discursive principles of the Analogies of Experience, this concerns the empirical rather than the pure use of the understanding. Time is directly involved in the synthesis of possible experience and can now, in the Postulates, become involved in how we think about experience. As we've seen, insofar as time is ruled by the categories it is the ultimate medium of anything that can be included in possible experience.

We've noted that Postulates are not involved in the pure use of understanding and we will now consider the implications of this for their role in Kant's architectonic. The Postulates do not precede what Kant calls the 'empirical use' of the understanding as the previous three components of the Table of Principles do (ibid.: A218/B265-6). The pure use of the understanding marks out a priori the space and time where empirical understanding can then be at work by providing the magnitudes and the relations that form part of possible experience. It is then in this empirical use of the understanding that we are faced with questions of possibility, actuality and necessity. Possibility, the first Postulate, must make us think in terms of time as *sum total*, about what is possible in time and according to the categories that it realizes as principles. Kant writes of the impossibility of anyone possessing the concept of a figure enclosed by two straight lines (ibid.: A220/B268). The figure is not negated in thought because it is not contradictory and yet it is an impossible figure in experience because it cannot be constructed in space. This refers us back to the building up of objects in extension that was the concern of the Axioms of Intuition. We are ultimately referred to how, through time and its relation to the categories, objects emerge only if they can be constructed in space. Equally, it would not be possible for two opposite determinations to belong to one object simultaneously, carrying forward the concern of the Anticipations of Perception to account for the production of degrees of reality. Something cannot be both 'too hot' and 'too cold' if it is to have a real and productive role in possible experience. This becomes a condition of possibility in the context of time as 'sum total' where, as the Anticipations showed, different magnitudes are not simultaneous in the same object but successive in their continuity. Thus, when in the schematism chapter the modal category of possibility is schematized, this excludes opposites as determinations of the same object at the same time. This schema is the harmony of any synthesis of the heterogeneous with time, with the conditions that time sets for the synthesis of possible experience (ibid.: A144/B184). This makes the schema of the category of possibility a source of the determination of objects of experience.

For Kant a great deal is realized in the Postulates despite their role being limited to the empirical use of the understanding. The postulate of possibility is a principle which demands that the concept of any object of cognition agrees with the a priori conditions of experience (ibid.: A220/B267). However, Kant is careful to be clear that the synthesis of experience necessary for the cognition of objects is achieved without the help of the Postulates. In other words, the Postulates refer to what is possible in experience according to how experience is synthesized. It adds nothing to this but makes possible the realization in empirical understanding of the work of a priori synthesis. The second and third postulates confirm this point when they draw upon the Analogies of Experience and the a priori rules they present in order to secure actuality and necessity in the context of *time sum total.* The Analogies are shown to be a source of coherence that makes experience possible and so must be postulated in all empirical use of the understanding. Kant argues using the following example. We cognize 'magnetic matter' as something that permeates objects on the basis of our perception of the attraction of iron fillings (ibid.: A226/B273). We can recognize the existence of this material despite our inability to directly perceive it. Here we have something more than possibility and yet something we can only perceive indirectly. Kant seeks to keep cognition in

touch with experience as something ultimately unified in time, in time as
sum total, even when perception is lacking. He refers to the coherence of
appearances whose laws are set out in the Analogies of Experience in relation
to time. These laws are to hold at all times or in time as sum total rather than
in particular cases. There is in this example coherence between the perceived
movement of bodies and the unperceived cause of that movement (magnetism).
It is a coherence that holds across all times and so for time as the sum total
of all relations that hold in experience and all magnitudes presented in
experience.

Necessity, the third Postulate, is also referred to the Analogies of Experience
and specifically to the role of cause and effect in the second Analogy (ibid.:
A227–8/B280). For Kant modality adds necessity to causality (ibid.: A228/
B281). This gives continuity to experience, making necessity a principle that
prohibits any leaps, breaks or gaps between appearances (ibid.: A228–9/B281).
This rules out the role of a vacuum in experience and its synthesis. If something
is not presented in time and under the category as part of a sequence of causes
and effects it is not a part of possible experience. The third Postulate thus
ensures that this rule is realized continuously in the thick of the empirical use
of the understanding. It ensures that the empirical understanding does not
speculate about voids or gaps in the unity of possible experience, that it is on
firm ground in the most concrete situations. It does this by taking forward the
concern of the previous three components of the Table of Principles with the
continuous synthesis of possible experience. Thus in the Anticipations of
Perception the role of negation was not to present us with a void or gap but
to keep the production of degrees of reality flowing and continuous. Kant is
primarily concerned that nothing gets in the way of the understanding and
the continuous realization of its concepts in the synthesis of experience (ibid.:
A229–30/B282). This ensures that the systematic realization of the Table of
Categories extends into the most concrete realms without being disrupted by
what we come across in the course of experience.

This positive presentation of the role of the schematized categories of modality
is still seemingly at odds with Kant's own apparently depreciating assessment
of their role (ibid.: A219/B266). We will now end this section by considering
whether the Postulates are out of place in the Table of Principles. This is important if we are to assess Kant's architectonic and it's supposed completeness and
integrity. What is at stake in the Postulates of Empirical Thought As Such
for Kant is the relation of the object of cognition to the cognitive power (ibid.:
A219/B266). The synthesis of experience has been secured but questions still
occur. Do we have a merely possible concept of an object or an actual one?
If it is actual is it also necessary? Georges Dicker questions the need for a
schematism of the categories of modality given that through them we only
reflect upon possible experience at a distance from its synthesis (Dicker 2004:
221). According to Dicker's reading, the Postulates concern only the attitude
of the judger towards the judgements they are making: '. . . they simply pertain

to the attitude one holds toward the application of a concept to something, toward the linkage of two or more concepts in a proposition, or toward the linkage of two or more propositions to each other' (ibid.). Thus the Postulates counsel against having a speculative attitude. We must not speculate about things that exceed the bounds of coherent and continuous possible experience, such as about gaps or voids in the determination of experience in time and under the categories.[7]

Another concern is that, in the Postulates of Empirical Thought As Such, Kant is again brief in his presentation and arguments. He presents the three Postulates in terms of our most general ways of thinking about time and makes limited appeal to examples and concrete cases. W. H. Walsh complains that:

> It is not enough to say that what is really possible must agree with the formal conditions of experience; he must show, in particular instances, how what look like genuine possibilities are not such because they conflict with those conditions. Otherwise Kant runs the risk of appearing to be merely dogmatic, dismissing speculation of one type on the basis of convictions which are equally speculative and equally unargued. (Walsh 1975: 150)

I've sought to show throughout this book that Kant employs an internalizing method. He therefore does not look at the a priori synthesis of possible experience from the outside. He does not in this unfolding of his architectonic stop to seek proofs using examples of how we actually distinguish the possible from the impossible. Rather than what is given in experience, the product, his concern is with the process of accounting for experience. It follows that the principles of modality refer us only to the production of concepts by the 'cognitive power' (CPR: A234/B287). We must remember that the cognitive power is, at the stage of the a priori synthesis of possible experience, the transcendental unity of apperception which I touched upon in Chapter 3 of this book. The Postulates draw upon this cognitive power that was developed over the preceding pages of the Transcendental Analytic as the transcendental unity of apperception. They form part of an argument that is not based upon what is given in experience in order that we do not presuppose what is to be accounted for. Therefore, any talk of a cognitive power has nothing to do with a personal or psychological 'attitude' that we form over the course of experience or observe in inner sense. It has everything to do with the impersonal elements of an a priori account of experience. These elements are referred to in the Postulates because they are involved in the realization of the categories in time as sum total. This is affirmed by the Postulates as much as it was affirmed in the Metaphysical Deduction and the rest of the Analytic of Principles. As we saw in Chapter 3 of this book, the synthesis of possible experience realizes conceptual rules that are given all at once in the abstract in a Table of Categories. Having been given all at once they will unfold in a similarly decisive fashion, eschewing dryness and tedium in a way that is unsatisfying for readers like W. H. Walsh.

However, we've seen that for Kant we cannot develop these rules at our leisure. We again find that we cannot make sense of Kant's progress unless we take the time to consider his singular mode of argument.

Conclusion

In this chapter I have put Kant's move from abstraction to concreteness in his Analytic of Principles in the context of his architectonic. This, I argued, was the only way of making sense of Kant's rejection of the dry and tedious just as in the Metaphysical Deduction it is behind his concern with the brief and solid. The decisive affirmation of the Table of Categories in the schematism chapter is followed by the unfolding of the Idea of the whole that this table embodies in the schemata and principles. It culminates in the affirmation of *time sum total* as the horizon in which categories are realized as the conceptual rules of synthesis that make experience possible. At the end of the previous chapter we saw that having appropriated and revised his notion of schematism, Deleuze appears to take his leave of Kant rather than following him in his architectonic mode of presentation and argument. The schematism was useful for Deleuze and in this chapter we saw that he also finds the Anticipations of Perception useful. However, I've argued that these meeting points do not exhaust their relations, that listing aspects of the *Critique of Pure Reason* that Deleuze makes use of restricts our potential understanding of how these two thinkers relate. I therefore sought to follow Kant's architectonic strategy in order to understand it more fully. We saw that this can lead us to think about the mutual presupposition of the abstract and the concrete in the context of Kant's architectonic. Here an abstract Table of Categories is to be realized in the concrete synthesis of possible experience. I have sought to follow Kant's strategy and see where this leads us in order that I can then make a deeper comparison between Kant and Deleuze. This will involve, not isolated parts of the whole, but Kant's architectonic and its problematic Idea of the whole. In the next chapter I will be concerned with the full implications of this strategy for exploring their relations.

Chapter 6

Deleuze's Categories

In this chapter I will seek to relate our reading of Kant's *Critique of Pure Reason* to Deleuze's account of experience. We've seen that Kant's account of experience is organized by a Table of Categories. I will not, however, be holding up each of Kant's categories in turn in order to ask what relevance it has to Deleuze's work. As we have seen, Deleuze is concerned with an account of 'real experience'. He rejects Kant's attempt to provide conceptual forms that are applicable to sensation and always given in advance. However, I will seek to show that Kant's Table of Categories is not a point at which his relations with Deleuze are exhausted. In order to do this I will build upon the methodological common ground uncovered in Chapter 2 of this book. I will add to their common concern with problematic Ideas a concern with arguments that are founded upon problematic Ideas. We've seen that Kant's Metaphysical Deduction of the Table of Categories is such an argument but can we characterize Deleuze's method in the same way?

In order to explore the relevance of Kant's Table of Categories to Deleuze's project I will first seek to consider how Deleuze and Kant share a common problem. Kant's concern to relate the abstract and the concrete will be shown to resonate with Deleuze's thought. This common ground will then be tested by being put in the context of Deleuze's critique of Kant's philosophy. The second section of this chapter will consider Deleuze's reading of Kant's categories and how he proposes to relate categories to character and mood. In the third section I will relate this interpretation of the categories to Deleuze's emphasis upon sensation in his account of experience. We will see that, while Deleuze's categories differ from Kant's, they have similar ways of arguing for the role of categories in an account of experience. This will allow me, in the final section of this chapter, to argue that by considering the role of categories in Deleuze's account we can better understand his concerns. The main contention of this chapter will be that Deleuze himself gives a productive reading of Kant's categories and opens the way for establishing a necessary role for a Metaphysical Deduction in his own project.

A Common Problem

In order to grasp the role of Kant's Table of Categories in Deleuze's thought I have to first show that they share common concerns and that this table is Kant's response to these common concerns. In Chapter 2 of this book I focused upon the methodological common ground to be found in Kant and Deleuze. Can we develop this further and say that they share a common problem that unifies their accounts of experience? James Williams seeks to capture a problem at the heart of Deleuze's thought and uses this to assess his relations to other thinkers. This is the problem of attaining both openness and reach:

> I define openness in metaphysics as a relation that does not impose restrictions on future transformations and events. A metaphysics that sets down the path of the world from now to some final judgement day, or a metaphysics indebted to a particular science or set of laws, or one that sets out fundamental onto-logical forms and elements would not be open. (Williams 2005: 4)

We can see from the work that we've done so far that Kant and Deleuze share a concern to provide a full account of experience. In Chapter 2 of this book we saw that they are both concerned with how a problematic Idea can open up experience. Sensation must continue to add to experience although this 'openness' to sensation is realized in different ways by these two thinkers. However, both argue that we must not look outside of experience to find the ends of inquiry. To seek such ends is an approach that Deleuze describes as 'filling in' experience. We 'fill in' openness rather than allowing openness to be realized in different ways (DR: 170). Our inquiry must be synthetic because we are seeking to uncover the synthesis of experience and not what is given in experience. Thus rather than filling our account with givens of experience we must keep it open to synthesis.

James Williams points to the danger that openness and reach can cancel each other out unless we relate them in a way that realizes them both (Williams 2005: 5). To secure reach there needs to be a way of determining experience such that things we are open to can be distinguished from one another. We must not be permanently overwhelmed by sensation, unable to distinguish what is met with in experience. Thus, to be simply open is to fail to be dynamic or in any way successful in dealing with what arises through synthesis. Nothing is distinguished and so we really aren't open to anything that has any signifi-cance or effect upon us. In openness alone we have something that cannot be called experience if experience involves, by definition, distinct and significant things. However, we must also avoid the danger that openness is sacrificed because our ways of reaching different parts of experience lead us to neglect the concrete particularities that sensation has to offer. At stake then is the need for openness and reach to be realized through one another. In other words, a concern with reach alone sacrifices openness to synthesis and openness alone produces nothing worthy of being called experience. This reflects Kant's concern to relate the synthetic and the a priori. However, when we consider how reach is to be secured, Kant and Deleuze differ strongly. I will now consider whether the differences that emerge here undermine the relations between these two thinkers.

If the problem of openness and reach seems to be of common concern we find that Deleuze is also concerned that we attain an 'internal' account of experience that rules out aspects of Kant's account. In Chapter 2 of this book we understood this as the incarnation and realization of the intelligible in the sensible. For Deleuze this ensures that we do not represent experience in terms external to sensation but encounter its own ways of determining things. We do not 'fill in' experience but remain open to its synthesis, to what sensation has to offer. For Deleuze openness is being sacrificed, rather than secured, through Kant's categories or pure concepts of the understanding. He develops this critique when he writes that Kant's mistake in the *Critique of Pure Reason* is to '. . . leave external what is separated . . .' (DR: 170). In other words, openness is not realized through the sensible synthesis that accounts for experience. We leave external what could actually provide this internal account, the differences that are involved in the synthesis of sensation. As we saw in Chapter 2 of this book, for Deleuze problematic Ideas lead us to learn from sensation or from the differences internal to it. In Kant something external is added to complete the account of experience rather than allowing sensible synthesis to provide an internal account. In Chapter 2 we also considered how moments of concrete synthesis make us idiotic so that we learn about experience from sensation rather than relying upon our concepts. Insofar as it is unintelligible, synthesis extends our reach over experience, as we learn more about experience in these moments than in moments when things are intelligible. For Deleuze then Kant proceeds by assuming something external in order to make up for the lack of an internal account of experience. He does not grasp what sensation can do through its own resources and therefore has to rely upon concepts that do not reflect what sensation has to offer.

How important is this critique of Kant to Deleuze's approach to the *Critique of Pure Reason*? Deleuze suggests that although both he and Kant are concerned with accounting for experience, with securing openness and reach, something quite different is at the centre of his account:

> Transcendental empiricism is meaningless indeed unless its conditions are specified. But the transcendental 'field' must not be copied from the empirical, as in Kant. It must be explained on its own terms: 'experienced' or 'attempted' on its own terms (but it is a very particular type of experience). (Deleuze 2006: 362)

When in Chapter 2 of this book we considered unintelligible moments of synthesis, we uncovered the role of our encounters with sensation in Deleuze's account. He argues that instead of applying conditions to sensation we must learn from our 'experiences' or 'attempts' to be open to concrete synthesis.

We must then develop our reach by being open to experience, by learning from sensation. This takes us to the heart of Deleuze's critique of external presuppositions and concern to secure an internal account of experience. His critique of Kant includes the charge that his categories, these allegedly pure concepts of the understanding, are 'copied' or 'traced' from the empirical. In this sense they are given in experience rather than being significant in how experience is accounted for. This helps him to give a positive definition of a transcendental field that is to be 'experienced' or 'attempted'. What is 'experienced' or 'attempted' is something actually involved in accounting for experience. We engage with the sensible synthesis of experience and in Chapter 2 we saw how we are made idiotic by unintelligible moments of this synthesis. For Deleuze this brings us closer to an internal account of experience by involving us in the synthesis by which sensation accounts for experience as such. We encounter the synthesis through which experience is given. This is to 'experiment' with the ways in which sensation itself stages experience. James Williams argues that this is something that we can '. . . only experiment with, rather than grasp' (ibid.). Deleuze's approach is to be contrasted to one that seeks to 'grasp' experience since this carries the expectation, an external presupposition, that experience will always be 'graspable' in a certain ways. For Deleuze, if experience becomes unintelligible then this is positive, it allows us to learn more about it or to experiment. Does this put him at odds with Kant? In the previous chapters of this book we have seen how Kant is concerned to relate the a priori to synthesis or to relate reach to openness. Synthesis is the process through which experience is given but is not to be confused with what is given in experience. Thus, while Deleuze rejects Kant's categories as external to the synthesis of experience, he shares Kant's concern to relate our ability to reach experience to an openness to experience in its synthesis or production.

   Can we develop links between Kant and Deleuze's projects without their similarities being too vague or too general to be significant in how we understand their work? The problem of openness and reach which we began with, which is in a very real sense the concern of any and every philosopher, must be shown to have a common meaning and common outcomes in their two projects. Like Deleuze, Kant is concerned that openness to synthesis is realized. He takes rapid and definite steps to secure this in the Metaphysical Deduction. We saw, in Chapter 3 of this book, how he takes decisive action to defeat the sceptic. This means that our openness to synthesis does not, as it does for Deleuze, account for the abstract ways we are able to reach experience. He does not account for the a priori through openness to sensible synthesis but first secures the a priori and then relates it to the synthetic. We have then a common problem but a markedly different solution. Let's remind ourselves of why Kant argued that openness to experience could only be secured if we formulated a Table of Categories once and for all. His concern here is with how situations are grasped or secured in the most basic ways. Thus we have the proliferation of empirical concepts like 'body', 'house', 'table', 'landmass' and 'cosmos' which reach across different presentations of objects but rely upon the more basic reach or unity provided by categories or pure concepts. Kant is here asking: What is behind this diversity of empirical concepts? What makes it possible in the first place? Categories together provide the basic forms of unity and embody the transcendental horizon in which these empirical concepts can arise. We have then categories that hold together situations in the most basic ways so that objects of cognition can multiply and develop because empirical concepts can always reach diverse sensations. Like Deleuze Kant is concerned to realize openness to the concrete in the reach of the abstract. We will now consider how, despite this common concern, Deleuze's emphasis upon sensation distinguishes him from Kant. This will allow us to situate their common ground within their different projects.

In *Difference and Repetition* Deleuze writes:

It is true that on the path which leads to that which is to be thought, all begins with sensibility. [. . .] The privilege of sensibility as origin appears in the fact that, in an encounter, what forces sensation and that which can only be sensed are one and the same thing, whereas in other cases the two instances are distinct. (DR: 144–5)

This is a privilege earned by sensation insofar as it provides an internal account of experience. If sensation were brought into experience by something external, if its force is derived from how categories always unify sensations, then it would not provide an internal account. However, we've seen that for Deleuze we must be open to sensation's own synthesis of experience. This is a force involved in accounting for experience that can only be sensed because it is internal to sensation and relies upon nothing external. We saw that Deleuze does not want difference to be left external. In the sensible synthesis of experience it is made internal and this privileges sensation as the source of an account of experience. The encounter with sensation is therefore with a force that is entirely its own. It involves being open to a synthesis that does not obey the rules of the understanding. Therefore, while in Kant's Metaphysical Deduction we encountered understanding's abilities, its forms of judgement, for Deleuze we must instead come face to face with what sensation alone can do.

How does this concern with sensation separate Kant and Deleuze? James Williams writes that '. . . a distinction must be drawn between Kant and Deleuze. For the former, abstracted universal forms are seen to presuppose pure transcendental forms. For the latter, singular events in sensibility are seen to presuppose pure transcendental forms' (Williams 2005: 10). This captures the role of encounters with the sensible synthesis of experience that we've just considered. For Kant an encounter with an object of cognition may well lead us in thought to conceptual conditions of possible experience. It would bring us to what is most basic in experience, what secures openness to possible experience prior to any encounter with it. However, for Deleuze the encounter with the sensible must lead to an account of experience internal to sensation. Levi R. Bryant argues that Deleuze moves decisively away from Kant's project because he seeks to learn through encounters with sensation about how it accounts for experience: 'It is precisely this dogma [held by Kant], this assumption of the non-productivity of intuition, of its lack of intelligibility as opposed to the rational structure of concepts, that Deleuze's transcendental empiricism is designed to overcome' (Bryant 2008: 8). This presents us with the contrast between their sharing a common problem, that of openness and reach, and their lack of common ground when it comes to sensation. On the reading we have been giving, Kant formulates an open-ended Idea of the whole, an Idea of the cognition which the understanding is capable of, thanks to its a priori judgements and categories. This horizon opens up only because it is secured once and for all in the Metaphysical Deduction. It seems that Deleuze could not share his concern to secure the reach of categories or pure concepts in advance of experience because he wants to learn from sensation how it, and not the understanding, accounts for experience. Despite this we will seek to show, in the next section of this chapter, that Deleuze's way of responding to the problem of securing openness to the concrete does resonate with Kant's project. Kant may turn to the understanding rather than sensation to secure this, but how he does this, the form of argument he employs, is relevant to Deleuze's own attempt to secure openness and reach.

Deleuze on Categories and Moods

Deleuze presented Kant's account of experience in an original way during a seminar on 14 March 1978. This presentation is more positive than those that we have so far considered but the question we must answer is whether it has any relevance for his own project. In this seminar Deleuze seeks to explain the nature and role of the categories or pure concepts of the understanding in the *Critique of Pure Reason*. He takes the example of a rose which for Kant would first of all be referred to using empirical concepts. All roses form a set that is part of a broader set formed by all flowers and is also distinguished from those flowers that are not roses. However, Deleuze then locates the role of categories or pure concepts: 'When I say "all objects have a cause", am I not in another domain completely?' (KS1: 3). This a priori predicate-concept is what allows us to be certain that something is an object and thus part of experience. It is a category or pure concept of the understanding because it is one of the basic forms of experience, something that must be given prior to experience in order to make experience possible in the first place. Deleuze argues that '. . . it is thus via the notion of conditions of experience that the idea of a whole of possible experience will take on a sense. There is a whole of possible experience because there are predicates or pseudo-predicates which are attributed to all possible objects and these predicates are precisely what are called categories' (ibid.).

Here Deleuze stages the move from the empirical to the transcendental, to the horizon or Idea of the whole that envisages experience on the basis of categories. For Kant, it is the categories that secure openness to experience because, as we've seen, they are involved in its synthesis. Does this, as well as aiding Deleuze's presentation of Kant's philosophy in this seminar, have a basis in his own project? We must be careful not to assume a degree of similarity that is in fact blocked by Deleuze's critical concerns. Thus we find Deleuze writing here that Kant is concerned with an 'idea of the whole of possible experience' and the role of possibility contrasts with his own concern to account for 'real experience'. He understands possibility as an external presupposition, as something traced from experience rather than accounting for it. For Deleuze the encounter that brings us closer to an account of experience is always an encounter with sensation. However, we will pursue Deleuze's understanding of how Kant attains the level of the transcendental or of an Idea of the whole. If Deleuze rejects Kant's Table of Categories how can his thought relate to the move from the empirical to the transcendental that they involve?

We find that Deleuze goes beyond the mere exposition of Kant's account of experience in this seminar: 'I could define the categories in the simplest way as being the predicates of any object whatever. Thus you can yourself make your list of categories according to your mood, according to your character . . . what would be good would be to see if everybody came up with the same list of categories' (ibid.). The exercise that Deleuze suggests involves asking '. . . what is for me predicable of any object whatever' (ibid.). This is what we might call Deleuze's version of Kant's Metaphysical Deduction although we have yet to establish its nature and whether it is relevant both to Kant's deduction and to Deleuze's own project. A mood can be expressed briefly but can everyone understand the outcome of this deduction? It will certainly be a brief deduction, like Kant's, but does this make it a solid one given that moods are liable to constant and sudden change? As an argument it seems to fail to meet the criteria set by Kant's architectonic method. It relies upon mood and character, things apparently given in experience, and would thus appear to draw upon empirical psychology, which for Kant studies fluctuating inner states rather than conditions of possibility for experience. If the basis of the deduction of categories is found in moods and character, then they would seem to be too open to experience to be able to secure it, to realize both openness and reach. However, if categories respond to mood and character, we find that for Deleuze these are not in fact things which are given in experience. For him moods are the valid foundations for accounting for experience, for providing arguments that establish categories. Deleuze's thinking on mood and character actually makes them a potential non-empirical starting point for a Metaphysical Deduction rather than things that are given in experience. We must try to work out in what sense, according to Deleuze, mood and character actually account for experience without presupposing what is given in experience. It will be important to remember that in this seminar Deleuze has not merely equated categories with mood and character but also discussed their necessary and universal role. He writes that '. . . there is a level where the whole of possible experience takes on a sense, it is precisely because there are universal predicates which are attributed to all things, which is to say are attributed to any object whatever' (ibid.: 4). Therefore, Deleuze is not playing the role of the sceptic when he bases categories upon character and mood. He is not saying that we cannot have a priori, necessary and universal, categories. Instead he is seeking to find the source of such categories in character and mood.

In order to understand how Deleuze accounts for categories through character and mood, we will return to the emphasis upon sensation that characterizes his account of experience. As we have seen, sensation provides the object of the encounter through which we learn about the sensible synthesis of experience. If sensation is to provide the moods and characters that account for categories it must be the non-empirical starting point for a Metaphysical Deduction of the conditions of real experience. We have seen Deleuze writing that '. . . what would be good would be to see if everybody came up with the same list of categories' (ibid.: 3). We also saw that he recognizes the universal and necessary role of categories, something that demands that mood and character are not things given in experience. Character and mood are encountered as somehow involved in the way in which sensation itself is at work in accounting for experience. We've noted already that Deleuze finds resources in sensation that for Kant could only be secured given the role of the understanding in providing the judgements and categories behind cognition. Sensation alone is to be the source of a deduction of the categories. However, we will argue that despite his emphasis upon sensation to the exclusion of Kant's concern with the understanding he is seeking to develop a Kantian form of argument. This argument is a Metaphysical Deduction which starts with the non-empirical and secures categories with brevity and solidity. For Kant the non-empirical starting point is the pure use of the understanding while for Deleuze it is sensation and the moods and characters we encounter in it. This will lead us to focus upon the form of argument both Kant and Deleuze employ. In the next section of this chapter we will consider how Deleuze's emphasis upon sensation gives rise to a Kantian form of argument, a Metaphysical Deduction of categories that has its starting point in encounters with sensation.

The Being of the Sensible

Deleuze emphasizes sensation in his account of experience by talking about 'the being of the sensible'.[1] What does it mean to say that sensation has a 'being'? Miguel de Beistegui argues that Deleuze is concerned to avoid mediating sensation through concepts: 'What escapes us is the thing in its difference or *nuance*. And this we can achieve by following the real in its self-differentiation, by pursuing the thing all the way to its internal difference, at the stage at which it becomes a "this". Yet the empiricism in question is further qualified as *transcendental* empiricism, and one that, in the process, becomes a *superior* empiricism' (Beistegui 2004: 242). It is in this sense that the move that we have already observed in Deleuze's critique of Kant is central to his own theory of sensation. This is the move from talking about or representing sensation to what sensation itself does, to its own syntheses. This invokes its 'self-differentiation' or the internal differences that are at work in its synthesis. Insofar as this synthesis can provide an internal account of experience it is elevated to a transcendental and superior status. This is something that we encounter in sensation, as its own 'being' or role. We saw in Chapter 2 of this book that Ideas are dramatized in sensation without this process relying upon an author, actor or subjects. Sensation does not need such external conditions to account for experience. However, if sensation is to account for experience through its synthesis, how does it account for the reach we have in experience? How do we, through sensation, grasp individual things or objects of experience? This leads us to consider Beistegui's reference to 'the thing in its difference'. This concerns how we understand and envisage a thing as being determined and distinguished solely through the sensible synthesis of experience. This 'thing in its difference' does not need conceptual forms of determination to be what it is but instead we are referred to its own difference and the synthesis through which this arises. Thus something is different or individual insofar as it is nuanced or distinguished by sensation itself. 'The thing in its difference' is the individual given in and through sensation and through a difference that makes it individual. This brings us to Deleuze's account of individuation. This is something we must explore further because it will bring us significantly closer to the categories that concern Deleuze. These categories are involved in an account of individuation that is internal to sensation.

In response to the problem of securing openness and reach we have arrived at a conception of a 'thing in its difference'. We need to be able to both encounter and reach different individuals and for Deleuze we can do this because sensation individuates or differentiates experience. In a seminar entitled 'The Method of Dramatization' Deleuze considers how this process can be formulated (DI: 94–116). We will compare this to his presentation of Kant's categories. The focus is upon sensation and the way it accounts for experience. In 'The Method of Dramatization' Deleuze seeks to formulate the questions that are staged in the very individuation of experience through sensation. He presents these questions as forming a universal system which . . .

> . . . sketch[es] out the multiple coordinates which correspond to the questions *how much? who? how? where? and when?*, and which gives such questions their transcendent consequences, beyond empirical examples. These determinations as a whole indeed are not connected with any particular example borrowed from a physical or biological system, but articulate the categories of every system in general. [. . .] It happens all the time that dynamisms which are

qualified in a certain way in one domain are then taken up in an entirely different mode in another domain. (ibid.: 98)

In contrast to Kant's account, 'the categories of every system in general' cannot be set out in advance of sensation. However, they must be set out in advance of what is given in experience and provide an account of experience. As we've seen, they concern 'the being of sensation' or sensation's own synthesis. We see that Deleuze is concerned here with what he calls 'determinations as a whole' that are to precede and make possible 'every system in general' (ibid.). These are what 'the being of the sensible' must be able to secure in every case of experience, just as for Kant understanding must secure certain basic concepts in every case. Like Kant, Deleuze rejects the idea of a list of categories and opts instead for a 'whole set of determinations'. To list determinations would be to take one's bearings from things arising in experience, things which are listed as and when they arise, rather than from what is involved in accounting for experience. Kant and Deleuze both reject any notion of looking outside a process always already underway. Instead they seek to secure these determinations 'as a whole'. Thus while for Kant the understanding is the source and for Deleuze it is sensation, brevity and wholeness are valued in both cases. The method by which categories are secured must not leave time for any external additions, external to sensation for Deleuze and external to the understanding for Kant. Categories should then be given all at once and as a whole on the basis of what sensation, or understanding, is capable of. Thus we have an argument that is internally focused, that is brief in order to provide an internal account of experience. This reflects Kant and Deleuze's methodological common ground, something that relates them despite their differences when it comes to the origin of the categories.

If the questions that Deleuze presents are involved in accounting for experience, we need to consider how this secures a 'thing in its difference', something we found to be a necessary feature of Deleuze's account. We ask *Who?* in order to grasp the individual that is a necessary determination in any case of experience. Sensation asks this question in order to secure the individual or 'thing in its difference' and what this individuating difference entails. This is not a question of grasping situations by seeking a stable individual or a way of classifying individuals. Instead, sensation is able to secure a 'thing in its difference' that is unmanageable and something to be approached instead, as we saw earlier, through 'experiments' and 'attempts' to harness or realize this difference. In other words, we have a question that seeks to capture the role of difference in a situation in such a way that it presents the ongoing role of sensation in a process that Deleuze calls individuation. We encounter a 'thing in its difference' as something undergoing individuation, as animated by a difference whose outcomes are open-ended for a process of individuation. Deleuze is concerned that we interrogate this process correctly: 'The question

What is this? prematurely judges the Idea as simplicity of the essence; from then on, it is inevitable that the simple essence includes the inessential, and includes it *in essence* and thus contradicts itself' (ibid.: 95–6). This would involve asking questions in order to better manage or understand sensation rather than to learn from encounters with it, to experiment with differences that are individuating in oneself and in others. We must approach a 'thing in its difference' rather than considering how things remain the same. By doing this we get closer to an account of experience, we focus upon individuation through sensible synthesis. *What is this?* is a question that does not focus on the individuating difference of a thing on the grounds that this would leave our grasp of it incomplete. However, for Deleuze we need to grasp a thing in its ongoing individuation, something that is always incomplete or unfinished. Only in this way do we learn about its synthesis and about how experience is accounted for. We consider a thing 'in its difference' or in terms of its individuation through difference. For Deleuze we must include this determination in the categories of 'every system in general' (ibid.: 98).

How is the question *who?* involved, like Kant's categories, in the synthesis of every case of experience? The individual or 'thing in its difference' can also be understood as a 'force' to be played out in a situation. Why use the term 'force' here? It enables us to distinguish the individual or 'thing in its difference' from any subject or any object that we grasp on the basis of experience. We have something that is impersonal and non-empirical, something not given in experience. It can therefore be involved in the synthesis of experience. In this way we do not presuppose something already given in experience but uncover something involved in accounting for it. This is an individuating difference or force that is at work in subjects and objects but is not to be confused with them. For Deleuze we need to have a force that is individuating in a situation and to be open to the ways this force can be realized given the obstacles and means that the situation provides. This leads us to the other questions that Deleuze poses in his account of experience. We ask *who?* and grasp an individuating difference or force, but what does this individual relate to?

Other questions expand individuation, putting it in context so that we have situations in which individuals develop, experiment and interact. As we saw, the full set of questions are: *how much? who? how? where? and when?* Deleuze brings these into play when he talks about 'the characteristic or distinctive trait of a thing in general':

Such a trait is twofold: the quality or qualities which it possesses, the extension which it occupies. Even when we cannot distinguish actual divisible parts, we still single out remarkable regions or points; and it is not only the internal extension that must be examined, but also the way in which the thing determines and differentiates a whole external space, as in the hunting grounds of an animal. In a word, each thing is at the intersection of a twofold synthesis: a synthesis of qualification or specification, and of partition, composition, or organization. (ibid.: 96)

The distinctive trait or character of a thing, secured by what we've described as its ongoing individuation, is related to its environment as an animal is related to its hunting grounds. We see that 'the being of the sensible', through the questions it poses, provides the determinations that mark out and develop 'hunting grounds'. First there is the role of the *who?* question in the individuation of the hunter. The hunter is not a hunter because it is distinguished from its prey but because it is a 'thing in its difference'. It expresses an individuating difference provided by sensible synthesis, something that plays a part in marking out 'the hunting grounds of an animal'. The question *who?* is a condition of this and every other situation because it determines this situation by locating a particular character or mood within it. This makes individuation one of a number of determinations that we saw Deleuze referring to as 'determinations as a whole' (ibid.: 98). The situation is also determined by various ways of occupying space and time. The term Deleuze uses is 'spatio-temporal dynamisms' (ibid.: 96) and these are to be behind the emergence of hunter and hunted, and the development of the practice of hunting over time. Thus *where?* and *when?* refer to spatio-temporal dynamisms that determine how the force expressed in the individual is actually realized in a situation. We could say that they externalize individuation so that a 'thing in its difference' faces an outside world, a *where* and a *when*. This introduces clashes between highly individual forces, such as we witness in the hunting field of the animal between the hunter and its prey. We also ask *how much?* and this brings into play the amount of force of each individuation in a situation. Then we ask *how?* so that the ways hunter and hunted occupy space and time allow them to experiment, to respond dynamically and strategically to this situation. In this way Deleuze's 'whole set of determinations' has the power to explain an open-ended variety of situations by specifying only the basic ways in which individuals occupy space and time. As we saw with Kant's Table of Categories, the aim is to account for experience but without over-determining it. Deleuze seeks to provide conditions that make experience possible, 'a whole set of determinations', but not to determine it any further.

We will now explore the nature and role of Deleuze's categories by further expanding upon his reference to 'the hunting grounds of an animal'. Here there are basic co-ordinates that situate the animal in relation to its prey. We ask *how?* at the same time as asking *where?* and *when?* so that these times and places become obstacles or means of capture or escape. Here (*where?*) and now (*when?*) there are certain obstacles and certain means that give rise to questions of strategy (*how?*). This allows an individual (*who?*) to experiment with how thingsare determined over the course of experience. This experimentation can have lasting results for a species, such a distinguishing a species like the zebra that has never been domesticated because it is so dangerous to humans after a certain age (Diamond 2005: 171–2). It is distinguished by an individuating difference, by a violent character and mood, and how this is expressed in space and time, and in relation to other individuals. Zebras cannot be confined so as to be selectively bred and developed in captivity through human intervention. Unpredictable behaviour and aggression are then ways of occupying space and time that overcome the forces of individuation expressed in human attempts at domestication. Human beings fail in their attempt to experiment with the individuating differences they encounter in zebras, to remove through selective breeding the differences that make them wild and exploit their other characteristics in a domestic setting. The way (*how?*) in which this animal occupies space (*where?*) and time (*when?*) allows it to sustain and develop an individuating difference that has resisted all human intervention. We find that solitary and territorial species are less likely to have been domesticated, exceptions among territorial mammal species being the cat and the ferret (ibid.: 173). In the case of herd animals, attempts at domestication can be undermined if, for example, herds have exclusive territories which they protect against other herds. They occupy space and time in such a way that if they are penned in, a strategy of domestication used by human beings, they will not behave in ways that can be predicted or managed. These examples give us a sense of what is at stake in Deleuze's account of individuation.[2] They help us to show how the categories are at work in any case of experience. The clash of individuating differences or forces takes place in space and time. We do not ask *what is x?* but rather concern ourselves with places and times where individual forces clash, and with the strategies that they employ – *how much? who? how? where? and when?*. In our example this gives continuity to the story of the zebra's relation to human beings over thousands of years. This is the history of the clash of individuating differences. We find an individuating force or difference in zebras that has consistently opposed human experimentation, something that emerges in a time and space where strategies of domestication are met with strategies of resistance. We have then a sense of the way in which for Deleuze the individual '. . . determines and differentiates a whole external space . . .' (DI: 96). This exploration of Deleuze's categories has revealed their role in an account of experience. However, we now need to consider the relation they have to mood and character if we are to understand how such categories are formulated.

Deleuze enlightens us further about the *who?* question and also relates it to the singular reading of Kant's Table of Categories that we found in his 1978 seminars on Kant. He does this when he names the individual who is sought by this question 'the larval subject'. Deleuze argues that . . .

> . . . it is not enough to ask the question: 'what is the true?' As soon as we ask *who wants the true when and where, how and how much?*, we have the task of assigning larval subjects (the jealous man, for example) and pure spatio-temporal dynamisms (sometimes we cause the very 'thing' to emerge, at a certain time, in a certain place; sometimes we accumulate indexes and signs from moment to moment, following a path that never ends). (ibid.: 98)

This allows us to understand how the larval subject is the non-empirical starting point for a deduction of the categories. Deleuze illustrates this using the example of 'the jealous man'. This larval subject is no one and yet it can be expressed by anyone or everyone. It can be the mood of you or I, or indeed of both you and I in a case where it forms the mood of a crowd of which we both form a part and in whose mood and character we participate.[3] This distinctive larval subject might have been absent a moment before, a moment at which space and time is not occupied by a crowd or person animated and held together in what they are doing by jealousy as their dominant larval subject. Deleuze's singular reading of Kant's categories proposed a deduction of categories based upon mood and character. In 'the jealous man', as a larval subject, we are dealing not with empirical manifestations of mood or character but with something involved in an account of experience that is internal to sensation. Thus Deleuze describes the questions staged in actualization as '. . . the dynamisms of inquisition or admission, accusation or inquiry, silently and dramatically at work, in such a way as to determine the theoretical division of the concept' (ibid.: 99). These secure a larval subject but specify this subject not as a person but as a mood or character that dominates a person or a crowd. The character or mood Deleuze is concerned with is secured as part of a process of posing questions that accounts for experience. It emerges through the sensible synthesis of experience that also secures the *how much? how? where?* and *when?* of different cases of experience.

In the example we used to explore Deleuze's account of experience we suggested that the zebra has never been domesticated because the ways in which it occupies space and time are not predictable or manageable. The individuating force or larval subjectivity that is dominant in situations where it is penned in overwhelms human strategies of domestication. For Deleuze this would show that even a domesticated individual, one predictable enough to be domesticated, exceeds our grasp when considered as a 'thing in its difference'. The ways in which they occupy space and time can be experimented with, giving rise, for example, to domesticated animals that are smaller or larger than their wild ancestors or with less developed organs because they no longer rely upon these to escape from wild predators (Diamond 2005: 159). However, this does not give us a concept of an animal species that exhausts their individuation, which gives us a complete picture of the ways in which they might occupy space and time. For Deleuze individuation is never finished or complete and so the success of domestication is not an end to the process. While we can affect their individuation in many ways, by providing a new environment or through their selective breeding, human beings can never understand what domesticated animals might become in quite different situations. This shows how the questions involved in accounting for experience ensure that we do not sacrifice openness when we seek to secure an understanding of sensation. We will now consider an objection to Deleuze's understanding of how the larval subject, as an individuating difference or force, is the starting point for a deduction of categories.

The issue that we must now consider is that individuation can seem to take place in an inner and excessively individual realm. If we consider a 'thing in its difference' this can appear isolating insofar as we do not look outside of this thing. We focus on its individuating difference or larval subject. Thus while we saw that Deleuze is focused upon 'the hunting fields of an animal', the danger is that by beginning with individuation he cannot avoid neglecting the external world. James Brusseau draws this conclusion in his book *Isolated Experiences*. He argues that for Deleuze '. . . difference is both the genesis of being and limited in its scope with respect to being. [. . .] Difference is a restricted ontology. If difference explains a certain event, then understand and deploy difference in that one slim place' (IE: 13). In this sense the individual is the playing out of individuating differences or larval subjects and this is an excessively individual process. It has no need of a shared world because it is only concerned with its own private dramas. Thus the individual is caught up in the mood or larval subject it is possessed by to the detriment of its relations to other individuals. This shows how the emphasis upon individuation in Deleuze's work runs the risk of preventing him from providing a full account of experience. This seems to be the case in *Difference and Repetition* when Deleuze invokes the name of Narcissus. He writes that '. . . we are all Narcissus in virtue of the pleasure (auto-satisfaction) we experience in contemplating, even though we contemplate things quite apart from ourselves' (DR: 74).[4] What is most different, or 'quite apart from ourselves', provides the resources for what is most individual. It is therefore the object of a Narcissism that is a condition of our ongoing individuation. Deleuze makes the external world something through which the individual seeks to extend and deepen their own individuation. This process is thus outward looking only insofar as this serves the purposes of individuation. While we contemplate things quite different from ourselves, we are narcissistic and ultimately inward looking. Brusseau proceeds to look for cases that fit into Deleuze's limited account of experience: 'I am looking for cases of unilateral distinction, of being generating its own limits' (IE: 17; cf. DR: 28). If Deleuze concentrates on isolated individuals, the locations where individuation takes place, he neglects relations between individuals (IE: 158). Brusseau's worry is that Deleuze turns the individual into a solitary location where individuating differences or larval subjects occur rather than situating it in the midst of experience and a shared world.

The individual is in splendid isolation, a Narcissus who only relies upon the world for the differences that animate and extend its inner life. This allows moods or larval subjects to play out individually and avoid the distractions and obstacles found in a shared world. One example Brusseau offers is of a life that seems to represent the ideal of Deleuze's account of individuation, the life that it is best able to account for.[5] It is the example of a wretched existence made up of aimless travelling. Brusseau takes this as an illustration of a world where relations to other individuals and things are neglected in the name of one's own individuation: 'For her, every separation from everybody else becomes a measureless distance' (ibid.: 194). We have an individual who has opened herself fully to the differences expressed in her as larval subjects, but who relates minimally to outer experience. We have openness to a process of individuation but little reach beyond an inner life. The life in Brusseau's example ends in suicide. It is a life without other people or things, a life in which they do not figure in a way that could make this life worth living or extend it further. Thus the individual would eat food as a minimal relation to the external world but would never relate to other individuals through this. They would be a solitary diner with no interest in the social and professional practices related to food. For Brusseau this extreme case of alienation leads to suicide as the final and inevitable renouncement of everything external in the name of individuating difference: 'The ultimate scene of [her] possession, and the highest display of her alienation from any need in common, from any shared world, and finally, from any other, is her sinking herself in rushing flood waters' (ibid.: 195). This is the ultimate fate of an individual who '. . . wallows in the solitude of difference' (ibid.: 191). This critique must be answered if Deleuze's account of experience is to be shown to be full and convincing. Has the emphasis upon an individual source of the deduction of the categories created a gulf between the individual and the external world?

We appear to have a highly individual Metaphysical Deduction of categories that depends upon non-empirical moods or larval subjects that do not join or contribute to shared worlds. This seems to be the outcome of Deleuze's presentation of categories that depend upon our mood and character in his 1978 seminars on Kant. However, there are two key points that Brusseau's account neglects when it paints this picture. The first point is that the individual is not to be confused with a personal or psychological self, such as the hunter or the farmer in our previous example. A process of individuation may result in, and continue to sustain, the life of a hunter or indeed the life of the solitary and doomed individual of Brusseau's example. However, this is always the outcome of a wider process. We must again qualify the individual as the individual difference or force behind things given in experience. For Deleuze the individual must be something non-empirical insofar as it is one of the 'determinations as a whole' involved in accounting for experience. We do not then have a larval subject who is located in isolation from a world outside but a determination involved in accounting for experience along with certain other determinations. We have a 'whole set of determinations' and not a dominant determination to which the others are subordinate. Thus if a deduction of the categories depends upon our mood or character, this refers to a non-empirical larval subject, to something bound up with other determinations that are involved in accounting for experience. For this reason the individual is

not alone. Contrary to Brusseau's account, the question *who?* is bound up with
the questions *how much? how? where?* and *when?.*

The Situations and Strategies of Proust's 'Jealous Man'

How can we test the explanatory power of Deleuze's account of experience that
makes use of categories? By turning to literary examples provided in Marcel
Proust's *In Search of Lost Time,* I will seek to explore the role of certain questions
in providing a 'whole set of determinations' or categories in every case of
experience. A deduction of the categories that proceeds by considering the
mood or character at work in a situation will be tested using this novel. In his
Proust and Signs, Deleuze argues that for Proust: 'The beloved appears as a sign,
a "soul"; the beloved expresses a possible world unknown to us, imprisoning
a world that must be deciphered, that is, interpreted' (PS: 7). This energizes
the activity of the narrator in *In Search of Lost Time* and this literary example will
be useful in showing that individuation takes us beyond the narrow account of
experience Brusseau claims to find. Indeed, the 'jealous man' is an individual
who is expressed in Proust's narrator but who could not be understood in
isolation, any more than the hunter could emerge in isolation from the hunted
in our previous example. Deleuze writes that for Proust: 'To fall in love is to
individualize someone by the signs he bears or emits' (ibid.). In the second
volume of *In Search of Lost Time* we are presented with the individuation of
Albertine, the narrator's future lover, from among a group of girls he sees
for the first time from his hotel room window at Balbec.[6] This may appear
to involve only a lack of recognition, the inability to affix diverse features and
characteristics to a single and unified self. However, for Proust this experience
is inseparable from the individuation of the narrator as the 'jealous man'
through his relation to Albertine. Seeking to know her is integral to this
process. On first seeing the group, the inability of the narrator to distinguish
one girl from the other is thus found to be significant in itself: 'And this want,
in my vision, of the demarcations which I should presently establish between
them permeated the group with a sort of shimmering harmony, the continuous
transmutation of a fluid, collective and mobile beauty' (WBG: 428). This is not
an error or lack of anything but refers to the process by which an individuation
is staged. In fact, never knowing Albertine, her motives and thoughts, is to
know her truly. As an object of jealousy and in her own ongoing individuation
she is never someone who can be known. She is most truly 'fluid' and 'mobile'.
The 'jealous man' that the narrator becomes again and again is a larval
subject brought to the surface by a relation to the many Albertines that the
narrator finds in his experience and memory of her, in his ongoing attempt
to know her.

Deleuze finds here a truth about the process individuation, whether it is
the individuation of another person or one's own individuation in relation to

another. Proust shows the narrator realizing this truth in volume five of *In Search of Lost Time* that: '. . . none of us is single, that each of us contains many persons who do not all have the same moral value, and that if vicious Albertine had existed, it did not mean that there had not been others, . . .' (CF: 605). Thus what is significant in the process of individuation, what gives rise to all kinds of situations in experience, is this lack of a single, unified self. Instead there are larval subjects like 'vicious Albertine' that are part of a process of individuation through which there also arises again and again 'the jealous man' as the individuating difference that dominates the narrator. The search for a single self behind these many selves is fruitless and futile and yet this is what jealousy most truly is. We can then chart the two series of moods or larval subjects in *In Search of Lost Time* and see how they are played out in the way these characters occupy space and time in relation to one another.

If we return to 'The Method of Dramatisation' we may remind ourselves of the whole set of questions that allow us to assign the categories of any situation:

> As soon as we ask *who wants the true when and where, how and how much?*, we have the task of assigning larval subjects (the jealous man, for example) and pure spatio-temporal dynamisms (sometimes we cause the very "thing" to emerge, at a certain time, in a certain place; sometimes we accumulate indexes and signs from moment to moment, following a path that never ends). (DI: 98)

'The jealous man' is a larval subject that emerges in the midst of actual situations and this may well conflict with what is already the case and with the ongoing individuations of another person. An incident that takes place in volume five of *In Search of Lost Time* may help us see how this helps us to account for experience. We will ask each of Deleuze's questions in turn in order to see whether they fully interrogate the process through which this incident comes about. *Who?* 'The jealous man' is the larval subject that is realized in and through the narrator in this situation. The narrator is situated by his love for Albertine, which is inseparable from the continued emergence of this larval subject. It is his encounter in memory and in outer experience with the different selves of his beloved that makes 'the jealous man' dominant in him. He is also situated by the scenarios that arise in his search for the truth about Albertine, implying further questions. *Where?* In the apartment where Albertine is staying with the narrator and where she finds herself a captive and under surveillance. Here the narrator finds himself a spy and gaoler as a result of the friction between their conflicting larval subjects. *When?* After the musical evening attended by the narrator at the Verdurin's house. A septet by Vinteuil is performed that is new to the narrator and yet the music contains a 'little phrase' that he has heard before in the composer's work. In his sonata it had a different effect in the sensations it gave rise to.[7] The narrator now listens to the septet:

> . . . all of a sudden, I found myself, in the midst of this music that was new to me, right at the heart of Vinteuil's sonata; and, more marvellous than any girl, the little phrase, sheathed, harnessed in silver, glittering with brilliant sonorities, as light and soft as silken scarves, came to me, recognisable in this new guise. (CF: 281)

This experience of the same phrase gives rise to different sensations and we therefore do not recognize it as identical or similar to a previous experience. However, it does still take us beyond the particular case because it is the same 'little phrase' that structures the sensations the narrator undergoes in each case. The encounter with it ultimately revives the narrator's jealousy rather than leading him to continue the meditation on artistic creativity that he at first entered into in response to the 'little phrase'. It now resonates with the object of his jealousy because in seeking the same self, he meets many Albertines just as he undergoes different sensations in response to the 'little phrase'. It thus captures the truth behind Albertine as the object of his jealousy: 'Alas! Albertine was several persons in one' (ibid.: 384). She is never to be individuated as an object of knowledge, as a single self, and this is precisely how jealousy proceeds. This is how sensation works in both of these cases, whether in the case of love or art. However, in the novel it is the artwork that is closer to this truth than jealousy because it is created in the knowledge that its object is multiple and it makes use of this.[8] Art is creative because it draws upon the variety of sensation while jealousy is frustrated because it continues to search for a single self that it can never find.[9] We have then a truth of individuation discovered in art, making art a worthwhile pursuit and showing jealousy to be futile.

We find that the 'little phrase' that unifies and differentiates Vinteuil's music resonates with and revives the object of the narrator's jealousy because both express the multiple nature of individuation through sensation. It reveals the truth of individuation that larval subjects occur in our experience of ourselves and of others. Albertine's continued mystery, like that of the phrase of music that the narrator had heard in Vinteuil's compositions, is essential to her ongoing individuation for the narrator. It sustains the narrator's love for her just as the 'little phrase' continues to animate Vinteuil's music in different ways and with different results. However, the force of jealousy, of 'the jealous man' as a larval subject, means that the narrator is tormented again by his inability to know Albertine as a single, unified self. This recurrence of 'the jealous man' as dominant larval subject is behind his renewed search for this knowledge of Albertine.[10] Rather than, as will later be the case, leading him to pursue his vocation as a writer, this 'little phrase' returns him to the world of jealousy: 'The fact is that jealousy is as a rule partial, intermittent and localized, . . .' (ibid.: 253). Thus it is upon returning home from this musical evening that the narrator is confronted by Albertine who is angry at not having been told where he was going and is feeling oppressed by her captivity. Now her own mood or larval subject challenges his jealousy. Answering the *when?* question has brought us to the collision of two larval subjects.

How? This question brings us to strategies of jealousy. In his attempt to know the self of his beloved the narrator seeks to maintain the captivity he hopes will make this possible. He pretends that he wants to end their relations right away and this is a strategy prompted by Albertine's anger at his having attended the Verdurin's musical evening without telling her. He fears her attempt to escape her captivity. The larval subject that has become dominant in her is something that could have enough force to prompt a course of action that would overpower the force of his jealousy. He intends that she should be overcome with tender feelings for him at the sudden prospect of their separation, that a different larval subject should then become dominant in her. Having extracted maxim distress from Albertine, as planned, he relents upon his decision that they should separate. However, he is left with the feeling that the problem has not been solved, something that reflects his continued inability to know what Albertine thinks, to know her as a single self. He cannot tell when the same larval subject will occur again in her, something that is likely to result in a strategy of flight. As we've seen, the selves that compose her are multiple and become dominant in different situations. Finally we ask *How much?* 'The jealous man' is a mood or larval subject that overpowers Albertine's desire for flight as the expression of her own, forceful larval subject at this moment. It is the dominant force in the situation, partly thanks to the strategy that the narrator employs and also because of its own degree of force as an individuating difference. When Albertine eventually employs a strategy of flight, packing her things in the night and leaving before the narrator is out of bed, it is the larval subject dominant in her at that time which is most forceful (CF: 473f.). In this way certain questions provide a 'whole set of determinations' or categories that map out a situation but only in order to make possible the open-ended course of experience.

We've seen that there is no single Albertine and so questions must be dynamic enough to cope with a succession of larval subjects rather than seeking a single, unified self. Unlike in James Brusseau's account we find that an individual is preoccupied with an external world, seeking to keep up with the individuation of another by devising strategies and engaging extensively with things other than themselves. In Proust's novel this is the case even when his beloved is no longer alive. After her death in a riding accident, Albertine lives on in the narrator's memory because he is still in love with her. 'The jealous man' is activated as he remembers things she had said and done, seeking the truth behind them. However, this still leads him to engage widely with the external world. Until his love is at an end, he seeks the truth about Albertine, even commissioning research into her activities when she was alive but not in his company.[11] The larval subject is therefore to be found in the midst of experience, bound up with other questions.

Conclusion

Our exploration of literary examples from Proust's novel has allowed us to consider what is distinctive about Deleuze's account of experience, how it draws upon the role of sensation, and also how its concern with categories resonates with Kant's thought. Kant sought to involve categories in the synthesis of possible experience as such. We've seen how for Deleuze the role of categories in cases of experience is secured by always asking the same questions. We secure the larval subject (*who?*) and then on the basis of the mood in question add further categories in response to further questions (*how much? how? where?* and *when?*). On the basis of a mood or character, we populate situations with categories that allow this larval subject to develop over the course of experience in unpredictable ways. If we can speak of a Deleuzian Metaphysical Deduction, it will be in this sense. Categories emerge through the synthesis of sensations that accounts for experience. These deductions are multiple for Deleuze so that, unlike for Kant, we do have different categories according to the mood we are in. Thus we might find ourselves in the same time and place (*when?* and *where?*) but new strategies (*how?*) could arise in this situation in response to a new larval subject (*who?*) that has arisen within it. However, it is always the same questions that are answered in securing categories. These basic questions echo the role of Kant's Metaphysical Deduction insofar as they set out the basic categories of any case of experience. It is this concern to ensure that experience is accounted in basic ways, that it has a 'whole set of determinations', that relates Kant and Deleuze in their accounts of experience.

In comparing the categories that are involved in these two accounts of experience, there is a danger of overlooking the significant differences between Kant and Deleuze, and of pointing to common concerns that are too vague to be significant in how we relate them. However, by locating a concern with a deduction that is brief and solid, and with its non-empirical starting point, we find that significant links can be made between the ways in which Kant and Deleuze account for experience. Deleuze does not embrace Kant's Table of Categories or his attempt to locate categories in the understanding. However, we have seen that there is much more than this to the Metaphysical Deduction. We saw that Deleuze takes an interest in Kant's move from the level of the empirical to the level of the transcendental. This invokes an Idea of the whole or a problematic Idea of the relation of openness and reach. This relation is to be realized by providing categories for any case of experience which are able to combine openness to the synthesis of sensation, to emerging larval subjects, with the reach provided by a 'whole set of determinations'. For both Kant and

Deleuze, a deduction of categories must hold together a situation without borrowing from experience. This concern contributes to their respective philosophical accounts of experience that nevertheless have strong points of divergence. Deleuze's own Metaphysical Deductions may be multiple, unlike Kant's, but they express the same concern to secure and elaborate, without borrowing from experience, cases of experience in all their most basic determinations: *how much? who? how? where?* and *when?*.

Conclusion

Debates in Kant and Deleuze Studies

In this conclusion I will seek to contribute to key debates in Kant and Deleuze studies on the basis of the work I've done in this book. In Chapter 1 I defined transcendental arguments, which have been much debated recently, according to a particular reading of the *Critique of Pure Reason*. In the first section of this conclusion I will engage with the contemporary debate over the nature and scope of transcendental arguments. I will argue that the way in which we read Kant's text provides the key to formulating and assessing transcendental arguments. They are to be made convincing insofar as they embody the criteria of Kant's architectonic method rather than being understood in isolation from his account as a whole. Thus while formulations of transcendental arguments have become more modest in their ambitions, and those who formulate them have sought to escape the alleged subjective origins of Kant's account, I will take a different approach. I will argue that they would benefit by relating to Kant's *Critique of Pure Reason* more closely. In the second section of this conclusion I will consider the debate in Deleuze studies over the relation of the actual and the virtual. Deleuze's account of experience suffers if the actual is neglected in favour of the virtual. He can seem to reduce the role and importance of the actual insofar as the virtual does not resemble it and appears to be superior in various respects. I will show that the reading of Kant's *Critique of Pure Reason* I've developed provides resources for meeting this challenge to Deleuze's thought. On the basis of the relation between Kant's architectonic method and Deleuze's concern with individuation, something I established in Chapter 6 of this book, I will seek to conclude that Deleuze's thought needs to be developed along Kantian lines.

Transcendental Arguments

Let's remind ourselves of the challenge faced by any formulation of transcendental arguments. The scope of such arguments is particularly challenging. Ralph C. S. Walker writes that: 'If transcendental arguments are not capable of exhibiting factors that must be shared by all experience at every time, they degenerate into observations about how we do think, not arguments about how we must think' (Walker 2006: 254). We saw in Chapter 1 of this book that this form of argument emerged from Kant's architectonic method. It refers to all of experience at all times. We also saw that some arguments are too limited to be transcendental in the sense that Kant would recognize. We will now seek to apply these lessons to the contemporary debate over the nature and scope of transcendental arguments. P. F. Strawson rejected Kant's transcendental idealism while re-formulating his account of experience. According to his formulation, transcendental arguments refer only to reality 'for us' and never to an 'in itself' reality.[1] They refer to that which is involved in the ongoing cognition of possible experience. Strawson writes: 'If, therefore, our experience is to have for us the character of objectivity required for empirical knowledge, our "sensible representations" must contain some substitute or surrogate of the real, unknown object' (Strawson 1966: 91). This substitute is the 'rule-governed connectedness of our representations' which distinguishes the natural world from 'the subjective order of our perceptions' (ibid.). We only experience subjective perceptions but the rule and order they exhibit allows us to argue that they are objective. This sets the scene for formulations of transcendental arguments that start with the world as it is 'for us' and not with truth-claims concerning an external or independent reality. However, when we review the debate for which Strawson set the terms, it seems that an external remainder to the process of cognition is unavoidable. A gap remains between reality as this is captured by cognition and the external reality of objects of experience. Thus while we don't talk about a 'thing in itself' after Strawson, an object beyond our experience or in a second world of objects, something remains of this in the notion that there is a reality external to our concepts. This leaves us wondering if we actually refer to objective reality when we secure the subjective conditions of experience using transcendental arguments. If these arguments cannot close the gap they become more modest but, as we shall see, for some commentators this is a positive thing. In the introduction to this book I considered the 'two-world' or 'two-object' reading of Kant's account of experience and suggested reasons for rejecting it. In the following chapters I sought to show that my approach was supported by the internal focus of the architectonic method. I argued that Kant never looks outside of cognition in order to account for it. The conclusions we can draw from this reading will now be used to assess accounts of transcendental arguments that assume that Kant is ultimately unable to avoid postulating an unbridgeable gap between appearance and reality. I will question the notion that for Kant theoretical reality was ever anything other than what is internal to the process of cognition.[2]

Strawson argued that we can defeat scepticism by focusing on the way in which any argument makes sense. For experience in general to make sense, he argues, we must have a certain conceptual scheme (Strawson 1959: 15). This will provide the rule and order that subjective perceptions need if they are to refer to something objective. It follows that we can only think about particular, objective things in experience on the basis of this scheme. For example, we make sense of experience because there are objective particulars in the world and some of them are independent of us (ibid.). This is a condition without which all our talk about experience would be meaningless. Like Kant, Strawson seeks to implicate even sceptical statements and arguments in a reliance upon this conceptual scheme. He writes of the sceptic that: 'He pretends to accept a conceptual scheme, but at the same time quietly rejects one of the conditions of its employment. Thus his doubts are unreal, not simply because they are logically irresoluble doubts, but because they amount to the rejection of the whole conceptual scheme within which alone such doubts make sense' (ibid.: 35). Thus a sceptic might argue that there are not particular things in the world of experience that are independent of us and exist when there is no one to perceive them. However, this argument makes sense only because this conceptual scheme holds true and we can therefore make sense of the notion of independently existing things. The sceptic has used a conceptual scheme to state their argument but has then denied its existence. They have denied the necessary conditions for their own argument making sense.

Barry Stroud seeks to undermine this formulation of a transcendental argument when he argues that Strawson has invoked 'an additional factual premiss' (Stroud 1982: 122). This is a serious concern for us because we've argued that for Kant any reference to the facts or givens of experience would undermine a transcendental account. Stroud argues that the unacknowledged use of a verification principle secures this hidden factual premiss. Without this, he claims, the argument would not be convincing. He agrees with Strawson that the notion of independently existing objective particulars makes sense to us. It follows that we can 'sometimes' know certain conditions which imply that objective particulars do or do not continue to exist unperceived (ibid.). Thus in any number of cases we can verify the conclusion that objective particulars exist independently. In this way he limits the conclusions we can draw so that: 'We sometimes know that the best criteria we have for the reidentification of particulars have been satisfied' (ibid.: 128). Understood in this way, an apparent transcendental argument relies upon a verification principle for its force. It is now limited to certain cases, as all arguments based on a verification principle are, and thus forms a narrower argument than Kant demands. If transcendental arguments are made superfluous, because they are shown to rely upon a narrower form of argument, we have to admit that we cannot make such general arguments about experience. The only progress we can make is with narrower verificationist arguments. Stroud makes transcendental arguments superfluous insofar as bridging the gap between our concepts and an external reality turns out to rely upon a verification principle. We know that objects exist unperceived in some cases and we can verify this without being able to make a transcendental claim about experience in general. This is a far cry from the arguments we located in Kant's architectonic method. Before turning to Kant's concern to locate both our concepts and any external reality within the architectonic we will consider how other scholars have responded to Stroud's challenge.

Robert Stern recognizes the difficulty of formulating transcendental arguments that allow us to make knowledge claims about an external reality (Stern 1999b: 47). We cannot secure a conclusion general enough to rule out the possibility that we are in error concerning the conditions of experience. His response is to accept that this ambitious aim cannot be met.[3] He argues that Stroud has weakened transcendental arguments because he has shown that there is a gap between external reality and our beliefs concerning that reality (ibid.: 49). We cannot set conditions applicable to this reality because of the gap between our concepts and something independent of them. This seems to leave two alternatives. We can give up transcendental arguments and accept the limitations of a verification principle. The other alternative would be to embrace idealism but for Stern this would abandon any sense of our being in touch with reality (ibid.). We either limit our conclusions to particular cases or lose touch with the reality we are trying to secure. However, in our reading of the *Critique of Pure Reason*, the synthetic and the a priori were seen to articulate possible experience through their relations. An external reality was ruled out by the architectonic method but all aspects of the real were to be accounted for and included in its unfolding, from the most concrete to the most abstract. We saw that for Kant the object of cognition secured by synthetic a priori judgement is to embody reality without remainder. Stern seeks to hold onto, or keep in touch with, reality by considering how norms or beliefs about reality form a coherent system and are made objective and real by their very coherence. He quotes F. H. Bradley who writes that the test for the truth of a belief is whether '. . . to take [it] as error would entail too much disturbance of my world' (Bradley 1914: 212; cited in Stern 1999b: 54–5). This coherence theory of truth can support beliefs insofar as their coherence with one another secures the reality and objectivity of the world we inhabit. Stern argues that the second Analogy of Experience in the *Critique of Pure Reason* embodies this criteria. It argues that we must accept the belief that A caused B, making it a norm for all experience, in order to relate A and B in time and treat them as events (ibid.: 51). This norm is to make experience possible and to do so by being coherent with itself and with other norms like the inherence of a substance in both A and B, allowing us to recognize them over time. Stern names such arguments 'belief-directed' transcendental arguments as opposed to those that are 'truth-directed' or that seek to know reality independently of our cognition of it (ibid.). This echoes the argument I uncovered in Chapter 2 of this book where for Kant a coherent system was to guarantee the objectivity of experience. It has the internal focus that his architectonic method demands and realizes in a system. Similarly, Stern wants to focus upon the coherent system of beliefs and norms that structure our experience and not upon an external reality. However, his account lacks the ambitions we uncovered in Kant's *Critique of Pure Reason*. We will now consider why Stern lacks this confidence given our understanding of why for

Kant transcendental arguments are 'in touch with reality' while also being concerned with the concepts we use.

Stern's account is modest because he is not claiming to be able to defeat a sceptic who doubts our claims to knowledge of an independent or external reality. Such a sceptic looks outside of our system of beliefs and norms to a world that they must correspond to and challenges this correspondence. For Stern we can never bridge the gap between appearance and reality, and thus defeat this type of sceptical challenge. However, he is claiming to be able to defeat a sceptic who doubts things that are internal to our belief-system. Such a sceptical challenge doubts norms that make our experience possible and does not refer to what is external to this system of beliefs (ibid.: 52). Stern writes of such a sceptic that:

> His position is instead thoroughly 'internal' to our practice: that is, he takes the norms that constitute our practice as given, accepting that practice itself is well formed, whilst claiming that the belief in question nonetheless fails to conform to any of those 'standards and procedures', as we take them to be. (ibid.: 53)

The sceptic is once again caught in the trap of something that makes sense of his own statements. Something doubted is shown to be necessary to ensure the integrity of a belief-system that is shared by the sceptic who doubts it. Neither the sceptic nor the transcendental philosopher refers to anything external to this system. Both refer to a coherent system of beliefs and norms, and argue in ways that make sense only on the basis of this system. In this way Stern preserves Strawson's concern not to refer to what is external to our experience but he also avoids Stroud's challenge by referring not to particular cases of experience but to a system that is general enough to encompass all our experience. He avoids doubt over whether we refer to reality by making reality relative to our beliefs and norms, things that are real insofar as they structure our experience coherently. As I've noted, this move to secure coherence in a system echoes our reading of the *Critique of Pure Reason* in Chapter 2 of this book but we can now register a crucial difference. I argued in Chapter 2 that Kant's system offered a third way between an 'order of being' and an 'order of thought'. This insight can now be brought to bear on this debate over the nature and scope of transcendental arguments. Kant does not want to refer to anything external to cognition in the argument he makes and yet he wants to account for experience in all its reality. How would he respond to Stern's formulation of transcendental arguments?

Scott Stapleford accuses Stern of neglecting Kant's intentions, of missing the ambitions and concerns that animated his thought:

> One could even go so far as to speculate that the shift away from questions of truth and of the conditions of experience, to questions of the 'rational

legitimation' of beliefs and the related matter of assigning beliefs to the appropriate norms of belief formation that cover them, are notions so far removed from Kant's immediate concerns he would have had a hard time in even understanding what they mean. (Stapleford 2008: 22)

This criticism of Stern is supported by the conclusions we can draw from our reading of the *Critique of Pure Reason*. There is something missing in Stern's account insofar as it neglects the internal and inclusive nature of the architectonic method. This ensures that all dualisms are accounted for rather than being presupposed in giving an account of experience. Rather than seeking to deal with the gap between our concepts and an external reality, Kant seeks to deal with the relations between the elements of his architectonic through which all knowledge of reality is to arise. The synthetic and the a priori are to secure the reality that Stern wants to keep in touch with. As we saw, the a priori must be involved in the synthesis of possible experience rather than providing ways of making sense of an external reality. The a priori is related to synthesis before we are aware of it, before we encounter sensations. Thus rather than an 'order of being' or an 'order of thought' we have a system that makes possible these two sides of reality, the objective and the subjective, in the first place. We saw in Chapters 4 and 5 of this book that a priori concepts were not beliefs concerning sensation but directly involved in the synthesis of sensation prior to experience and in the midst of experience. Kant argues that reality is shaped or constructed in this way and that these necessary conditions make it possible rather than only being a way in which we respond to sensation. Thus he only recognizes a reality produced through the relations of the synthetic and the a priori in an ambitious architectonic account. Stern's use of a coherence theory of truth is useful and reflects Kant's understanding of the architectonic as the art of constructing systems. However, for Kant a system is to make reality possible and is made up of conditions of possibility rather than beliefs about reality. In Chapters 4 and 5 we saw how reality is secured in such processes as the counting of parts of space that mark out concrete situations in the a priori synthesis of possible experience. Therefore, if a system makes experience possible then for Kant it does this in the fullest sense, not simply as a reality relative to us but as one in which we find ourselves.

In response to Stern's account Scott Stapleford argues that for Kant transcendental arguments must relate abstract concepts through their reference to concrete experience. Although we cannot refer to the givens of experience in transcendental arguments we can still make reference to the concrete: 'As strange as it may sound, the stuff that binds concepts in philosophical proofs is *possible* experience or *possible* intuition' (ibid.: 43). This reflects the reading we have given, according to which the relation of the synthetic and the a priori takes priority over the dualisms that it must account for. These include the dualisms of subject and object, self and world, and appearance and reality, which occupy Strawson, Stroud and Stern so very deeply. We saw in Chapter 3 of this book that synthetic a priori judgements are part of a transcendental or material logic that refers to the concrete synthesis of possible experience in order to relate a priori concepts. Such a logic was to mark out situations in which dualisms arise. It makes possible the distinction between self and world by providing categories through which this is first cognized. Thus if we distinguish a self as the cause of certain events in the world and as effected by causes found in the world this is because categories have already been at work and secured cause and effect as an a priori form of synthesis. These are not beliefs or norms but provide a very material logic for concrete situations. They mark out the dualisms that we recognize so consistently. Thus rather than arguments that reflect upon an external reality, Kant seeks arguments that account for all cognition of experience, outside of which there is no external reality to be reached by theoretical cognition. This should not suggest that there are no problems or challenges in Kant's system. As we've seen, the opposite is the case. However, it helps us to understand how for Kant the problems of relating very different things are positive rather than negative. His architectonic is animated not by a lack of reality but by the problem of relating the synthetic and the a priori through which the cognition of experience is to be made possible.

Quassim Cassam's assessment of transcendental arguments continues to develop the reading of Kant's *Critique of Pure Reason* that has set the terms for this debate. We saw Stern pursuing an internal focus in his account but this was limited to a belief-system and its norms. As we've seen, this modesty helps those formulating transcendental arguments to avoid making assumptions about an external reality while holding onto beliefs that are real. Cassam develops this understanding of transcendental arguments when he talks of the 'subjective origin thesis' (Cassam 1999: 89).[4] This characterizes Kant's arguments concerning the a priori conditions of experience. These proceed on the basis of the subjective origin of the conditions of possibility they seek to establish. This would explain why the thinkers we've considered struggle to deal with a gap between appearance and reality in formulating transcendental arguments. Cassam traces this back to Kant's formulation of arguments in his account of experience. He argues that:

> To say that the categories have subjective origins in Kant's sense is therefore to say that the understanding is their 'birthplace'. It follows that '*a priori* conditions of the possibility of experience' in Kant's sense are not just necessary conditions. They are conditions which are wholly subjective in origin. (ibid.: 91)

This means that for Kant origins confer legitimacy on the conditions of experience and this has led to the problem of relating something with a subjective origin to something that arises in experience and thus has an objective origin. It follows that transcendental arguments have struggled to get over this difficulty ever since, something which was inherent in their first formulation. Cassam understands Kant as arguing that if conditions of possibility are not located in experience, in the object, they must be located in the subject. This allows Stroud to challenge such arguments because they cannot close the gap between the subjective and the objective or what is internal to cognition and what is external to it. Cassam writes: 'This argument assumes that in the case of concepts such as *substance* and *cause*, there are only two mutually exclusive options: either they are derived from sensation, or they are wholly subjective in origin and therefore quite ideal' (ibid.: 97). He distinguishes what he calls 'world-directed' and 'self-directed' transcendental arguments on these grounds (ibid.: 85). They arise because we must find the origin of a priori conditions either in the subjective or the objective. We must either look inwards to the self and its cognitive apparatus or outwards to the world. Is this background to transcendental arguments inescapable? I will suggest that given the reading of the *Critique of Pure Reason* I've presented in this book, Kant does not in fact argue against this background.

Cassam's solution, as articulated in his book *The Possibility of Knowledge*, involves replacing a concern with 'conditions' with a concern with 'means'. Unlike Stern he does not seek beliefs and norms because this would give rise to another self-directed argument and he wants to provide a world-directed account. He wants to break with the focus on the subject that he traces back to Kant. His alternative is to argue that: '. . . specifying appropriate means of coming to know is an appropriate means of explaining what empirical knowledge is' (Cassam 2007: 81).[5] Such an argument is world-directed because it provides an open-ended list of means to know objects of experience. These means are different ways of connecting with the world, of expanding our knowledge of its objects. We note that Cassam does not share Kant's concern with a complete and indispensable account of experience. He sees this as necessarily relying upon subjective origins and invoking self-directed arguments because completeness is never given in the world. In the world there are only different means of knowing and these can be added to in ways we cannot predict. We also note that Cassam wants to know what empirical knowledge is, rather than how it is possible, giving up any ambition to provide an architectonic account. Rather than exploring his approach further, here we will consider whether he is right to argue that Kant invokes a subjective origin. If Kant's arguments do not face an inevitable choice between subjective origins and an external reality there will be no reason to seek a different account. We've argued that Kant does not accept that the subjective and the objective are given in advance or that 'self' and 'world' are the two possible directions that transcendental arguments can take.[6] The architectonic method of the *Critique of Pure Reason* mustn't be seen as taking certain things for granted. It is a context-independent argument or one that accounts for the contexts where cognition takes place, like the one where self and world are distinct because the categories allow us to recognize their distinctness. Only on the basis of this account can we define empirical knowledge by talking about the means by which it can be achieved. The reading I've presented suggests that for Kant the need to include all of possible experience in this account is overwhelming. This shows the importance of considering Kant's thought carefully before reformulating transcendental arguments. In this book I have argued that those who seek to respond to his apparent neglect of an external reality fail to engage with his architectonic method. Until this is taken seriously and explored in depth the *Critique of Pure Reason* will not be able to play its full role in contemporary philosophical debates.

The Actual and the Virtual

In turning again to Deleuze's thought I will be concerned with how Kant can add constructively to his account of experience. In the introduction to this book I noted that much work has been done on how Deleuze adds to our understanding of Kant. On the basis of the readings I've given I will show how a major criticism of Deleuze's account of experience can be met using the resources I've uncovered in Kant's *Critique of Pure Reason*. A major debate has been taking place over the relation of the actual and the virtual in Deleuze's thought. Does the unique nature of the virtual lead him to neglect the actual which it does not resemble? How can two such different things relate and contribute to one another such that their relation is one of reciprocal determination? This is a crucial debate because the reciprocal determination of these two poles of experience will ensure that both are accounted for and have a role in experience. For Deleuze, reciprocal determination is inseparable from complete determination. If the actual and the virtual determine one another, this must give rise to a complete account of experience rather than being one-sided. As we saw in the debate over transcendental arguments, there is much current concern to safeguard all the real aspects of our experience. Commentators on both Kant and Deleuze worry that in accounting for very real problems and objects of experience we risk undermining their reality and significance. How can Kant help Deleuze meet these challenges? According to the criteria of the architectonic method the abstract reach of the a priori must not lead it to neglect the particularities of the concrete that would be left behind if the abstract was only concerned with itself. Likewise, the abstract can only be realized in the concrete, in the sensible synthesis of experience, because, as Scott Stapleford puts it, '[t]he concepts that feature in philosophical proofs are little more than logical shells before perception saturates them with intuitive content' (Stapleford 2008: 48). My investigation of this problem in Kant's *Critique of Pure Reason* helped us to think about Deleuze's account of experience and the problems that characterize it in Chapter 6 of this book. On the basis of this reading I will consider critical concerns over whether Deleuze relates the actual and the virtual in a way that accounts for experience fully and convincingly.

It may seem odd that I have neglected the terms 'actual' and 'virtual' until this late stage of the book. The reason for doing this is that by not foregrounding two dominant terms in many readings of Deleuze I have been able to approach his thought in a new way. I sought to approach it in terms of his relation to Kant rather than, for example, approaching it in terms of his relation to Henri Bergson whose work is the source of the term 'virtual' for Deleuze (DR: 327, n23). The virtual is always in danger of crowding out other parts of Deleuze's account and distracting us from his relation to different thinkers.[7] By approaching his thought through our reading of Kant's *Critique of Pure Reason* I sought to show that Deleuze is concerned, like Kant, with the integrity of an account of experience. In such an account the virtual would play its part but not overpower or dominate other elements. Deleuze writes about the virtual in the following terms in *Difference and Repetition*:

> The virtual is opposed not to the real but to the actual. *The virtual is fully real in so far as it is virtual.* Exactly what Proust said of the virtual: 'Real without being actual, ideal without being abstract'; and symbolic without being fictional. (DR: 208; cf. Proust 2000b: 224)

It is the reality of the virtual that leads Alain Badiou to fear for the reality and integrity of what Deleuze calls 'the actual'. This embodies the concrete particularities of experience and the means by which experience proceeds. These include abstract relations between objects and between objects and subjects. Such relations and particularities make it possible, for example, for a threat to be real and for us to have real means of dealing with this threat. Badiou fears that only the virtual is real in Deleuze's account. This can seem a strange complaint when, as we've seen, Deleuze emphasizes the concrete and seeks to explore concrete cases. Badiou acknowledges Deleuze's concern to think 'under the constraint of cases' but wants to put this in the context of his account of experience as a whole (Badiou 2000: 20). He argues that while Deleuze is concerned with ever different cases, rather than with generalizing about experience, this is based upon the notion that Being is One. It is the Being-One of reality that thought reflects and extends when it thinks about very different cases. Thought reflects the dominant power of the virtual to produce different cases of experience rather than reflecting the integrity and importance of particular cases. For Badiou this is Deleuze's way of unifying reality by thinking about the power of the virtual to differentiate it. The equality of being follows from this, with all of reality being equally an expression of the virtual (ibid.: 21). Everything is equally a product of the virtual rather than being anything important in itself.

Philosophy's task is now understood in the following terms: 'When thought succeeds in constructing, without categories, the looped path that leads, on the surface of what is, from a case to the One, then from the One to the case, it intuits the movement of the One itself' (ibid.: 40). According to Badiou, the virtual dominates thought, distracting philosophy from the actual and its concerns because the actual only tells us what the virtual can do and makes little contribution itself. Thus, while the equality of all actual beings in expressing virtual Being might seem to empower the actual, for Badiou this is not the case. It means that nothing actual stands out or makes a difference because it is only a sign of the many different things the virtual can bring about. The virtual is therefore the ground of the actual, the source of its complete determination (ibid.: 43). We can understand this by referring to Deleuze's concern with a groundless ground: 'To ground is to metamorphose' (DR: 154). This ground makes sure that all cases are different, it 'ungrounds' experience in order to produce very different cases of experience. In other words, it grounds the actual by differentiating it rather than by preserving resemblance across cases. For Badiou this only shows what the virtual can do and distracts us from the actual. Everything actual is equally a product of the virtual and nothing significant in itself. Thus: '. . . [if] the virtual is the deployment of the One in its immanent differentiation, then every actualization must be understood as an innovation and as attesting to the infinite power of the One to differentiate itself on its own surface' (Badiou 2000: 49). It follows for Badiou that the actual and the virtual are only a formal distinction or a nominal opposition (ibid.). They describe what the virtual does, its ability to give rise to actualities, by formally distinguishing actual products from their virtual production. However, the reality of the product is subsumed by the superior reality of its production. It follows that when we account for the production of the actual we concern ourselves less and less with the actual itself, we reduce it to the outcome of something more interesting and more productive.

Peter Hallward also mounts a defence of the actual and brings to the fore the concerns of those who see the virtual as a threat to the integrity of the actual. He writes: 'That something is *actual* means that it exists in the conventional sense of the word, that it can be experienced, perceived, measured, etc' (Hallward 2006: 36). He defines the virtual as something that does not resemble this at all. It is not objective, perceptible or measurable. It is not present or presentable because it does not make an *actual* difference, in the *here and now*. For Hallward the actual is what is useful and indeed necessary to human life while the virtual is not. The virtual refers to the whole of time rather than a present moment of time. This whole is limited or constrained when it relates to the actual as one of the present moments that characterize the temporality of actual experience (ibid.: 32). It is in the present that human beings act and react, that they encounter actual things and use them to do things. Hallward concludes that for Deleuze being concerned with the present is less important than relating to the virtual or time as a whole (ibid.: 32–3). What isolates human beings from the virtual are 'the needs of the moment' or the priorities of human life (ibid.). These needs or priorities cut us off from the virtual that relates all of time regardless of whether it is relevant or useful to the actual. It follows that actual conditions must be disrupted so that the whole of time can be thought.

Hallward writes 'If the actual is sustained by the interests of action then virtual insight will require the paralysis of actions and the dissolution of the actor' (ibid.: 34). His critique echoes Dr Johnson's response to the philosophy of Bishop Berkeley. We encounter forceful individuations that make a significant difference in actual experience. Accordingly, Dr Johnson kicked a stone in order to refute Berkeley's idealism.[8] He encountered a forceful individuation in the sense I explored in Chapter 6 of this book. There is friction between two individual forces, between the stone and Dr Johnson's foot. We saw how this also arose between Proust's 'jealous man' and the other conditions of actual situations: *how much? who? how? where?* and *when?*. Insofar as the virtual doesn't resemble these conditions it surely cannot be relevant to them. However, we saw that Deleuze shares Kant's concern to account for experience without presupposing the forms it takes. We encounter actual objects and experience proceeds by means of these but how do we account for forceful individuations like the stone that stops our foot or will break a window when thrown at it with sufficient force? Could it be that something that does not resemble the actual intervenes in the course of actual experience in a way that makes it possible and is deeply relevant to it? In response to the defence of the actual mounted by Badiou and Hallward we will turn to the shared concern of Kant and Deleuze to account for experience without presupposing it.

What if we understand time as a whole in the sense we developed in Chapters 4 and 5 of this book? We saw that for Kant time is involved in the schematism of the categories. It is a very concrete and actualizing force, thanks to its four modes that mark out concrete situations. We saw that counting is a process that presupposes the involvement of time in situations and responds to problems that arise in the course of experience. Contrary to Peter Hallward's understanding we find that time as a whole can be deeply relevant to the actual and to the present moments that concern it. How does a Kantian reading of Deleuze allow us to respond to the apparent shortcomings of his account of experience as a whole? Keith Ansell Pearson argues that . . .

> . . . [t]he notion of individuation plays a crucial role in the unfolding of the psycho-biology of *Difference and Repetition* since it serves to mediate the virtual and the process of actualisation. [. . .] Deleuze stipulates that evolution does not simply progress from one actual term to another, or from general to particular, and this is precisely because there is the intermediary of an individuation which creates a realm of difference between the virtual and its actualisation. (Ansell Pearson 1999: 94)[9]

Ansell Pearson's reading of Deleuze's account of individuation draws upon the biological theory that he engages with (ibid.: 4). I took a different course when I explored individuation in terms of the literary models Deleuze develops. However, both biological and literary models relate the actual and the virtual in a way that is Kantian. They both introduce a 'realm' that is between the actual and the virtual. This realm secures the conditions of actual situations, it makes the virtual relevant to the actual while preserving and realizing their difference. Thus a forceful individuation is relevant to the actual but can change it in fundamental ways. A larval subject plays a very full role in actual situations and yet when and where it will occur is not predictable. We also saw that individuation relates the actual and the virtual in a way that allows them to reciprocally determine one another. It ensures that the actual can make a difference to the virtual. Thus the larval subject is a category of any situation and this category draws upon both the actual and the virtual. It draws upon the power of the virtual to make things different without specifying this in actual ways. It also draws upon the actual ways in which it is realized as a larval subject, such as in the actual relations and strategies of jealousy. Thus, while the actual decisions made by someone who is jealous do not fully account for experience, they do contribute to this account by making it possible for a larval subject to be realized in specific ways. We saw that while the course of experience is unpredictable, because a new larval subject can occur at any time, the choices of someone afflicted by jealousy can affect the course of jealousy. There is then a balance to be struck between specific details that enrich the actual and the pure virtual emotions that do not specify anything but are always realized in specific ways in actual situations. This helps avoid Badiou's conclusion that the actual is collapsed into the virtual, that it is devalued and neglected because it has no reality in itself and thus no significant contribution to make. It helps keep the actual and the virtual in play as non-resembling but necessary conditions of experience through their shared project of individuation. We saw in Chapter 6 that this aspect of Deleuze's account can be developed using Kant's way of arguing in his architectonic method. Now we are able to form conclusions about how this does not simply develop an aspect of Deleuze's account of experience but contributes significantly to his account as a whole. We can now see that Deleuze's version of Kant's Metaphysical Deduction ensures that the conditions of actual situations are not swept away by the virtual. In the face of challenges by Badiou and Hallward, the integrity of Deleuze's account as a whole can be defended using a Kantian form of argument.

I sought to justify my textual focus in the introduction to this book. I argued that the *Critique of Pure Reason* needs to be presented on its own terms and that these terms are outlined in the architectonic method. This has led me to present a distinctive reading of the text and question the approach of commentators who isolate parts of the whole. I argued that certain limitations commonly identified in Kant's account of experience can be traced to the reading strategy we employ. Such things as the relation between disjunctive judgement and the category of community were shown to be convincing insofar as they were related as parts of a wider whole. I also argued that this strategy would allow us to relate Kant and Deleuze with positive results for our understanding of how Deleuze's account of experience is to be further integrated and made more convincing. I allied these two thinkers on the basis of their methods, the problem-setting and forms of argument they both engage in. Similarities emerged that led me to focus upon and develop one aspect of Deleuze's account of experience, his notion of individuation, allowing me to conclude that the virtual does not undermine his account as a whole. I have been able to develop the role that Kant's methods and forms of argument can play in contemporary philosophical debates. It therefore seems that reading Kant's *Critique of Pure Reason* on its own terms is a worthwhile undertaking, one that can make a significant contribution to both Kant and Deleuze studies.

Notes

Introduction

1 In this book I will follow the convention of referring to Ideas with a capital 'I' in order to distinguish the philosophical use of the term from its more common use. As we shall see, in Kant's philosophical account of experience Ideas play a role alongside concepts and sensations.

2 For example, Peter Hallward argues that Kant's influence is insignificant because the role of thinkers such as Spinoza and Leibniz largely exclude Kant. See Hallward 2006: 12.

3 In this book I will argue that Kant allows Deleuze to understand the relation between time as a whole and concrete cases of experience. We will not explore the relation between the influences of Kant and Bergson on Deleuze's thought because this would be a considerable undertaking and would prevent us from investigating Kant's role in sufficient depth. However, we may note that the understanding of time that Deleuze locates in Bergson involves the 'coexistence' of the whole of the past and the 'leap' we make when we place ourselves in the past (Deleuze 1991: 61). In Chapters 4 and 5 of this book I will argue that Kant contributes an understanding of time's role in the present, in concrete cases, rather than considering time as it exists in itself. This means that we do not need to 'leap' into the past to discover time but discern it through its role in the present.

4 This claim is also made by Constantin Boundas (2005: 261), Ray Brassier (2008: 7) and Joe Hughes (2009: 11).

5 For example, Michael Bowles develops the implications of the Anticipations of Perception for our understanding of the nature and role of matter in the *Critique of Pure Reason* as a whole (Bowles 2000: 1–18).

6 A 1963 essay by Deleuze entitled 'The Idea of Genesis in Kant's Esthetics' proposes that '. . . the *Critique of Judgment*, in its esthetic part, does not simply exist to complete the other two Critiques: in fact, it provides them with a ground. The *Critique of Judgment* uncovers the *ground* presupposed by the other two Critiques: a free agreement of the faculties. Every determinate agreement can be traced back to the free indeterminate agreement which makes the others possible in general' (DI: 58). Deleuze also proposes this reading in his *Kant's Critical Philosophy* (KCP: 68) and in the fourth of his formulas in 'On Four Poetic Formulas That Might Summarize the Kantian Philosophy' (ECC: 33–5).

7 Joe Hughes takes this approach, arguing that '[i]n the third Critique, everything changes' (Hughes 2009: 3–4).

Chapter 1

1   The 'external' for Kant would also refer to what is outside of experience. As I noted in the introduction to this book, Kant refers to this as the 'thing in itself' as opposed to the 'appearances' that are actually involved in, or internal to, the formation of objective knowledge through the cognition of experience. My focus in this chapter will be upon how Kant seeks to avoid relying upon what is given in experience so that we can understand the form of argument he proposes. However, in the conclusion to this book I will return to the distinction between appearances and an 'in itself' reality in order to show that, on the basis of the reading I am here developing, this distinction is not in fact presupposed in Kant's account of theoretical cognition in the *Critique of Pure Reason*.

2   In the *Critique of Pure Reason* the term 'possible experience' is often used negatively. It tells us what cognition must restrict itself to, possible experience, and what it must not inquire into, that which is outside of possible experience. However, its positive meaning is found in the fact that all cognition is to be realized within it (CPR: A146/B185). As we shall see, possible experience is restricted to certain conditions of possibility but for Kant this is what makes experience possible in the fullest sense. It is this positive meaning that we will be focusing upon and exploring in this chapter. Also of note in the phrase 'cognition of possible experience' is the use of the term 'cognition' rather than 'knowledge'. Cognition (*erkenntnis*) in Kant's account needs to be distinguished from knowledge (*wissen*) because while knowledge is a finished product of cognition, cognition is an ongoing process. Knowledge is produced by cognition; it relies upon the sufficiency of the judgements made by cognition. Furthermore, for Kant we can give a complete account of cognition and thus re-found this process once and for all while knowledge is something that can always be extended. This will become clearer as we explore his account.

3   Kant argues in favour of this conclusion in his second Analogy in the Analytic of Principles of the *Critique of Pure Reason*. We will explore this in the fifth chapter of this book as part of the unfolding of the architectonic.

4   'By *organon* namely we understand an instruction for bringing about a certain cognition. This implies, however, that I already know the object of the cognition that is to be produced according to certain rules. An organon of the sciences is therefore not mere logic, because it presupposes the exact knowledge of the sciences, of their objects and sources' (L: 15).

5   In his *Metaphysical Foundations of Natural Science* Kant gives us a further sense of the wider meaning of the term architectonic. He argues that all 'proper' natural science must have a 'pure' part in order to provide the basis for 'apodictic certainty' (MF: 5). This pure part is distinguished from what is empirical or based upon experience, something which denies the certainty Kant values in genuine sciences. Whether or not a discipline has a pure part will determine its place in Kant's architectonic. Two instructive examples are chemistry and psychology. In the preface to the *Metaphysical Foundations of Natural Science* Kant associates the purity and apodictic certainty of a genuine or proper science with systematic and unified cognition (ibid.: 4). On these grounds he denies chemistry the status of a genuine science, citing the empirical basis of its methods which make it

'. . . a systematic art rather than a science' (ibid.). It would seem that chemistry is downgraded because in Kant's time it had not been given a rigorous mathematical foundation. I will seek to show that mathematics is key to providing the apodictic certainty and purity Kant seeks at the basis of all proper or genuine sciences. Psychology is our second example. Kant describes empirical psychology in his *Anthropology from a Pragmatic Point of View* as '. . . a methodological compilation of the perceptions in us, which deliver material for a diary of an *observer of oneself*, and easily lead to enthusiasm and madness' (A: 20). Empirical psychology is not founded upon a priori concepts and principles because it is unable to rigorously analyse the situation it finds itself in: '. . . the situation with these inner experiences is not as it is with *external* experience of objects in space, where the objects appear next to each other and *permanently* fixed. Inner sense sees the relations of its determinations only in time, hence in flux, where the stability of observation necessary for experience does not occur' (ibid.: 22–3). Kant's view of empirical psychology is something fundamental to his account and cannot be explained by the state of this discipline in his time. I will explore the importance for Kant of the psychological subject being passive because it is situated in time. This will show us why empirical psychology cannot play a role in accounting for experience.

6 This is an assertion I would justify by pointing to the absence of the term 'architectonic' in the indexes of many more recent books on Kant's *Critique of Pure Reason* (e.g. it is absent from Altman 2008). When it does appear it does not play a prominent role and does not unify the reading that is given (in Buroker 2006 it is referred to on only two pages).

7 Kant's concern with this issue is clear when he is discussing the right of philosophy to examine the foundations of other faculties in *The Conflict of the Faculties*. He argues that other disciplines become 'miracle-workers' if philosophy is not allowed to publicly challenge the notion that they can provide all the answers. This would prevent people from relying upon such disciplines while failing to engage in thought and activity themselves (Kant 1992: 51). One could argue that this concern is highly relevant today when disciplines are increasingly specialized and this undermines attempts to gain a broader view of knowledge.

8 In the introduction to *Kant Trouble* Diane Morgan writes that '. . . this book does not try to sum up Kant and his philosophy. Instead, it contents itself with highlighting an ongoing problematization within the Kantian system of the possibility of founding the progressive Enlightenment project securely in the here and now' (Morgan 2000: 2). This is the problem that the here and now, in all its concrete detail, escapes or exceeds the attempts to unify knowledge and universalize the principles of cognition that the Enlightenment represents. Thus instead of the foundation of a secure and complete system we have a construction characterized by what escapes it, by problems that are at work in systems without this being explicit to their authors.

9 The similarity between this presentation of Kant's architectonic method and Hegel's dialectical method must be noted. Everything is internal to the relation of two opposite poles of experience, echoing strongly Hegel's following presentation of his dialectic: 'Everything around us can be regarded an example of dialectic. For we know that, instead of being fixed and ultimate, everything finite is alterable and perishable, and this is nothing but the dialectic of the finite, through which

the latter, being explicitly the other of itself, is driven beyond what it immediately is and overturns into its opposite' (Hegel 1998: 172). In this dialectic relations between opposites move thought and understanding forward and the cognition of experience is internal to this movement. However, the role of negation in this dialectical relation distinguishes Hegel's account of experience from Kant's architectonic method. As we shall see, the relation of the synthetic and the a priori makes it possible to include more and more of the concrete in the abstract structures of cognition. Kant's account is focused upon this positive problem rather than upon how negation determines the extension of experience. Thus Hegel will write that when: '. . . the result is conceived as it is in truth, namely, as a *determinate* negation, a new form has thereby immediately arisen, and in the negation the transition is made through which the progress through the complete series of forms comes about of itself' (Hegel 1977: 52).

¹⁰ Kant argues that we should value equally the abstract and the concrete aspects of our experience, the way we are affected by objects and our ability to think these objects (CPR: A51/B75).

¹¹ In his lectures on logic Kant argues that concepts must be relevant to and engaged with the concrete if we are to account for our cognition of experience through concepts: 'The expressions of the *abstract* and the *concrete* thus refer not so much to the concepts in themselves – for every concept is an abstract concept – as rather to their use only. And this use again can have varying degrees, according as one treats a concept now in a more, now in a less abstract or more concrete way, that is, either omits or adds a greater or smaller number of determinations. Through abstract use a concept gets nearer to the highest genus; through concrete use, however, nearer to the individual' (L: 105–6). Here also Kant argues that abstract and concrete are of equal value. He argues that since we cognize little in many things through abstraction and much in fewer things through concretion, they both have something unique to add to cognition (ibid.: 106).

¹² Roger Scruton argues that Kant does rely upon a theory of innate ideas in giving his account of the role of the a priori (Scruton 1982: 26). In response Quassim Cassam points to Kant's words in his essay 'On a Discovery According to which Any New Critique of Pure Reason Has Been Made Superfluous by an Earlier One': '. . . the *Critique* [*of Pure Reason*] admits absolutely no divinely implanted or innate *representations*' (Kant 1973: 135; cited in Cassam 1999: 92 n18). However, even if Kant does not invoke an innate component of the mind, his presentation of the role of the a priori has led different commentators to argue that the a priori must have a 'subjective origin'. There is surely nowhere else for the a priori to be located if it is not on the side of sensation. However, I will argue that this concern to 'locate' elements of Kant's account of cognition in experience presupposes what is to be accounted for. In recognition of the importance of this issue in Kant scholarship I will return to it in the conclusion to this book. This treatment will be delayed in order to first build up a case for reading Kant's account of the a priori without recourse to subjective origins.

¹³ Whether or not Kant indulges in psychologism in his account of experience has been the subject of a major and ongoing debate in Kant studies. Gary Hatfield asks whether Kant was forced to rely upon psychology despite his concern to avoid presupposing what he is trying to account for (Hatfield 1992: 213). Did he

use psychological concepts and modes of explanation when such things are what he needs to account for (ibid.: 214)? I will seek to follow the progress of the architectonic method in order to present Kant's response to these critical questions.

14 Béatrice Longuenesse uses the phrase 'silent judgement' in order to capture the work of the a priori before we are aware of it (KCJ: 122f.).

15 Morris Kline sketches the view of mathematics current in Kant's time: 'As of 1800 [Kant died in 1804], mathematics rested upon two foundations, the number system and Euclidean geometry' (Kline 1981: 445). He adds that '. . . mathematicians would have emphasized the latter because many facts about the number system, and about irrational numbers especially, were not logically established or clearly understood. Indeed, those properties of the number system that were universally accepted were still proved by resorting to geometric arguments, much as the Greeks had done 2500 years earlier. Hence one could say that Euclidean geometry was the most solidly constructed branch of mathematics, the foundation on which many other branches were erected, the surest body of knowledge man possessed' (ibid.).

16 By formalism in the foundations of mathematics we mean the view that axioms are not seen to have any meaning or to be open to interpretation. There is a syntax that ensures that these propositions are well formed but no semantics as there is in Kant's understanding of the foundations of mathematics, according to which axioms have a well-founded physical meaning. For Kant they find their meaning in how space is constructed or synthesized. Morris Kline argues that the axioms of Euclidean geometry were seen as self-evident because what they tell us about physical space is supported by immediate experience (Kline 1981: 446).

17 In this book I will argue that Kant makes it a virtue of any argument that it is not dry and tedious. Despite his self-criticism in the *Prolegomena* he does seek to present arguments that are neither dry nor tedious at key points in the unfolding of the architectonic of the *Critique of Pure Reason*. In Chapter 3 of this book I will consider how the Metaphysical Deduction can be understood in this light.

18 Stern's first example in the above quotation is the argument that forms Kant's 'Refutation of Idealism' in the *Critique of Pure Reason* (B275–B279). It argues on the basis of the work on time-determination that precedes it in the Analytic of Principles which itself relies upon the Table of Categories established in the Metaphysical Deduction. Therefore, this transcendental argument relies upon Kant's systematic account of experience as a whole to argue that inner experience and outer experience are inseparable. This account is something we will continue to explore in Chapters 2, 3, 4 and 5 of this book.

Chapter 2

1 The notion that imagination is a faculty or power is in fact rejected by Kant in the second edition of the *Critique of Pure Reason* (Kant 1996: 191, B152). I will discuss this in Chapter 4 of this book, which will be concerned with the imagination's power of schematism. However, in both editions of the text Kant refers to its role in mediating concepts and sensible intuitions through schematism.

2 Deleuze argues that Friedrich Nietzsche goes beyond Kant in pursuing an immanent and total critique, and that this necessarily culminates in destruction: 'Critique
   is destruction as joy, the aggression of the creator. The creator of values cannot
   be distinguished from a destroyer, from a criminal or from a critic: a critic of
   established values, reactive values and baseness' (NP: 87).

3 If we ask who has priority or most influence on Deleuze's theory of Ideas among
   the many names mentioned in Chapter 4 of *Difference and Repetition* we will find
   many answers in the secondary literature. These include Leibniz and structural-
   ism (Patton 1994: xii), Kant and Jung (Kerslake 2007: 70) and the mathematician
   Albert Lautman (Bogue 1989: 59).

4 Christian Kerslake develops such an approach when he writes that: 'I don't want
   to suggest that everything important in Deleuze comes back to Kant – but I
   do think that none of his explorations of other philosophers (Spinoza, Hume,
   Leibniz, Bergson) is comprehensible without a framework of Kantian and post-
   Kantian questions' (Kerslake 2002: 33, n4). If we consider Kant's account as
   a whole, how it is unified by setting problems and arguing in a certain way, this
   will enable us to locate a Kantian methodological framework that is shared by
   Deleuze.

5 Deleuze contrasts Kant and Foucault in these terms: '. . . Foucault differs in certain
   fundamental respects from Kant: the conditions are those of real experience
   (statements, for example, assume a limited corpus); they are on the side of the
   "object" and historical formation, not a universal subject (the *a priori* itself is
   historical); all are forms of exteriority' (Deleuze 1988: 60). We see Deleuze con-
   trasting Kant to a thinker who emphasizes real rather than possible experience
   and does this on the basis of an a priori that is not internal or located in the
   subject but external and historical. This means that experience can be extended
   through its real relations, through Ideas incarnated in sensation, rather than on
   the basis of subjective conditions of possibility that are imposed upon it. Like
   other readers of Kant that we've so far encountered Deleuze argues here that
   Kant's account has 'subjective origins'. This is something I will challenge in this
   thesis as well as seeking to locate their common ground in the methods they
   employ in accounting for experience.

Chapter 3

1 The chapter is entitled 'On the Guide for the Discovery of All Pure Concepts of
   Understanding'. Subsections 11 and 12 were added in the second edition of the
   Critique of Pure Reason.

2 Thomas Kaehao Swing is equally blunt: 'Kant never explains how the Table of
   Categories is derived from the Table of Judgements. He simply presents the two
   tables one after the other, apparently assuming that the derivation of one from
   the other is obvious. But it is one of the most baffling affairs in the *Critique* [*of Pure
   Reason*]' (Swing 1969: 19).

3 It follows that singular and infinite judgements are to be left out of Kant's Table
   of Judgements (ibid.: 159). As we will see, they were included because this table
   is concerned with securing an object of cognition. For Frege we should reject
   the role of ordinary language in logic and, according to Béatrice Longuenesse,

this would rule out Kant's categories of relation which he understands as being reducible to the grammar of sentences: 'And ordinary language itself is governed by the subjective, psychological intentions and associations of the speaker addressing a listener' (ibid.: 158; cf. Frege 1970).

4 In their introduction to Kant's lectures on logic, Robert S. Hartman and Wolfgang Schwartz write that '[c]ompared to a textbook in symbolic logic the Kantian *Logic* shows a marvellous philosophical richness. In particular, we find fully treated here the fundamental concept of any logic, the concept of concept, which cannot be found in a modern text on symbolic logic – just as one cannot find the concept of psyche in a modern psychology text' (Hartman and Schwartz 1988: xx–xxi).

5 Cited and translated by Henry E. Allison (KTI: 86).

6 See previous note.

7 This is not to suggest that these things are not objects of cognition but to focus upon them is to simplify the notion of an object of cognition and borrow from the habits and practices of a scholar. These are quite different from, for example, those of a mountain climber for whom the mountain is his overwhelming object of cognition.

8 However, Swing does not see this as a positive aspect of Kant's Metaphysical Deduction: 'We have repeatedly noted that there is a generic difference between formal and material concepts. Kant mistook their generic difference for a mere functional one. The entire Metaphysical Deduction hinges on this mistake' (ibid.: 43). We will argue that Kant formulates a transcendental and material logic not through neglect or ignorance of the nature of logic but because he seeks to account for experience in this way.

9 We note that this passage comes after the Metaphysical Deduction and at the beginning of the first edition Transcendental Deduction. However, Kant here speaks of 'deduction' rather than specifically of 'transcendental deduction'. We may therefore apply this to the Metaphysical Deduction in order to understand it better.

10 'The most admired deduction writer of Kant's time was J. S. Pütter, professor of law at Göttingen and coauthor of the textbook that Kant used in his frequent lectures on natural law' (ibid.: p. 33). Henrich argues that Kant seems to have learnt from Pütter's method of deduction writing. Pütter followed one of his legal deductions with a note entitled 'Brief Outline of the Zedwitz Case'. This method of presentation is echoed in Kant's second edition Transcendental Deduction which is followed by a similar summary entitled 'Brief Outline of the Deduction' (Ibid.: 34; CPR: B168–9).

11 Henrich attributes the description to a legal text from 1752 but gives no further reference.

12 Arthur Hassell writes that 'Germany was divided into some 300 petty states, the rulers of each of which had the right not only to tax, to impose custom duties, but also to make treaties, and to decide upon the form of religion to be professed within their respective dominions. [. . .] The [Holy Roman] Empire has become a nominal federation of independent princes, and the victory in the long struggle between the centrifugal and centripetal tendencies, between monarchy and aristocracy, rested with the centrifugal principle. [. . .] Germany, at the beginning of the eighteenth century, has lost all national feeling, a degradation of manners

had set in, and the dominant tone in the small states was fatal to the domestic life which, previous to the Thirty Years' War [1618–48], had proved the strength of the country' (Hassell 1929: 10–11). What's more 'All sense of German unity was lost; the French had taken Strassburg and Alsace; they were about to take Lorraine. The Imperial army could neither defend Germany from attack, nor could the Imperial forces put down internal disorder. The Seven Years' War [1756–63] exemplified the weakness of the Germanic body, the utter decay of the Holy Roman Empire, and the general confusion prevalent among all the Imperial institutions' (ibid: 13).

13 Georges Dicker contrasts Kant's notion of substance with the 'bundle theory', for which '. . . a thing is nothing but a collection of coexisting properties. By contrast, the substance theory says that a thing is composed not just of its various properties but also of a substance (often also called "substrate" or "*substratum*") distinct from all those properties, to which the properties all belong' (Dicker 2004: 73). Kant's notion of substance will be explored further in Chapter 5 of this book.

14 See CPR: A111. Werner S. Pluhar translates *Gewühle der Erscheinungen* as *crowd of appearances* rather than *welter of appearances*. It would also be possible to translate it as *throng of appearances* and capture the threat posed to cognition by appearances. As I argued in the previous chapter, the relation between the synthetic and the a priori is always precarious or problematic.

15 Kant links the cognition of objects of experience to our awareness of an identical subject possessing the abilities and conceptual forms presented in the two tables (CPR: A108).

16 It will be noted that Chapter 2 of the *Analytic of Concepts*, which contains both Transcendental Deductions, is entitled 'On the Deduction of the Pure Concepts of Understanding'. However, the categories or pure concepts of the understanding that actually make up the Table of Categories are not specifically referred to. Therefore the Transcendental Deduction would be valid even if we revised the Table of Categories but the Analytic of Principles is organized according to this table. As we shall see in Chapter 5 of this book, the four parts of the third section of the second chapter of the *Analytic of Principles* correspond to the four divisions of the Table of Categories.

Chapter 4

1 It is interesting to note Deleuze's interest in Heidegger's reading of Kant. Christian Kerslake uncovers Deleuze's early interest in a tradition, stretching from Kant to Heidegger, which concerns itself with the ability of a system to be autonomously self-grounding. The source of this discovery is the transcript of a 1956 seminar entitled 'What is Grounding?' (Kerslake 2008: 30; lecture course available in French as 'Qu'est-ce que Fonder?' at www.webdeleuze.com/php/sommaire.html, I rely here on Kerslake's account of it). This reflects the shared concern of Kant and Deleuze with immanence, something that I considered in Chapter 2 of this book. We must not look for origins or starting points outside of the critical account of experience we are giving. Intriguingly, Kerslake reports Deleuze's interest in the architectonic method: 'Deleuze claims that Kant's own

approach to grounding is vitiated by his inability to settle on the side of method or system. Kant places his "Architectonic" of the realization of reason right at the end of the *Critique of Pure Reason*, when he should have placed the construction of the system at the beginning' (ibid.: 34). This leads Deleuze to favour Heidegger's Kant, a Kant concerned with a method for dealing with human finitude. Finitude is not dealt with by looking outside of experience but through autonomous self-grounding. This is something I will develop shortly by talking about the 'transcendence within finitude' that Heidegger locates in Kant's account of experience.

² In *Being and Time* Heidegger warns against understanding the world in terms of 'present-at-hand' properties, something that is informing his concern with an unknown common root in Kant's system. He argues that we must not approach the world with the attitude of a theorist, merely observing what is given or present in our experience of things. This would be to take things in abstraction from how they are given and how they exist in time more broadly construed so that: 'Entities are grasped in their Being as "presence"; this means that they are understood with regard to a definite mode of time – the *"Present"*' (Heidegger 1962: 47). If we disturb the involvement of things in the production of experience they are seen as present-at-hand rather than being what Heidegger calls 'ready-to-hand'. We gain merely a collection of present moments or present-at-hand things rather than an understanding of the givenness or production of experience that is always ongoing. We will see how relevant this is to Kant's understanding of the schematism as a unique and original ability that draws ultimately upon time in order to realize concepts in the synthesis or production of experience.

³ The addition of German terms in square brackets was made using the original German text (KVR: 77–8); cited in Caygill 1995: 210.

⁴ Howard Caygill refers to *Gemüt* as embodying certain capacities or faculties on the basis of an essay by Kant entitled 'From Soemmerring's *On the Organ of the Soul* (1796)'. Here Kant defines the two senses of the soul we are concerned with: 'By *mind* one means only the *faculty* of combining the given representations and effectuating the unity of empirical apperception (*animus*), not yet substance (*anima*) according to its nature, which is entirely distinct from that matter and form which is abstracted here; by this we gain that, with regard to the thinking subject, we must not cross over into metaphysics, which is concerned with pure consciousness and with the latter's *a priori* unity in synthesis (*zusammensetzung*) of given representations (i.e., concerned with the understanding); rather we are concerned with the power of the imagination, to whose intuitions, as empirical representations (even in the absence of objects), there can be assumed to correspond impressions in the brain (actually habits [*habitus*] of reproduction), which belong to a whole of inner self-intuition' (Kant 2007: 223, the addition in square brackets was made by the translator; cited in Caygill 1995: 210). We note that Kant is here concerned with the empirical use of the imagination and this is distinct from its pure or transcendental role. The empirical role of the imagination is made possible by its pure role insofar as this is co-ordinated with other faculties in a systematic process that accounts for the cognition of possible experience as such.

This passage also reflects the Aristotelian origin of the distinction between the two senses of the soul when it distinguishes *Gemüt* and *Seele* respectively as *Animus* and *Anima*. Empirical apperception or empirical consciousness is referred to as *animus* in a way that reflects Aristotle's understanding of the soul in *De Anima*: 'For if the eye was an animal, then sight would be its soul, being the substance of the eye that is in accordance with the account of it' (Aristotle 1986: 158). This definition reflects the analogy between an eye and Kant's Table of Categories which we considered in the third section of the previous chapter of this book. Rather than seeking the soul as an object Aristotle sees it as the centre of certain capacities that define and account for it. Thus he locates two capacities in the soul of an animal, those of discernment and locomotion (ibid.: 211). We can define what an animal *is* by considering what it *does*. He avoids asking 'what is the soul?' and as a result does not treat it as an object or substance but as a set of capacities or faculties that play a part in accounting for experience. We must not conflate the thought of Kant and Aristotle here but we can compare their methodological approaches to investigating the soul. We saw in Chapter 2 of this book that the architectonic method sets problems whose objects are undetermined rather than seeking to determine all objects of cognition in advance or ask questions like 'what is the soul?'.

5   Hence Kant's concern to deal with empirical psychology in his lectures on Anthropology and his 1798 book *Anthropology from a Pragmatic Point of View*. Kant also postpones his treatment of what he calls rational psychology and presents his critique of it in the paralogisms chapter of the Transcendental Dialectic of the *Critique of Pure Reason*. In contrast to the rich elaboration of the synthesis of experience he is concerned with when he talks about the schematism, he severely limits the role of rational psychology in accounting for experience. It's only material is the *I think* or transcendental unity of apperception which is a part of the account of experience that needs to be justified (CPR: A343/B401). This means that it is unable to locate a soul prior to the synthesis of experience that would be the location of powers or faculties like the imagination. Kant calls the *I think* an empty presentation (ibid.: A346/B404). Thus, while it might try to look for an object, rational psychology is only really able to reflect upon something that Kant considers to be the mere awareness of the unified activity of thought. It follows that empirical psychology is too full of things given in experience, and rational psychology is too empty, for either to be able to provide an account of the role of concepts in the synthesis of possible experience.

6   A word of caution is needed here because in referring to the imagination as a 'faculty' we ignore Kant's concern in the second edition Transcendental Deduction of the *Critique of Pure Reason* to understand the schematism as the understanding's action upon sensibility. We cited this in our discussion of Heidegger's reading of Kant earlier in this chapter. The implication is that, as well as not being original, the imagination's transcendental power of schematism is not a faculty alongside understanding and sensation. However, our reading of the schematism chapter has led us to understand it as a 'secret art' that responds to a problem internal to the architectonic. Thus while questions about its origin persist it is clear that Kant talks about it as an art or skill (*Kunst*) in the schematism chapter of the *Critique of Pure Reason* (KRV: 178).

7   In seeking to clear the ground of presuppositions about how experience is produced Deleuze wants to account for experience without presupposing what is given in experience. To this end he refers here to Antonin Artaud's notion

of a 'theatre of cruelty'. Artaud develops this notion in writings such as 'The Theatre of Cruelty: First Manifesto' (Artaud 1976: 242–51). Here Artaud writes that '[t]he question for the theater, then, is to create a metaphysics of speech, gesture, and expression, in order to rescue it from its psychological and human stagnation' (ibid.: 243). This is a theatre too cruel for psychological and human things like scripts, actors and spectators to survive, to undergo the spatio-temporal dynamisms that are here at work in producing experience. Rather than having to mediate human concepts and the sensations that situate human beings, a theatre of cruelty stages the direct communication of its elements so that, as Artaud writes, '[i]t flows into the sensibility' (ibid.). This is valued by Deleuze as a model for accounting for experience without presupposing what one is accounting for.

Chapter 5

[1] The role of time in Kant's *Critique of Pure Reason* is something that Deleuze often takes forward in his own thought. He begins the preface to the English edition of *Cinema 2* by acknowledging Kant's role in the philosophy of time he wants to draw upon: 'Over several centuries, from the Greeks to Kant, a revolution took place in philosophy: the subordination of time to movement was reversed, time ceases to be the measurement of normal movement, it increasingly appears for itself and creates paradoxical movements. Time is out of joint: Hamlet's words signify that time is no longer subordinated to movement, but rather movement to time' (Deleuze 1989: xi). He goes on to argue that a similar revolution took place in cinema after World War II (ibid.). This presents us with a selective reading of Kant because it takes forward his contribution to the philosophy of time which, as we've seen, develops only the concrete aspect or pole of his architectonic.

[2] Georges Dicker argues that '. . . Kant associates all three categories of quantity with only a single principle, . . .' (Dicker 2004: 62). From this it would seem to follow that the order of the three categories of quantity in the Table of Categories has no contribution to make to the formation of this principle. The Table of Categories thus ceases to be our systematic guide because we are guided by the process of counting or by the lessons of mathematics. For Dicker the Axioms of Intuition complements the Transcendental Aesthetic by showing that mathematics is capable of exhibiting a priori truths (ibid.: 63). This challenges the reading we've been giving because, in Chapter 1 of this book, we argued that such isolation arguments in the *Critique of Pure Reason* play a supporting role in its architectonic. The unfolding of the Analytic of Principles under the guidance of a Table of Categories in the Transcendental Analytic is part of a wider transcendental argument because it doesn't isolate the a priori but shows it to be a condition of possibility for experience as such. It can be supported in a unique way by the lessons of mathematics but we cannot substitute an isolation argument for a transcendental argument. We've just seen that Howard Caygill provides a response to Dicker's reading by showing how the three categories of quantity and their specific order are involved in the formulation of the Axioms of Intuition. Dicker's reference to the Axioms of Intuition being a single principle neglects

the more significant fact that three categories are involved. The Axioms of Intuition is certainly not split into three sections and three principles like the Analogies of Experience. However, the fact that Kant does not treat the role of each category separately or organize the Axioms of Anticipation into three sections does not mean that the Table of Categories and its tripartite structure ceases to be his guide.

3 We considered Kant's relation to mathematics in Chapter 1 of this book. We saw that his view of mathematics is 'intuitionist' or 'constructivist' because the foundations or truths of mathematics are for him established synthetically rather than purely formally and in abstraction from concrete cases. In the following passage from the *Metaphysical Foundations of Natural Science* he locates a truth about appearances that mathematics is well placed to reveal: 'At issue here is not the transformation of semblance into truth, but of appearances into experience; for, in the case of semblance, the understanding with its object-determining judgments is always in play, although it is in danger of taking the subjective for objective; in the appearance, however, no judgment of the understanding is to be met with at all – which needs to be noted, not merely here, but in the whole of philosophy, because otherwise, when appearances are in question, and this term is taken to have the same meaning as semblance, one is always poorly understood' (MF: 94). Appearances do not lack an object or 'thing in itself' that would complete them. We should not aim at truths behind appearances but at more productive ways of realizing appearances in the synthesis of possible experience. Mathematics treats objects in a revealing and truthful way when, as we saw, it understands them as a series of potential parts of objects. It does not take objects for granted, locating them behind appearances, but focuses upon the synthesis through which objects emerge. However, as we noted in Chapter 1, mathematics can only provide a supporting argument in Kant's architectonic. It reveals or isolates truths about how experience is to be accounted for but does not have the scope of a transcendental argument.

4 Kant argues that we can never meet an empty space and that this fullness is the source of variety in the degrees of reality or intensive magnitudes which characterize experience (ibid.: A174/B216).

5 Deleuze's use of Kant's account of intensive magnitudes tells us more about his closeness to, and distance from, Kant. We note that Kant limits his investigation of intensity to magnitudes or quantities. Deleuze has a wider view of the life and role of intensities. They actually account for extensity. Kant moved in this direction when he separated intensive magnitudes from magnitudes built up in extension. Deleuze wants to go further so that intensities are now qualitative as well as quantitative. Therefore, intensities will not only differentiate sensation in every way but also provide their own power to do so (DR: 222). However, Deleuze echoes Kant when he argues that a temperature is not composed of other temperatures or a speed of other speeds (ibid.: 237). It is not built up in extension but is indivisible because it is an irreducible difference. It is not made up of parts already given in experience. Deleuze, like Kant, is keen to avoid involving anything given in experience in accounting for experience but he will go to greater lengths to liberate intensity.

6 Melnick also factors in the coefficient of friction of the balls with respect to the billiard table (ibid.).

7 Although we are not considering Kant's 'Refutation of Idealism' section here we must note its place in the Postulates of Empirical Thought As Such, an addition that was made in the second edition of the *Critique of Pure Reason*. As we saw in the first chapter of this book, Kant uses a transcendental argument to draw out the conditions of possibility of something already accepted by his opponent. He notes that for an empirical or material idealist we are conscious of our own existence as something determined in and by time (CPR: B275). However, in order to avoid impoverishing possible experience for the empirical use of the understanding, we must not treat this as an isolated experience like the empirical or material idealist does. Such a thinker is plagued by doubt about the outside world rather than being armed with Kant's Postulates. Kant seeks to prove that a condition of the possibility of the truth accepted by the empirical or material idealist is the existence of things outside the self and the horizon of time as the ultimate form of the synthesis of possible experience. I am in fact conscious of my existence in time or of being determined in time. This is not an isolated experience but is included in a much wider process, the process of all temporal determination through the Table of Categories. In this way the horizons of the empirical use of the understanding are widened precisely because they remain within the bounds of possible experience. As we saw in Chapter 1, for Kant an inclusive and internalizing account of experience provides the fullest horizon of empirical cognition.

Chapter 6

1 Deleuze describes the term 'being of the sensible' as uniting the two senses of the 'aesthetic' which we can identify in Kant's critical philosophy. One is put forward in the *Critique of Pure Reason* in its Transcendental Aesthetic and the other in the *Critique of Judgement* in its Analytic of the Beautiful. The combination of these two senses of the Aesthetic provides another way of developing Deleuze's critical engagement with Kant's Table of Categories (see DR: 68). Deleuze seeks an account of sensation which provides this combination in order that we can account for experience from within sensation rather than having to rely upon an external Table of Categories. For him this is to recognize what sensation is capable of, to find the conditions of experience in sensation alone. I have been considering how Kant's account, when read in a unified way, can relate to Deleuze's thought. I am seeking to show that while he rejects the Table of Categories, Deleuze's project resonates with the method and form of argument that is behind it. My justification, as set out in the introduction to this book, for excluding the *Critique of Judgement* from the present study is that it allows me to pursue a new avenue in relating Kant and Deleuze. I argued that while Deleuze finds an account of the relations of the faculties in Kant's *Critique of Judgement*, we learn from the *Critique of Pure Reason* about the relation of the synthetic and the a priori. This allows us to consider the role of Kant's architectonic method and then relate what we've learnt to Deleuze's account of experience.

2 Another example put forward by Jared Diamond in his *Guns, Germs and Steel* is of the vicuñas, an Andean wild camel, which has never been domesticated.

The wool of this animal is very fine and light, making it a valuable commodity. Domestication would therefore be very worthwhile, especially because methods of shearing wild vicuñas involve trapping them or killing them. Diamond accounts for the failure to domesticate vicuñas by pointing to their '. . . long and elaborate courtship ritual before mating, a ritual inhibited in captivity; male vicuñas' fierce intolerance of each other; and their requirement for both a year-round feeding territory and a separate year-round sleeping territory' (ibid.: 170). Thus we find that the way space and time is occupied by these animals is what makes them individual in a very forceful way. When pitted against the individuating difference of these animals, the force that dominates in situations where it is trapped or in captivity, human strategies of domestication have failed.

3 Thus if we consider Elias Canetti's *Crowds and Power* we have many different types of crowd presented to us (Canetti 1973). However, they would have in common the individuating difference or larval subject that is dominant in each case. The dominant force gives rise to types of crowd depending upon what mood it expresses. The list of these is open-ended. There is the baiting crowd, fight crowd, feast crowd, slow crowd, invisible crowd and so forth, in Canetti's account. In itself this category, secured by the *who?* question, is empty, but it is realized in an open-ended way by the individuation of crowds over the course of experience.

4 Deleuze develops the role of narcissism in *Difference and Repetition* at page 75. This involves a concern with the individuation of the self through the accumulation of habits which are first of all found in the world but are then 'contracted' in a self. In the context of our present discussion this refers to the individuating differences that become habits which constitute the self.

5 This is in fact the historical example, used by Brusseau throughout the final section of *Isolated Experiences* (181–95), of Isabelle Eberhardt who was born in 1877 and died in 1904 (181).

6 'Although each was of a type absolutely different from the others, they all had beauty; but to tell the truth I had seen them for so short a time, and without venturing to look hard at them, that I had not yet individualized any of them. Except for one, whose straight nose and dark complexion singled her out from the rest, like the Arabian king in a Renaissance picture of the Epiphany, they were known to me only by a pair of hard, obstinate and mocking eyes, for instance, or by cheeks whose pinkness had a coppery tint reminiscent of geraniums; and even these features I had not yet indissolubly attached to any one of these girls rather than to another; . . .' (WBG: 427–8).

7 On the different structures of sensation that the sonata and septet give rise to, Proust writes: 'Whereas the sonata opened upon a lily-white pastoral dawn, dividing its fragile purity only to hover in the delicate yet compact entanglement of a rustic bower of honeysuckle against white geraniums, it was upon flat, unbroken surfaces like those of the sea on a morning that threatens storm, in the midst of an eerie silence, in an infinite void, that this unknown universe was drawn from the silence and the night to build up gradually before me. This redness, so new, so absent from the tender, pastoral, unadorned sonata, tinged all the sky, as dawn does, with a mysterious hope' (CF: 282). In the midst of this new landscape is the 'little phrase' but it is '. . . no longer the cooing of a dove as in the sonata . . .' (ibid.) but '. . . something like a mystical cock-crow, the ineffable but ear-piercing call of eternal morning' (ibid.: 283). Here the 'little

phrase' gives rise to a new structure of sensation for the narrator, showing its potential role in the artistic creativity which he is distracted from by the recurrence in himself of 'the jealous man'.

8   Thus in volume 6 of *In Search of Lost Time, Time Regained*, it seems that the work of art exemplifies the role of a larval subject. The narrator finds that '[i]t is our passions which draw the outline of our books, the ensuing intervals of repose which write them' (TF: 269). It is the activation of a larval subject, passion as a pure and basic determination, that provides the outline or the categories of works of art just as it had done for jealous scenes. However, this process has now become creative and the narrator becomes an artist rather than remaining in the world of jealousy.

9   In *Proust and Signs* Deleuze characterizes the stages of the search for 'lost time' as different worlds full of the 'signs' emitted by subjects and objects which are interpreted by the narrator. These are the world of worldly signs, the world of love, the world of sensuous impressions or qualities, and the world of art (PS: 3–14). The world of art is superior in the sense that at this stage the narrator interprets signs without seeking an object or subject behind them as the source of their meaning, and thus without associating them with anything recognizable or given in experience. There remains nothing that resembles the past and there is nothing empirically recognizable about the way these signs are incarnated: 'At the end of the Search, the interpreter understands what has escaped him in the case of the madeleine or even of the steeples: that the material meaning is nothing without an ideal essence that it incarnates' (ibid.: 13). Signs are treated as multiple without this signifying any lack, such as the lack of the single, unified self which is the illusion constitutive of jealousy, but are now the source of creativity in the work of art.

10 Thus when the narrator is assured of his knowledge of what Albertine is doing, assured of having her captive or under surveillance, he becomes indifferent to her because his jealousy loses its force. He falls in and out of love with her according to the emergence and disappearance of this larval subject as the reason behind his search for knowledge of her. Thus the narrator's suspicions and frantic concerns about Albertine's relations with Mlle Léa and her friends have behind them 'the jealous man', which is expressed in his schemes to prevent her meeting them. However, when such a scheme succeeds this larval subject is no longer dominant and behind his thoughts and actions: 'Whereupon, the danger of her renewing relations with them having been averted, it at once began to lose its importance in my eyes and I was amazed, seeing with what ease it had been averted, that I should have supposed that I would not succeed in averting it' (CF: 171–2). He continues: 'I no longer felt the slightest impatience to see Albertine. The certainty that she was at this moment engaged in shopping with Françoise, that she would return with her at an approaching moment which I would willingly have postponed, lit up like a calm and radiant star a period of time which I would now have been far better pleased to spend alone' (ibid.: 172–3).

11 After Albertine's death the narrator searches his memory for signs of the truth as well as questioning her friend Andrée (ibid.: 625–8, 686–9) and even asks Aimé, the headwaiter at the Grand Hotel in Balbec, to investigate the nature of her activities in Balbec (ibid.: 563) and in Touraine (ibid.: 598).

Conclusion

[1] 'In order to set limits to coherent thinking, it is not necessary, as Kant, in spite of his disclaimers, attempted to do, to think both sides of those limits [of possible experience]. It is enough to think up to them' (Strawson 1966: 44).

[2] We must again clarify this reality as theoretical for Kant because in the case of practical cognition something external is invoked. This does not involve possible objects of theoretical cognition but rather objects of practical cognition. These include a self who is free or unconditioned and undetermined by theoretical concepts like cause and effect. This postulate of practical reason allows us to think about the self as free in moral situations but must not interfere with our theoretical cognition of the self as subject to cause and effect and hence as conditioned. For Kant practical reason postulates things outside of experience solely in order to account for morality: 'These postulates are not theoretical dogmas but *presuppositions* from a necessarily practical point of view; hence, although they do not expand theoretical cognition, they do give objective reality to the idea of speculative reason *in general* (by means of their reference to the practical [sphere]) and entitle it to concepts of which it could not otherwise presume to assert even the possibility' (Kant 2002: 167, the addition in square brackets was made by the translator).

[3] Stern argues that transcendental idealism survives in his modest formulation of transcendental arguments only in form of the 'epistemological humility' it implies concerning 'things in themselves' (ibid.: 58).

[4] Quentin Meillassoux's critique of transcendental philosophy makes a similar move. He argues that it is marked by 'correlationism': 'By "correlation" we mean the idea according to which we only ever have access to the correlation between thinking and being, and never to either term considered apart from the other' (Meillassoux 2008: 4). The correlation between the knowing subject and the object known is imprisoning because anything 'outside' or 'external' is always something that is 'relative to us' (ibid.: 7). Meillassoux asks how a transcendental philosopher can account for something that no one has or ever could experience. This has opened a huge debate over the future of philosophy but, like debates over transcendental arguments, it is in danger of offering an inadequate reading of the founder of transcendental philosophy. While not engaging directly with Meillassoux, here we will engage with the reading he shares with those currently formulating transcendental arguments. Both assume that Kant invokes a subjective origin and is trapped by it, that he is always unable to reach an external reality that is therefore neglected by his account. This critique of transcendental philosophy is explored in the editorial introduction to a collection entitled *Thinking Between Deleuze and Kant.* Here the point is made that Meillassoux's reliance upon the mathematical data provided by science takes for granted the meaning that this information has for us. The case is made for following transcendental philosophy in seeking the conditions of meaning rather than assuming that it is simply given in scientific data (Willatt and Lee 2009: 9–10).

[5] Cassam writes that '[a] Means Response to a how-possible question regards the identification of one or more of the means by which something can come about as a means of explaining how it is possible' (ibid.: 6).

6 Thus we find Kant defining *world* in The Antinomy of Pure Reason in the *Critique of Pure Reason* rather than taking its definition for granted. It is to be distinguished from *nature* on the grounds that *world* refers to the mathematical wholeness or totality of appearances and thus to the quantitative outcomes of synthesis (CPR: A418–19/B446–7). Kant argues that nature is this same world but understood insofar as it is a dynamical whole, the unity not of an aggregate but of the existence of appearances. We notice that this distinction between world and nature carries forward the distinction between the mathematical and the dynamical that organizes the tables of judgements, categories and principles. This is because Kant is accounting for our understanding of a world on the basis of an account of experience which involves these tables. The world is defined as an aggregate because it is constructed out of quantities secured in cognition according to mathematical judgements, categories and principles. It is not given as a whole but as an Idea of the potential progression of experience, the notion that cognition will continue to increase through aggregation. Thus we have mathematical Ideas as well as mathematical judgements, categories and principles. Kant's strictly systematic account of experience determines how we understand and refer to a world in the first place. Therefore, for Kant the choice between being 'self-directed' and 'world-directed' in the arguments we make to account for the cognition of possible experience is a false choice.

7 James Williams argues that if we give priority to one part of Deleuze's account the whole would break down: '. . . he engineers systems where the concept of priority must not be confused with independence, separateness, abstraction or ethical superiority. As a good engineer, Deleuze's constructions are holistic as opposed to abstract hierarchies: if a crucial small, actual part perishes in a particular practical situation where it has a role to play, then it does not matter how much virtual power you have in reserve' (Williams 2008: 97).

8 'After we came out of the church we stood talking for some time together of Bishop Berkeley's ingenious sophistry to prove the non-existence of matter, and that everything in the universe is merely ideal. I observed, that though we are satisfied his doctrine is not true, it is impossible to refute it. I shall never forget the alacrity with which Johnson answered, striking his foot with mighty force against a large stone till he rebounded from it, – "*I refute it thus*" ' (Boswell 1993: 295).

9 James Williams makes a similar point when referring to the intensities or intensive differences involved in individuation: 'You have never finished with intensity. You are always working through the surface shared by actual depth and virtual height. Privilege one or the other and you have not understood your engine' (Williams 2008: 99). He argues that for Deleuze our embodiment is something we undergo, it is a shifting experience of the transformation of varying intensities (ibid.: 100). I touched upon Deleuze's account of intensities in Chapter 5 of this book and here we see how for Deleuze they embody the process of individuation, giving us a further sense of how it is a sensible 'realm of difference' that is not to be confused with the actual or the virtual.

Bibliography

Works by Immanuel Kant

Kant, I. (1882), *Reflexionen Kants zur kritischen Philosophie*, ed. B. Erdmann. Leipzig: Fues's Verlag.

— (1973), *The Kant-Eberhard Controversy*, trans. H. E. Allison. Baltimore: John Hopkins University Press.

— (1977), *Prolegomena to Any Future Metaphysics*, trans. P. Carus and J. W. Ellington. Indianapolis: Hackett.

— (1988), *Logic* (second edn), trans. R. S. Hartman and W. Schwarz. New York: Dover.

— (1992), *The Conflict of the Faculties*, trans. M. J. Gregor. Lincoln: University of Nebraska Press.

— (1996), *Critique of Pure Reason*, trans. W. S. Pluhar. Indianapolis: Hackett.

— (1997), *Lectures on Metaphysics*, trans. K. Ameriks and S. Naragon. Cambridge: Cambridge University Press.

— (2002), *Critique of Practical Reason*, trans. W. S. Pluhar. Indianapolis: Hackett.

— (2004), *Metaphysical Foundations of Natural Science*, trans. M. Friedman. Cambridge: Cambridge University Press.

— (2005), *Kritik der reinen Vernunft*. Paderborn: Voltmedia.

— (2006), *Anthropology from a Pragmatic Point of View*, trans. R. B. Louden. Cambridge: Cambridge University Press.

— (2007), *Anthropology, History and Education*, trans. M. Gregor, P. Guyer, R. B. Louden, H. Wilson, A. W. Wood, G. Zöller and A. Zweig. Cambridge: Cambridge University Press.

Works by Gilles Deleuze

Deleuze, G. (1978a), Seminar Transcript of 14 March 1978, trans. M. McMahon. http://www.webdeleuze.com/php/sommaire.html (last accessed on 3 March 2009).

— (1978b), Seminar Transcript of 4 April 1978, trans. M. McMahon. http://www.webdeleuze.com/php/sommaire.html (last accessed on 3 March 2009).

— (1983), *Nietzsche and Philosophy*, trans. H. Tomlinson. London: The Athlone Press.

— (1984), *Kant's Critical Philosophy: The Doctrine of the Faculties*, trans. H. Tomlinson and B. Habberjam. London: The Athlone Press.

— (1988), *Foucault*, trans. S. Hand. London: The Athlone Press.
— (1989), *Cinema 2: The Time-Image*, trans. H. Tomlinson and R. Galeta. London: The Athlone Press.
— (1991), *Bergsonism*, trans. H. Tomlinson and B. Habberjam. New York: Zone Books.
— (1994), *Difference and Repetition*, trans. P. Patton. London: The Athlone Press.
— (1998), *Essays Critical and Clinical*, trans. D. W. Smith and M. A. Greco. London and New York: Verso.
— (2000), *Proust and Signs*, trans. R. Howard. London: The Athlone Press.
— (2001), *Pure Immanence: Essays on A Life*, trans. A. Boyman. New York: Zone Books.
— (2004), *Desert Islands and Other Texts 1953–1974*, trans. M. Taormina. Los Angeles and New York: Semiotext(e).
— (2006), *Two Regimes of Madness: Texts and Interviews 1975–1995*, trans. A. Hodges and M. Taormina. Los Angeles: Semiotext(e).

Other Literature

Allison, H. E. (1992), 'The originality of Kant's distinction between analytic and synthetic judgements', in R. F. Chadwick and C. Cazeux (eds), *Kant: Critical Assessments*. London and New York: Routledge.
— (2004), *Kant's Transcendental Idealism: An Interpretation and Defense* (second edn). New Haven and London: Yale University Press.
Altman, M. C. (2008), *A Companion to Kant's Critique of Pure Reason*. Philadelphia: Westview Press.
Ansell Pearson, K. (1999), *Germinal Life: The Difference and Repetition of Deleuze*. London and New York: Routledge.
Aristotle (1986), *De Anima*, trans. H. Lawson-Tancred. Harmondsworth: Penguin.
Artaud, A. (1976), *Antonin Artaud: Selected Writings*, trans. H. Weaver. Berkeley and Los Angeles: University of California Press.
Aschenbrenner, K. (1983), *A Companion to Kant's* Critique of Pure Reason: *Transcendental Aesthetic and Analytic*. Lanham, New York and London: University Press of America.
Badiou, A. (2000), *Deleuze: The Clamour of Being*, trans. L. Burchill. Minneapolis: University of Minnesota Press.
Beistegui, M. de (2004), *Truth and Genesis: Philosophy as Differential Ontology*. Bloomington and Indianapolis: Indiana University Press.
Bogue, R. (1989), *Deleuze and Guattari*. London and New York: Routledge.
Boswell, J. (1993), *The Life of Samuel Johnson*. New York: Everyman's Library.
Boundas, C. V. (2005), 'The art of begetting monsters: the unnatural nuptials of Deleuze and Kant', in S. H. Daniel (ed.), *Current Continental Theory and Modern Philosophy*. Evanston: Northwestern University Press.
Bowles, M. (2000), 'Kant and the provocation of matter', in A. Rehberg and R. Jones (eds), *The Matter of Critique: Readings in Kant's Philosophy*. Manchester: Clinamen Press.
Bradley, F. H. (1914), *Essays on Truth and Reality*. Oxford: Oxford University Press.

Brassier, R. (2008), 'The expression of meaning in Deleuze's ontological proposition'. *Pli: The Warwick Journal of Philosophy*, 19: 1–29.

Brusseau, J. (1998), *Isolated Experiences: Gilles Deleuze and the Solitudes of Reversed Platonism*. New York: State University of New York Press.

Bryant, L. R. (2008), *Difference and Givenness: Deleuze's Transcendental Empiricism and the Ontology of Immanence*. Evanston: Northwestern University Press.

Buchdahl, G. (1992), *Kant and the Dynamics of Reason: Essays on the Structure of Kant's Philosophy*. Oxford: Blackwell.

Buroker, J. V. (2006), *Kant's* Critique of Pure Reason: *An Introduction*. Cambridge: Cambridge University Press.

Canetti, E. (1973), *Crowds and Power*, trans. C. Stewart. Harmondsworth: Penguin.

Cassam, Q. (1999), 'Self-directed transcendental arguments', in R. Stern (ed.), *Transcendental Arguments: Problems and Prospects*. Oxford: Oxford University Press.

— (2007), *The Possibility of Knowledge*. Oxford: Oxford University Press.

Caygill, H. (1995), *A Kant Dictionary*. Oxford: Blackwell.

Chipman, L. (1982), 'Kant's Categories and their Schematism', in R. C. S. Walker (ed.), *Kant on Pure Reason*. Oxford: Oxford University Press.

Diamond, J. (2005), *Guns, Germs and Steel*. London: Vintage.

Dicker, G. (2004), *Kant's Theory of Knowledge: An Analytical Introduction*. Oxford: Oxford University Press.

Frege, G. (1970), 'Begriffschrift, a formula language for pure thought, modeled upon that of arithmetic', in J. van Heijenhoort (ed.), *Frege and Gödel: Two Fundamental Texts in Mathematical Logic*. Cambridge, Massachusetts: Harvard University Press.

Gardner, S. (1999), *Kant and the* Critique of Pure Reason. London and New York: Routledge.

Guyer, P. (1987), *Kant and the Claims of Knowledge*. Cambridge: Cambridge University Press.

— (2006), *Kant*. London and New York: Routledge.

Hallward, P. (2006), *Out of this World: Deleuze and the Philosophy of Creation*. London and New York: Verso.

Hartman, R. S. and Schwarz, W. (1988), 'Translator's introduction', in I. Kant (1988), *Logic* (second edn). New York: Dover.

Hassall, A. (1929), *The Balance of Power 1715–1789*. London: Rivingtons.

Hatfield, G. (1990), *The Natural and the Normative: Theories of Spatial Perception from Kant to Helmholtz*. Cambridge, Massachusetts: MIT Press.

— (1992), 'Empirical, rational, and transcendental psychology: psychology as science and as philosophy', in P. Guyer (ed.), *The Cambridge Companion to Kant*. Cambridge: Cambridge University Press.

Heidegger, M. (1962), *Being and Time*, trans. J. Macquarrie and E. Robinson. Oxford: Blackwell.

— (1997), *Kant and the Problem of Metaphysics* (fifth edn), trans. R. Taft. Bloomington and Indianapolis: Indiana University Press.

Hegel, G. W. F. (1977), *Hegel's Phenomenology of Spirit*, trans. A. V. Miller. Oxford: Oxford University Press.

— (1998), *The Hegel Reader*, ed. S. Houlgate. Oxford: Blackwell.

Henrich, D. (1989), 'Kant's notion of a deduction and the methodological background of the first *Critique*', in E. Förster (ed.), *Kant's Transcendental Deductions*. Stanford: Stanford University Press.

Hughes, J. (2009), *Deleuze's* Difference and Repetition: *A Reader's Guide*. London and New York: Continuum.

Kemp Smith, N. (2003), *A Commentary to Kant's* Critique of Pure Reason (third edn). Basingstoke: Palgrave Macmillan.

Kerslake, C. (2002), 'Copernican Deleuzeanism'. *Radical Philosophy*, 114, 32–3.

— (2007), *Deleuze and the Unconscious*. London and New York: Continuum.

— (2008), 'Grounding Deleuze'. *Radical Philosophy*, 148, 30–6.

Kitcher, Philip (1998), 'Projecting the order of nature', in Patricia Kitcher (ed.), *Kant's* Critique of Pure Reason: *Critical Essays*. New York: Rowman and Littlefield.

— (2006), '*A priori*', in P. Guyer (ed.), *The Cambridge Companion to Kant and Modern Philosophy*. Cambridge: Cambridge University Press.

Kline, M. (1981), *Mathematics and the Physical World* (second edn). New York: Dover.

Körner, S. (1955), *Kant*. Harmondsworth: Penguin.

Kuehn, M. (2001), *Kant: A Biography*. Cambridge: Cambridge University Press.

Longuenesse, B. (1998), *Kant and the Capacity to Judge: Sensibility and Discursivity in the Transcendental Analytic of the* Critique of Pure Reason, trans. C. T. Wolfe. Princeton: Princeton University Press.

— (2006), 'Kant on *a priori* concepts: the metaphysical deduction of the categories', in P. Guyer (ed.), *The Cambridge Companion to Kant and Modern Philosophy*. Cambridge: Cambridge University Press.

Luchte, J. (2007), *Kant's* Critique of Pure Reason: *A Reader's Guide*. London and New York: Continuum.

Mackenzie, I. (2004), *The Idea of Pure Critique*. London and New York: Continuum.

Martin, J. C. (1999), 'Deleuze's philosophy of the concrete', in I. Buchanan (ed.), *A Deleuzian Century?* Durham and London: Duke University Press.

Meillassoux, Q. (2008), *After Finitude: An Essay on the Necessity of Contingency*, trans. R. Brassier. London and New York: Continuum.

Melnick, A. (1973), *Kant's Analogies of Experience*. Chicago: Chicago University Press.

Morgan, D. (2000), *Kant Trouble: The Obscurities of the Enlightened*. London and New York: Routledge.

O'Neill, O. (1992), 'Vindicating reason', in P. Guyer (ed.), *The Cambridge Companion to Kant*. Cambridge: Cambridge University Press.

Patton, P. (1994), 'Translator's preface', in Gilles Deleuze, *Difference and Repetition*. London: The Athlone Press.

— (2000), *Deleuze and the Political*. London and New York: Routledge.

Proust, M. (2000a), *The Captive, the Fugitive*, trans. C. K. Scott Moncrieff, T. Kilmartin and D. J. Enright. London: Vintage.

— (2000b), *Time Regained*, trans. A. Mayor, T. Kilmartin and D. J. Enright. London: Vintage.

— (2002), *Within a Budding Grove*, trans. C. K. Scott Moncrieff, T. Kilmartin and D. J. Enright. London: Vintage.

Scruton, R. (1982), *Kant*. Oxford: Oxford University Press.

Smith, D. W. (2006), 'Deleuze, Kant and the theory of immanent ideas', in C. V. Boundas (ed.), *Deleuze and Philosophy*. Edinburgh: Edinburgh University Press.

Stapleford, S. (2008), *Kant's Transcendental Arguments: Disciplining Pure Reason*. London and New York: Continuum.

Stern, R. (1999a), 'Introduction', in R. Stern (ed.), *Transcendental Arguments: Problems and Prospects*. Oxford: Oxford University Press.

— (1999b), 'On Kant's response to Hume: the second analogy as transcendental argument', in R. Stern (ed.), *Transcendental Arguments: Problems and Prospects*. Oxford: Oxford University Press.

Strawson, P. F. (1959), *Individuals: An Essay in Descriptive Metaphysics*. London and New York: Methuen.

— (1966), *The Bounds of Sense: An Essay on Kant's* Critique of Pure Reason. London: Methuen.

Stroud, B. (1982), 'Transcendental arguments', in R. C. S. Walker (ed.), *Kant on Pure Reason*. Oxford: Oxford University Press.

Swing, T. K. (1969), *Kant's Transcendental Logic*. New Haven and London: Yale University Press.

Walker, R. C. S. (2006), 'Kant and transcendental arguments', in P. Guyer (ed.), *The Cambridge Companion to Kant and Modern Philosophy*. Cambridge: Cambridge University Press.

Walsh, W. H. (1975), *Kant's Criticism of Metaphysics*. Edinburgh: Edinburgh University Press.

Willatt, E. and Lee, M. (2009), 'Editorial introduction: on the very idea of conditions', in E. Willatt and M. Lee (eds), *Thinking Between Deleuze and Kant*. London and New York: Continuum.

Williams, J. (2003), *Gilles Deleuze's* Difference and Repetition: *A Critical Introduction and Guide*. Edinburgh: Edinburgh University Press.

— (2005), *The Transversal Thought of Gilles Deleuze: Encounters and Influences*. Manchester: Clinamen Press.

— (2008), 'Why Deleuze doesn't blow the actual on virtual priority. A rejoinder to Jack Reynolds'. *Deleuze Studies*, 2.1, 97–100.

Index